VOLUME EDITORS

JESÚS ILUNDÁIN-AGURRUZA is Assistant Professor of Philosophy, and Allen and Pat Kelley Faculty Scholar at Linfield College, Oregon. He has published in the journals *Sports, Ethics, and Philosophy* and *Proteus*. He is a category 2 racer.

MICHAEL W. AUSTIN is an Associate Professor of Philosophy at Eastern Kentucky University, where he works primarily in ethics. He has published *Conceptions of Parenthood: Ethics and the Family* (2007), *Running and Philosophy: A Marathon for the Mind* (Wiley-Blackwell, 2007), and *Football and Philosophy: Going Deep* (2008).

SERIES EDITOR

FRITZ ALLHOFF is an Assistant Professor in the Philosophy Department at Western Michigan University, as well as a Senior Research Fellow at the Australian National University's Centre for Applied Philosophy and Public Ethics. In addition to editing the *Philosophy for Everyone* series, Allhoff is the volume editor or co-editor for several titles, including *Wine & Philosophy* (Wiley-Blackwell, 2007), *Whiskey & Philosophy* (with Marcus P. Adams, Wiley, 2009), and *Food & Philosophy* (with Dave Monroe, Wiley-Blackwell, 2007).

PHILOSOPHY FOR EVERYONE

Series editor: Fritz Allhoff

Not so much a subject matter, philosophy is a way of thinking. Thinking not just about the Big Questions, but about little ones too. This series invites everyone to ponder things they care about, big or small, significant, serious … or just curious.

Edited by Jesús Ilundáin-Agurruza
and Michael W. Austin

CYCLING
PHILOSOPHY FOR EVERYONE
A Philosophical Tour de Force

Foreword by Lennard Zinn

WILEY-BLACKWELL

A John Wiley & Sons, Ltd., Publication

This edition first published 2010

© 2010 Blackwell Publishing Ltd except for editorial material and organization
© 2010 Jesús Ilundáin-Agurruza and Michael W. Austin

Blackwell Publishing was acquired by John Wiley & Sons in February 2007. Blackwell's publishing program has been merged with Wiley's global Scientific, Technical, and Medical business to form Wiley-Blackwell.

Registered Office
John Wiley & Sons Ltd, The Atrium, Southern Gate, Chichester, West Sussex, PO19 8SQ, United Kingdom

Editorial Offices
350 Main Street, Malden, MA 02148–5020, USA
9600 Garsington Road, Oxford, OX4 2DQ, UK
The Atrium, Southern Gate, Chichester, West Sussex, PO19 8SQ, UK

For details of our global editorial offices, for customer services, and for information about how to apply for permission to reuse the copyright material in this book please see our website at www.wiley.com/wiley-blackwell.

The right of Jesús Ilundáin-Agurruza and Michael W. Austin to be identified as the authors of the editorial material in this work has been asserted in accordance with the UK Copyright, Designs and Patents Act 1988.

Library of Congress Cataloging-in-Publication Data

Cycling – philosophy for everyone a philosophical tour de force / edited by Jesús Ilundáin-Agurruza and Michael W. Austin; foreword by Lennard Zinn.
    p.   cm. — (Philosophy for everyone)
    Includes bibliographical references.
    ISBN 978-1-4443-3027-4 (pbk.: alk. paper)   1. Cycling—Philosophy.
I. Ilundáin-Agurruza, Jesús.   II. Austin, Michael W.   III. Title: Cycling – Philosophy for everyone.
    GV1043.7.C9 2010
    796.601—dc22

                                                          2010004888

A catalogue record for this book is available from the British Library.

Set in 10/12.5pt Plantin by SPi Publisher Services, Pondicherry, India
Printed in Singapore

1   2010

Michael would like to dedicate this to Karl, Jake, and the rolling hills of Kentucky.

Jesús dedicates this to the inventor of the wheel – who got us all on this path – and to his family, who patiently understands his cycling passion.

CONTENTS

FOREWORD

If you've picked up this book, there is no doubt that you adore bicycles and the freedom they offer. Whether you love the wind in your hair (okay, through the holes in your helmet), the sound of your own hard breathing and the persistent thumping of your heart as you climb steep mountains, the delicate maneuvering required to steer and power knobby tires through obstacles, the feel of countless impacts absorbed by your arms and your bike's suspension system on a rocky downhill, or the concentration of hours spent mastering a stunt, you also love the journey your mind takes while on the bike.

Riding bicycles takes us away from the frantic rat race as well as from the mundane and uninspiring. It at times gives us uninterrupted opportunities to muse at length and at other times demands all of our concentration and focus. We are in control of our destiny in the moment, not at the whim of the next interruption coming our way in our want-everything-right-now world.

Whether we are aware of it or not, we embark on a philosophical journey at the same time we embark on a physical journey every time we throw our leg over our saddle. And even when we ride with no particular destination in mind, we still are steering a more defined path on the physical journey than we are on the philosophical one. There are a finite number of places that the former will take us, whereas there is no telling where we will end up on the latter one. That's one of the reasons we ride, and that's one of the reasons you are reading this book.

The authors of each leg of the philosophical journey incorporated within these pages are beckoning you down a new road in your lifelong search for great rides. Jesús Ilundáin-Agurruza and Mike Austin have assembled an incredible group of tour guides to lead you down these roads, only accessible to those who travel on two wheels under their own power.

This journey will take you literally and figuratively to the ends of the earth. When it comes to commuting by bike as a way of life, John Harris and Robert Haraldsson could not be much closer philosophically, but geographically and meteorologically, Harris's Texas could not be further from Haraldsson's Iceland. Similarly, the leaderless common man declaring that he is not blocking traffic, but rather he *is* traffic in Zack Furness's discussion of the Critical Mass movement could not be further from the drive for supremacy of the heroes, quasi-heroes, and anti-heroes of Scott Tinley's, Gregory Bassham and Chris Krall's, and Raymond Belliotti's discussions of Lance Armstrong, Greg Lemond, and Marco Pantani. Finally, Belliotti's, John Gleaves's, and Bruce Dyer's discussions of how best to apply rules on doping and bicycle design to bike racing are about as far away as you can get from the gleeful childish discovery of balance and freedom and the adult embrace of suffering, life lessons, and a woman's touch found in the routes Jesús Ilundáin-Agurruza and Mike McNamee, Pete Hopsicker, Tim Elcombe and Jill Tracey, Steven Hales, Steen Nepper Larsen, Heather Reid, Catherine Womack and Pata Suyemoto, and Mike Austin take us on. And throughout, Patrick Vala-Haynes spices up the journey with creative signposts along the way, some of which leave us gasping for breath before we even embark on the next road that beckons.

The journey calling to you in this book is arguably one you have been on ever since you first got the taste for balancing on two wheels. Physical balance and the freedom to roam far and wide were immediately paired with a sense of emotional balance and the freedom to express the wide range of emotions you felt while riding. The flights of fancy on your bike, dreams of great personal feats as well as of being able to ride in a world where everyone rode and cars were nowhere to be seen, all took you partway along every single route in this book. Now these routes you've started on will be further enriched by the eloquent words of Austin's and Ilundáin-Agurruza's incredible group of authors. Enjoy the ride!

ACKNOWLEDGMENTS

No matter how dominant and great the cyclist, they all say the same thing: "Cycling is a team sport. Without my teammates I wouldn't have won." Well, this is even truer for the book you hold in your hands (which we hope feels as nice as a fine carbon handlebar, if a tad heavier). *Cycling & Philosophy* is an accomplishment that must be celebrated as the work of the *peloton* of contributors who have made it possible. They all took hard pulls, and no one skipped their turn at the front when we, the editors, put them to work, revision upon revision, with all kinds of big and minor adjustments to be made on the fly. And they all did this with a smile. This is truly their win.

The team at Wiley-Blackwell has been a formidable boon, not the least because they were willing to line up at the start line before anyone and then make sure we all crossed the finish line. Beginning with their fearless series editor Fritz Allhoff, who got the wheels rolling in the first place, following Brigitte Lee Messenger's steady lead, and not forgetting Tiffany Mok and teammates who, always the consummate professionals, worked with us to make sure we delivered on time and in style. A heartfelt thank you goes to them all (and our fit cyclist hearts can give a big thank you).

Neither of us had ridden a tandem before (sometimes called the divorce bike for a reason), working so closely on a project that took the better part of a year. But, in our case, rather than discord we have found that it has brought out a true collaborative spirit where we learned to work with each other's different talents. The only thing left is to decide whose turn it is to be the stoker now . . .

We also want to acknowledge our families for their unwavering support, cheering us on when we struggled, and never complaining when we went out to do "research" and work on the book, as we spun our cranks at the office or on the road. They were the perfect "team support car," and without their help we would have had to hitch a premature ride back on the bed of a farm truck.

There are some people who over the years have helped make us into the riders and thinkers we are today. The ride down memory lane would be too long – if pleasant – to reflect here, but we celebrate the many teammates, coaches, mechanics, mentors, colleagues, and even riders we have met in chance encounters, who have left an indelible mark and given us more meaningful reasons to be on the road, rain or shine. This is also their triumph.

And it is also yours, dear reader! You have picked this book up, and without a flicker of doubt are joining our group ride. We are honored to count you as a fellow thoughtful cyclist. Godspeed, and may you enjoy and find wisdom in this philosophical Tour de Force you are about to ride!

Jesús Ilundáin-Agurruza and Michael W. Austin

JESÚS ILUNDÁIN-AGURRUZA
AND MICHAEL W. AUSTIN

GETTING IN GEAR

An Introduction to *Cycling – Philosophy for Everyone*

Every time I see an adult on a bicycle I no longer despair for the future of the human race.

H. G. Wells[1]

Life is a like ten-speed bicycle. Most of us have gears we never use.

Charles M. Schulz[2]

Life is like riding a bicycle. To keep your balance, you must keep moving.

Albert Einstein[3]

Before the days of Wii's, iPods, and cell phones chock full of useless apps, a child's Christmas dream gift often was a bicycle. Given that you are reading these words, chances are that a (new) bike would *still* be your ideal "stocking stuffer." Or maybe it would be so for someone you know, and for whose sake you are checking out this book. Well, *Cycling – Philosophy for Everyone* is a lot cheaper than a new bike, especially now that pricey carbon is de rigueur for any cyclist worth her cleats. More importantly, it comes specked with readings that will set readers' minds on paths as liberating and full of surprises as those first two-wheeled escapades afforded. Indeed, for many our initial forays into freedom – often from parental oversight – rode on the sound of rubber on gravel, pavement, and dirt. The humble bicycle is a vehicle for enthusiastic independence and intellectually embodied inquisitiveness: pedal and probe, spin and delve, ride and discover. The world is a big place, geographically and existentially, and the view from the saddle is a valuable perspective that allows us to cover life's ways at humanly fit speeds that nurture reflection and bring satisfaction from our very actions. Wells's optimism in seeing adults on bikes is well founded and better saddled.

Cycling – Philosophy for Everyone takes fellow "cyclophilosophers" on an adventurous spin that explores life from that saddle. Perched on it, the wind on our face, we ponder *as* we pedal. Bicycles, cycling, and bike races are often the source of metaphors and proverbial quips. Isn't life like riding a bicycle or a ten-speed bike after all? Maybe. But riding a bike is not enough to understand what cycling is about, much less life. We need to shift to the reflective side of the road. Different disciplines are fond of or celebrate cycling for different reasons. Science loves cyclists. Their masochistic, hamster-like compulsive nature makes them ideal subjects to gather physiological data: put them on a trainer and have them go at it, the more pain the better. Literature finds it ripe for dalliances of many sorts, taking readers for sometimes wild, always fascinating, rides, be it Mark Twain's Yankee, Vladimir Nabokov's Ganin in *Mary*, Iris Murdoch's numerous suitors in *The Red and the Green*, or H. G. Wells's Hoopdriver in *The Wheels of Chance*. Even film finds it visually, dramatically, or comically rich, offering cult classics like *Breaking Away, American Fliers, The Flying Scotsman*, or *The Triplets of Belleville*. So, cycling has been around the block a few times, earning the respect of the arts and sciences. But philosophy? Doesn't this stretch the elastic to the snapping point?

Voicing this skepticism seems to start the ride on the wrong pedal and into a stiff headwind – reason enough to whine. But it only takes one fateful ride to realize the practical wisdom of riding out into the headwind to return with the tailwind. As we write this introduction, not only do we have the wind on our backs (wind? A gale!), but we are also drafting from a formidable train of cycling philosophers. This anthology's *peloton* of contributors shows that cycling genuinely engages the whole philosophical cogset: ethics, metaphysics, aesthetics, epistemology, and more. Indeed, this volume spins truer than a magic wheel by *Alchemy Bicycle Works*' Jeremy Parfitt. Cycling is not only a worthy subject matter for philosophic inquiry, but, as you will see, it also brings its own set of philosophic conundrums – some far worse than a chain-wrapped crank. Moreover, it is also a vehicle, metaphorically and literally, for a different and rich way to think – in fact, many an idea in this book has been spun on a saddle. Philosophy puts cyclists in command of the steering again.

The members of this *peloton*, a group as international and picturesque as the pro bunch, are philosophers and academics from cultural studies, kinesiology, literature, and political science, besides cycling insiders and former high-caliber athletes (sometimes the athlete has become a philosopher or the philosopher taken up competition). These are wheels you can trust to draft as close as a track pursuit team. Camaraderie is one of cycling's greatest boons, and by the time you finish this Philosophical Tour de Force they will be have become great riding buddies.

With its twenty-one rides, *Cycling – Philosophy for Everyone* is a veritable philosophical three-week Tour. This introduction is the Prologue by any other name. Just as three-week stage races divide into sectors according to terrain, our Tour splits and groups into six "stage segments" that contain routes of similar philosophic contours that offer shared and unique challenges and insights.

The foreword, our Tour's first ride, stars Lennard Zinn on top of the podium. Hardly needing introduction, we are very fortunate and grateful to be able to benefit from his legendary and towering, in many a sense, status within the field. A custom bicycle builder for the vertically privileged (he owns Zinn Cycles, Inc.), he has authored several books, such as the different editions of *Zinn and the Art of Bicycle Maintenance* (in road, mountain, and Triathlon versions), *Zinn's Cycling Primer*, or *Mountain Bike Performance Manual*, not to mention countless articles (particularly for *VeloNews*). To lace this with the least amount of spokes: he has made it possible for many of us to be much better mechanics and riders – particularly those of us who were shocked to find out wheels had nipples. Zinn's foreword makes for a very exciting opening to this Tour, and points our wheels in the right direction – once again. We couldn't have wished for a steadier wheel to get us started.

Spanish Tour de France winner Pedro Delgado used to remark on the big disparity between the number of kilometers set by Tour organizers and the kilometers actually ridden. What, with the warm ups, starting city neutral "parades," rides down mountain-top finishes, or back to hotels, the "ghost" kilometers add up very quickly. We have our own version of these here. Each of the six Tour stage segments suitably opens with a "warm up," a short narrative penned by Patrick Vala-Haynes, owner of Tommy's Bicycle Shop in McMinnville, Oregon. The point of contact between these vignettes and the ensuing sections is like that of good tires: minimal, fleeting, yet definitely gripping and opening possibilities. They will take you along for a ride on the wild side, to which

Vala-Haynes gives a fresh new meaning. Vala-Haynes is a Renaissance man: a great mechanic; an erstwhile racer who rides, runs, and plays soccer; and a talented writer who also teaches theater-stage fencing (a word to the wise: don't challenge him, for the face-off might not take place on the road!).

Nothing compares with the simple pleasure of a bike ride.

John F. Kennedy[4]

In the following three rides, the stage on *The Varieties of Cycling Experience*, shine the acrobats of the bicycle, fearless speed demons who create impossible openings with their balletic moves. We are all very aware that riding a bicycle is quite a unique experience, but that very familiarity shrouds the magic that lies behind every pedal stroke. What is it that makes a bike ride enriching, enjoyable, such a simple pleasure? Cycling has specific challenges that beg to engage our full range of intellectual and emotional gears. If successful, we are rewarded with the organic unity of body and bike gracefully parting space and time.

Pete Hopsicker, the next to stand on the podium, takes us back to those first pedal strokes, shows us how the magic works, and better yet, how to best understand the experience. Enlisting a bunch of riding companions that include literary greats like Mark Twain or philosophical powerhouses like Michael Polanyi, he deftly moves in the pack on his way to making our cycling experiences more transparent. The following race has Steen Nepper Larsen, self-proclaimed tallest Danish rider (at 6 ft 7 in. we won't argue with that), steering a phenomenological analysis of the cyclist's experience that gets us inside the mind and skin of the rider. As his narrative matches his supple cadence, he flies through legendary roads from the Alps to the Pyrenees, giving us insight on just what riding a bike feels like and how meaningful it can be. The third ride, a time trial, shakes things up as Bryce Dyer bolts down the ramp. A dedicated time trialist himself, he pares rig and arguments to their most efficient and aerodynamic expression, and celebrates the purity of the effort against the clock and its agonic challenge. He argues for completely opening the UCI's constricting brake levers that so tightly clamp innovative bicycle technology.

Age and treachery will overcome youth and skill.

Fausto Coppi[5]

JESÚS ILUNDÁIN-AGURRUZA AND MICHAEL W. AUSTIN

It is my thought that clean living and a strict observance of the golden rule of true sportsmanship are foundation stones without which a championship structure cannot be built.

Marshall "Major" Taylor[6]

Next up the road is *Velo Virtues*. The terrain becomes a tough "leg-breaker" of ups and downs that castigate muscles and minds in four grueling but fun and interesting jaunts. By now those in form show themselves, and we can observe the racers' ethos: their virtues and vices. Here we find heroes and villains being fatefully marked by actions and character as they write their story pedal stroke by pedal stroke.

With a "take no prisoners attitude," Gregory Bassham and Chris Krall deliver the next win with a careful assessment of Lance Armstrong's qualifications as a successful person. To determine his fitness in this regard, they pit him against some pivotal philosophical rivals hailing from ancient and medieval times, such as Aristotle or Aquinas, and especially a contemporary philosopher, Tom Morris, with his 3-D Approach to Life. The following sortie has Scott Tinley, former Kona Ironman champion, bringing us up close and personal with our heroes (or quasi-heroes). No outsider to celebrity status, Tinley gives us the conceptual tools to handle finicky fame: at the hub we find a solid analysis of heroism that laces his own narrative with LeMond's and Armstrong's personas. Amid the fray, Catherine Womack and Pata Suyemoto throw plans into disarray when they bring the female perspective to the front of the pack. In this outing, the beautiful gender drops the rough and gruff one with arguments and testimonial evidence that create new spaces within the bunch where the feminine perspective enriches the cycling experience for all. The last cavalcade in this portion of our Tour is led by Russell Arben Fox, who calms things down so we may safely navigate some of life's trickiest roundabouts (which seem to be sprouting like mushrooms in the rain nowadays). As complexity and a globalized market economy muck up our ability to make independent choices, he cleans the drivetrain and lubes things with "simplicity."

The bicycle is the most civilized conveyance known to man. Other forms of transport grow daily more nightmarish. Only the bicycle remains pure in heart.

Iris Murdoch[7]

In the stage of *Re-Cycling* we journey through the complex rapport between bicycle, environment, and urban landscape. What role is reserved to the bike amid the ecological crisis we face? There is more than one way to re-cycle, and pedaling our way through things is, if not a panacea, at least one of the most visible and ethically consistent: we ride the talk.

Robert Haraldsson is a philosopher who commutes yearlong in Iceland. As he picks his way through bad weather and worse arguments he takes away the grounds for any reluctance to commute. Mercifully, he also gives us the boon of realizing, as we follow his lead, that commuting under a range of meteorological and topological circumstances is rewarding and adds very worthy facets to our lives. Now, what excuse is left for the rest of us? Just in case, in the next foray John Harris takes the air out of car tires to put it in bicycles. He argues that we are actually morally obligated to swap steering wheel for handlebar. His refined arguments filter out our complacent ways, give us more breathing room, and promise cleaner air all around. The last course of this stage brings traffic to a halt as Zack Furness adds a social and political dimension when he takes on the polarizing Critical Mass rides – soon coming to an intersection near you. Furness, a passionate advocate, maneuvers his stance around the morass of today's clogged cities to open up spaces that free our minds and bodies from the constraints of a car-centered culture.

> *Cycling is just like church – many attend, but few understand.*
>
> Jim Burlant[8]

The big days in the mountains come next with three tough consecutive, but extremely rewarding, routes. At some point it is bound to happen; like getting a flat, the question pops up: Why pedal? *Spinning Wisdom* stops the heinous hissing of doubt quicker than a glueless patch. Better yet, and unlike a used patch that isn't good any longer, the resulting insights apply to many other aspects of our existence. These Socratic Team members teach us about ourselves as we read about *their* insights. Indeed, this is the sweetest kind of draft.

In the opening day, a hilltop finish, Heather Reid covers a lot of ground as she revisits a cycling career that saw her come within inches of an Olympic Team berth in the track sprint. The world may have "lost" a top cyclist when she hung up her racing wheels, but it gained a solid philosopher who

JESÚS ILUNDÁIN-AGURRUZA AND MICHAEL W. AUSTIN

learned how to philosophize on the bike. Her discerning words will certainly elicit epiphanies in our readers that, making Socrates proud, will make them wiser. In the next outing, Steven Hales pulls a gutsy and crazy solo breakaway through a bunch of passes, and regales us with a narrative that blends a trove of anecdotes with a veritable philosophic buffet where we can refuel with morsels from the philosophical greats that will power readers for many jaunts to come. In the third and last "date" in the mountains, Mike Austin swaps running shoes for pedals and brings a fresh and keen perspective to the spinning wheels. Clicking into a gear that dials back the obsession that possesses some of us to a sensible level, we learn to appreciate cycling within a larger context that makes it all the more meaningful.

The last time I'd ridden 200 miles, I felt awful the next day, like I'd been hit by a truck. After the Solvang race I woke up and felt hardly a touch of soreness. I also felt like I could easily ride another 200, and I realized that I'd entered another world, the realm of instant recovery. I'll be frank: it was a reassuring kind of world, and I could see why people might want to stay there.

Stuart Stevens[9]

Three cyclists, while hammering during a late-fall training ride, hit some black ice and fly off a cliff. As one cyclist opens his eyes, an angel asks him, "Who do you wish to be?" "Huh?" says the cyclist. "Look, in heaven, because you rode well and lived well, you get to transform yourself into any rider who ever lived." Just then a wool-specked racer whooshes by on a green bike. "Hey! That's …" says the cyclist. "One of your friends," the angel finishes. "He chose to be Fausto Coppi." As the angel asks, "Who do you wish to be?" The Cannibal rips by. "Maaan …" says the cyclist. "My other friend's taken Eddy already!" "Oh, no," says the angel. "Your other friend lived. That's just God. He wishes he were Eddy Merckx."[10]

By this point in our Tour the effort has taken such a toll on everyone, riders, readers, even viewers, that the temptation for a bit of extra "help" is *very* real. Well, choose a massage and a nice red wine instead. *Fair Play on Two Wheels* consists of three furious rollercoaster legs where we confront the issues of performance enhancement in cycling, and extreme competitiveness as embodied by Eddy "The Cannibal" Merckx. The former bunnyhops the challenges built to test us *as* cyclists that we're supposed to willingly abide by (these limit permissible means to achieve cycling's goals), whereas the latter may put too much tension on the spokes of the sport and beyond.

John Gleaves breaks away from the conformity of traditional views with a bold attack. He argues for a revision of our current attitudes and the punishments levied against "guilty" riders by the International Cycling Union (UCI) and the World Anti-Doping Agency (WADA). Gleaves takes advantage of inconsistencies, astutely distinguishes between penalties and punishments, and displays panache as he drops contending arguments and brings forth interesting, promising alternatives. For his part, Raymond Belliotti manages to police the front of the bunch with a rigorous analysis that, covering any reasons to which "would-be dopers" might resort, dissuades hopeful chasers from even trying. In his carefully argued piece, Marco Pantani's mercurial figure is the center of attention. With their contribution to the race the Belgian pair of Andreas de Block and Yannick Joye allow us to enjoy the joke about their countryman at a much deeper level, as they ponder whether The Cannibal may have taken his hunger for wins one bite too far. The resulting moral confrontation has the makings of an exciting photo finish: is trying to win at all costs a moral obligation that trumps other virtues such as friendship or generosity?

> *It is by riding a bicycle that you learn the contours of a country best, since you have to sweat up the hills and coast down them. Thus you remember them as they actually are, while in a motor car only a high hill impresses you, and you have no such accurate remembrance of country you have driven through as you gain by riding a bicycle.*
>
> Ernest Hemingway[11]

In *Pedaling Circles* we reach the end of the Tour. Although the standings in GC are set by now, these last three courses manage to keep the excitement with some atypical tactics and aggressive riding. Circling back, these explore alternative ways of understanding the cycling experience via unorthodox perspectives that, paradoxically, tighten any loose spokes.

Seth Tichenor brings an Eastern flavor to the Tour atop his *Bhagavad Gita* frame, specked with awesomeness, freedom, and yoga. Pedaling seemingly effortlessly, he calls forth cycling's potential for the awesome, and shows how deeply transformative and enriching riding can be.

JESÚS ILUNDÁIN-AGURRUZA AND MICHAEL W. AUSTIN

Next, Tim Elcombe and Jill Tracey take the inside line, and launch a vicious attack that puts the hurt one last but memorable time. Recounting their agonizing yet satisfying *Étape du Tour* experience, they bring out the joy of suffering on a bike to its most meaningful expression with the help of teammates like William James, John Dewey, Phil Ligget, and Paul Sherwen – all *sans* mind-numbing painkillers. Finally, in the closing ride to this Tour, Jesús Ilundáin-Agurruza and Mike McNamee come around for a surprise win (a tandem does make it easier!). Making the rounds through the various stages of life and cycling, they set in motion wheels within wheels that delve in, by now, familiar themes. They highlight the inherent worth of things cyclical and their unique contribution to a fun, rewarding life of the mind and on wheels. As Hemingway's lean and mean prose explains, we come to know certain things best on a bike.

In the name of all the members of the *peloton*, we, as the editors and organizers of this philosophical ride, wish to thank you for joining this Tour. With the open road ahead, just like before a promising ride, these pages will transport you to new places or help revisit old haunts with fresh eyes, savoring that pleasure without equal that a bike brings to those who come to worship at its temple. Soaring to new intellectual heights on mechanical steeds, we take the inspiring view from the summit, meander our way through tricky switchbacks, and flat out fly, whether it be on silky tracks, smooth and rough roads, or on dirt. Best of all, the fun is had in the riding and reading itself. At the end of the road, this is about getting the most out of this passion we share, and which makes our lives go around. Happy and meaningful pedaling!

NOTES

1 Bill Strickland, *The Quotable Cyclist* (New York: Breakaway Books, 1997), p. 18.
2 Charles M. Schulz, *Life is Like a Ten-Speed Bicycle* (New York: HarperCollins, 1997).
3 From www.quotegarden.com/bicycling.html (accessed September 14, 2009).
4 kba.tripod.com/quotes.htm (accessed September 14, 2009).
5 kba.tripod.com/quotes.htm (accessed October 5, 2009).
6 kba.tripod.com/quotes.htm (accessed October 5, 2009).
7 James E. Starrs, *The Literary Cyclist* (New York: New York, 1997), p. 33.

8 kba.tripod.com/quotes.htm (accessed September 14, 2009).
9 Stuart Stevens, "Drug Test," *Outside Magazine*, November 2003. Available online at outside.away.com/outside/bodywork/200311/200311_drug_test_1. html (accessed November 13, 2003).
10 Adapted from kba.tripod.com/quotes.htm (accessed September 14, 2009).
11 James E. Starrs, *The Literary Cyclist* (New York: Breakaway Books, 1997), p. 38.

THE VARIETIES OF CYCLING EXPERIENCE

CHAPTER I

WARM UP

A Surreal Ride

"I'm a vegetarian, you know," Jon announced.

"You are not. They aren't even mammals."

"They have faces."

"So you think they have souls?"

The creatures were so tiny we at first mistook them for spiders. Not even spiders, just a shimmer, a trick of light.

We curled into the cocoon of wet forest, cedar, and maple, thigh-high ferns. There was no reverberation of sound here. The whisp of tires on the wet backroad, ca-chink of a gear change, my laughter and Jon's constant blather – nothing bounced back. Rather, we simply propelled ourselves into the next moment, past the next mile, through broken light, over rippled pavement. The air smelled like ice, the threat of winter. The leaves had not yet begun to change, and wouldn't in any dramatic fashion. Not here in the North Cascades, so close to the Canadian border. Just a slow fade from green to lighter green, then yellow and … they would fall. Nothing of great drama. Hardly the proclamation of a new season.

Beneath the glowering trees, Mosquito Lake Road disappeared into bracken and rotted cedar. A wooden post warned us to *YIELD*.

"Who puts a *YIELD* sign in the middle of the road?"

Jon was right. There was a *YIELD* sign planted in front of us. Ten miles in on a single-lane paved road, not a single intersection or home nearby, and someone had planted a *YIELD* sign.

Jon stopped.

"What's wrong with you?" I asked.

"A citizen has responsibilities. I obey the law."

I rolled up beside him and slid off the saddle.

"Do you see?" He pointed past the sign.

I did see, the faint shift of the road from west to east.

"Maybe I should have stayed away from the mushrooms," he said.

"You didn't tell me you had mushrooms. All I had were eggs and potatoes."

"In the navy. 1969. It was probably the beer more than the mushrooms. Portabella, I think."

"You don't experience hallucinations from eating Portabella mushrooms." I continued to look down the road.

"The road's moving."

"Maybe we're moving."

"It's all relative. Motion is relative," Jon said.

He stepped on his pedal and slid fifteen feet past the YIELD sign. "See? Relative."

I pulled alongside him. As far as we could see, the strip of pavement was crawling, bouncing, tilting, sliding. We both remounted and pedaled a few more strokes.

"At first I thought it was spiders," he said.

Ping. Ping. Ping. Ping. The road came alive, little masses of green creatures churned through my spokes, some luckier than others. The road *was* alive. No, not like some bad dream, but actually alive, green with stuff that moved. Not moss, or bouncing rain or scattering leaves, but frogs. A flood of frogs. Frogs?

"Frogs!" I screamed. Frogs everywhere, blanketing the road, hippety-hopping from one side to the other.

"You're awfully excitable today. Of course they're frogs," Jon said. "What did you expect? Just ride slow. Don't make any sudden movements. Ooh, you got one."

The frogs continued to pour from the forest. A river of them. We rode more carefully than we ever had. Jon refused to stop smiling. After more than a hundred yards, the creatures began to thin. The road tipped upward.

"Do you have a block plane?" Jon asked. The flow of his conversation was as normal as ever.

I knew Jon was about to offer me his block plane. Not because I'm perceptive, but because Jon was giving away things today. He was dying

PATRICK VALA-HAYNES

and he needed to give stuff away. I already had a good plane my father had given me. But Jon's plane would be better, even if the handle was cracked.

"I could use a good block plane," I lied.

"You want mine?"

"Didn't I just say that?"

"This road makes no sense. It dead-ends on top of the ridge. But the bridges are backwards."

"How can a bridge be backwards?"

"The first one we crossed was dated 1949."

"So?"

"The last one said 1947. That means the road was built from the top down. That's stupid."

"No, that's Zen."

"That's what I said." He smiled.

Simplicity and banality. That was the beauty of the moment. There were frogs. And for the moment there was Jon, growing no closer to his death. Teasing me about my sincerity. In love with ironies. Allowing me to steal his block plane.

"I'm really not a vegetarian, you know. I just like frogs."

CHAPTER 2

LEARNING TO RIDE A BIKE

Two-Wheeled Sensations

Every type of cyclist – novice to expert, enthusiast to racer – started their journey to being a bike rider in the same way. We straddled the bike, grasped the handlebars, pushed the pedals, and entered a foreign world defined by an elevated center of gravity, a continuous service to balance, and a constant forward motion. While often a durable and memorable moment, descriptions of initial attempts to ride a bike frequently elude verbal explanation.

This is not to say that descriptive attempts have not been made. Indeed, many cyclists have tried from a variety of perspectives. Some have resorted to spiritual metaphors. "You look for that magic moment that makes the duo stay up when it should go down," one cyclist recalls. "And then one morning ... the miracle had taken place. I was riding. I never wanted to put my feet back down for fear that the miracle wouldn't happen again."[1] Others used more worldly accounts, describing the initial sensations of riding a bike as being "supported by nothing ... but mysterious forces and dumb luck."[2] Still others noted failed attempts at scientifically explaining "how a six-year-old child rides a bike."[3]

Perhaps our inability to describe the learning-to-ride-a-bike experience contributes to the lack of philosophic attention given to this almost universal phenomenon. The cycling literature is thick with stories of perfect rides, paceline strategies, physical training programs, and competitive drama. But the inspection of the cycling experience foundational to all of these – that of learning to ride a bike – remains neglected.

Obviously, probing the learning-to-ride-a-bike phenomenon exposes the core physical skills of cycling – the manipulation of a two-wheeled velocipede through the acts of balancing, pedaling, steering, and braking. Yet learning to ride a bike reveals more to us than these practical skills. The bicycle, through its uncomplicated, consistent design and almost universal usage, has become a seminal human tool that catalyzes our "physical" education to what Scott Kretchmar calls "the sensuous life." Simply, the bicycle provides us a means of confronting more profoundly our aesthetic, sensory-rich existence – an existence filled with fragrances, feels, forms, colors, sounds, rhythms, tensions, climaxes, and resolutions.[4]

It is this sensory-rich physical world that we must experience, learn, and embody from the time we are born. How else could we negotiate the challenges in our lives without such a "physical" education? Yet this education is not a birthright. It is something we must discover, develop, and maintain. Ironically, it is also something that we do not have to pursue. Recent advancements in communication, travel, and production often limit our sensuous interaction with the world, which in turn creates a "discrepancy between our sensory potential and our failure to develop that potential." Kretchmar warns that such technological luxuries can dull the human ability of having "the eyes to see, the fingers to touch, or the muscle memory to feel" sensual experiences.[5] The potential result: human advancement, while not inherently evil, sometimes limits our physical education and, by default, restricts our access to the sensuous life.

Being truly physically educated, however, requires that we develop rich and numerous experiences in diverse feels, tastes, sights, sounds, and smells. It is an education that requires not only initial, sporadic, and novel experiences but also routine maintenance and practice for the embodiment of those experiences. It is an education to our world that begins in our youth. It is an education that, for many of us, can be continuously developed and expanded through riding a bike.

What follows is an examination of the bike-riding activity – descriptions of those being physically educated to the sensuous life of cycling – the movements and feels, the distances and speeds, and the sights and sounds. Relying on David Sudnow's method in *Ways of the Hand*, I use personal description to delineate this education. Similar to Sudnow,

"My concern is description and not explanation, a phenomenologically motivated inquiry into the nature of [the human body] from the standpoint of the performer."[6] This will reveal not only the initial skills necessary to negotiate the bicycle itself, but also the intensified changes in our sensual perceptions. It is these newly heightened components of our sensuous world that change us from being simple pedestrians to being different sorts of beings – cyclists that have been "physically" educated to a more "sensuous life" through the bike.

The "Bicycling Method"

The bicycle's ability to reveal a richer understanding of the sensuous world begins with our initial attempts to ride the machine. As noted above, however, modern-day writings of this learning-to-ride-a-bike experience are few and far between. Yet there is an untapped source of writings that describe these early learning attempts in a very raw fashion – those inaugural cyclists of the late nineteenth century who were completely ignorant of the workings of this novel invention.

American essayist Mark Twain was one of those early cyclists and he, as well as other riders, was strongly challenged by the operation of this foreign device.[7] Attempting to ride the two-wheeled contraption for the first time, these original cyclists had no "how-to" books or well-tested teaching methods required for success.[8] Not surprisingly, most riders resorted to sheer determination as the key learning strategy in mastering the machine. They simply bought a bike out of curiosity, brought it home with the person who sold it to them or the friend who convinced them to purchase it, and then, at the direction of this person, proceeded to get on and fall off the bike at regular intervals until acquiring the skill simply through trial and error.

Through this "bicycling method," as Twain called it, the basic skills of riding a bike quickly became known: balancing upon the machine, propelling it, steering it, mounting it on your own (the most troublesome step for Twain), and finally, mastering the "voluntary dismount" – as opposed to the "involuntary dismount" at which, Twain admits, he was naturally proficient.[9] Indeed, combining these skills into a smooth, complete ride initially proved treacherous. Using words like "weaving," "tottering," "uncertainty," "slowness," and "lumbering," one early rider likened his first attempts at riding to "a drowning man clutching a plank, wobble it never so wildly [*sic*]."[10] Often riding only a few feet at a time before "involuntarily dismounting," some novices found themselves "measuring their length upon the ground" or repeatedly "having the pleasure of a renewed acquaintance with the soil" rather than spending any quality time in the saddle.[11] They were simply not yet physically educated to the ways of the bike.

Their descriptions, however, highlight one of the core physical education lessons of cycling. Learners had to conquer their natural feels and impulses and replace them with the bike's sensuous paradoxes. Twain highlights the prominence of these ironies. "Whatever the needed thing might be (to ride the bike)," Twain writes, "my nature, habit, and breeding moved me to attempt it in one way, while some immutable and unsuspecting law of physics required that it be done in just the other way." It is these initial paradoxical feelings of balance and imbalance that challenge new riders the most. Twain further details his struggles. "If I found myself falling to the right, I put (the handlebars) hard down the other way, by a quite natural impulse, and so violated a law, and kept on going down. The law required the opposite thing – the big wheel must be turned in the direction in which you are falling."[12] Of course, successful cycling requires riders to conquer the natural impulse to turn away from their fall. Rather, riders need to turn into the loss of balance – into the direction they are falling – in order to place the bike back under the rider's center of gravity.

An "ah-ha" moment often accompanies the successful overcoming of this bicycle-balance paradox – a moment that is, perhaps, the most profound memory in a budding rider's progress. Described by one rider as a "genuine experience ... (that) impresses a man so vividly that he never forgets the place where it struck him," this "ah-ha" moment marks the point when the bike-riding skill becomes suddenly and wonderfully easy to perform.[13] A spontaneous and unpredictable occurrence, it is the experience that marks the embodiment of being upright, balanced on two aligned wheels, and constantly moving forward. It may also be the key happening in our cycling physical education that initially opens our eyes to a richer, sensuous world.

From this initial physical "ah-ha" sensation of achieving a state of balance, other feelings and relationships become felt and recognized. Through his cycling adventures, Twain described his progressing physical education to the sensuous life. He begins to realize that the bicycle informed him of formerly hidden nuances in his environment such as the grade of the street, the consistency of the road, and the distance between himself and the curb or passing carriages. "I had been familiar with that street for years, and had always supposed it was a dead level," Twain writes, "but it was not, as the bicycle now informed me, to my surprise ... (The bicycle) notices a rise where your untrained eye would not observe that one existed; it notices any decline which water will run down." From his new vantage point, Twain's perception of the world changed from that of a pedestrian to that of a cyclist.[14]

Other riders also highlighted their awakening to the more finite qualities of their common environment. "I knew I lived in a slightly undulating country," one rider explains, "but never before had dreamed that I lived all up-hill ... except where it was down, and who could say which was worse."[15] Awakenings similar to these have not disappeared with time. Modern riders also note the distinctions in how some roads "look flat ... but when your legs are the engine, you feel every uphill and every downhill."[16] Through these examples, it is apparent that riding a bike quickly and clearly reveals some intimate nuances and feels of the roads previously imperceptible by the rider.

These musings reveal considerable insight into how the bicycle physically educates us to a richer, more sensuous world. First and foremost, the bicycle teaches lessons in balance. Obviously balance is needed to keep the bike upright, but it also teaches the balance needed in our attentional awareness among several skills – those of balance, pedaling, steering, braking, mounting, and dismounting. Through learning the overall skill of riding a bike, one must learn how to jumble and coordinate the multiple sub-skills necessary for success. This coordination may not be that dissimilar to learning other complex skills like driving a golf ball or serving in tennis or downhill skiing. However, when acquiring any of these other skills, we are more likely to find ourselves saying that their achievement was "just like riding a bike." The "ah-ha" moment of balancing on a bike is experientially more profound, more shaping than these others.

Secondly, once able to ride the bike, Twain and the others began noticing the nuances of their environment – the uphills, the downhills, and the accompanying changes in heart rate and breathing patterns when traveling over both. This is the beginning of their physical education beyond the simple usage of the bicycle and is usually the next lesson in a continuous series of lessons provided by the bike. To illustrate this continuing education, I will examine some of my own personal experiences from the saddle as a modern and advanced example of how the bike can physically educate one even further to the sensuous life.

PETER M. HOPSICKER

Lessons from the Saddle

Accurate memories of our first attempts at riding a bike can prove cloudy. Perhaps like other riders, I have a spotty recollection of the sensations accompanying this experience. However, I do remember bits and pieces. One detail of my initial lessons remains clear in my mind and highlights how learning to ride a bike profoundly opened my eyes to a new world of time and distance, of heart rates and muscle power, of effort and elevation, and of speed and wind.

My lessons took place on the sidewalk directly in front of my house. Like Twain and the others, my initial rides were more of survival than cycling. Zigzagging back and forth between the sidewalk's two edges – randomly changing speeds and alternating between balance and imbalance – I focused on using the bike. Strangely, the construction and consistency of the sidewalk remain a very clear memory for me. The sidewalk was segmented into square yards separated by two-inch-wide grooves. Not only did these grooves add to my trepidation of staying balanced and steering straight, they also became indicators of my speed and traveled distance. As my speed increased, the frequency between each subtle bump decreased. Not only could I count each crack to determine my distance, I could also listen to the *thump-thump* rhythm of my rolling wheels to judge my speed. Indeed, my early success as a cyclist was most accurately measured one yard at a time.

Although this may seem to be an odd memory, it indicates an early enrichment in my sensuous world. When walking or riding in a car, apart from counting my steps, noting the auto's odometer, or marking the time, I judged distance and speed simply on a point A to point B basis. I left from one spot and arrived at another – distance measured in its most superficial form. In contrast, the bicycle revealed to me that the same distance had more distinct qualities. No longer was my bike ride around the block only measured by my success of arriving safely back home. Now, all the points in between the end points were brought to my attention – slight jolts from the tires rolling over the cracks and other imperfections in the sidewalk; the rhythmic sound of rolling over the segmented yards; the intensity of the wind echoing in my ears; the freewheel humming; my heart rate pounding in my chest; the temperature of my skin heated with effort and cooled with speed. The bike provided a more intimate relationship between me and my physical environment. It helped etch these sensuous experiences into my memory – something that continues to happen even today when I experience one of those "favorite," "perfect," or "beautiful" rides.

Three decades later, the bike continues to help me experience the sensuous life in distinct ways. Several years ago, I committed to riding my first century. I had not been riding much at the time. In other words, I was essentially a pedestrian. My first training ride for this event consisted of 25 miles on a nearly flat Rails-to-Trails bike path.[17] I started out too hard and my legs quickly turned to rubber. My labored breathing echoed from my gasping mouth. My heart beat pounded in my chest and thumped in my ears. My visual focus oscillated between a spot 20 feet ahead of my bike and the bike computer that unsympathetically measured my toil one-tenth of a mile at a time. My training strategy disintegrated into simply keeping the bike moving forward. Two and a half hours later, I had completed my first lesson in cycling distance. Demoralized, I realized that I was on pace to finish those 100 miles only after ten hours of pedaling! Clearly, my concept of distance as a pedestrian did not match the concept of distance I needed to survive in long-distance endurance cycling. I was still measuring my rides one sidewalk square at a time.

Yet that seemingly insurmountable distance of 25 miles (let alone 100 miles) was soon replaced with a new appreciation for the distinct feels of endurance cycling. With training, I became physically educated to the details of longer rides. My legs became stronger, my fitness level increased, and I became a smarter rider, focusing more on creating consistent feelings of exertion rather than reacting to the highs and lows of effort and recovery. I became less and less overwhelmed and overpowered by the sensations of my body working on the bike. More astutely, I began to use the feelings of my pounding heart and the sounds of my breathing in my ears as a gauge for my training pace. I became more aware of the subtle nuances of the trail – sensuous landmarks along the way which segmented my ride: a washed-out bend in the path that hugged the river; the pocket of cool air caught in a hollow shrouded in pine trees; the smell of those pine trees, wild flowers, decaying vegetation; the sounds of the flowing river, the wind in the trees, the trail surface grinding against the tires. The time it took me to complete the rides steadily decreased. I eventually finished the century in slightly less than seven hours.

In contrast to my physical education in the flats, climbing and descending have taught me somewhat different lessons. When facing a tough climb, physiological lessons begin immediately. My ride becomes one of "tough love" – one of rationing muscle, oxygen, and calories. I can almost

PETER M. HOPSICKER

feel each muscle in my legs make its individual contractions. My breathing fills my ears in a rhythmic series of inhalations and exhalations. My heart pounds in my chest. My eyes are watering slits. My shoulders and arms ache from pushing and pulling on the handlebars. My nostrils flare as my body desperately seeks just a little more oxygen. The workings of my body dominate the sensations of this experience. It is a physical education rarely felt in my non-cycling life.

With time, I began noticing some other unique qualities of climbing. My visual focus, for example, adapts to the strenuousness and slower speeds. My vision narrows considerably as the broader, gestalt perception of less strenuous riding slowly deconstructs into detailed fragments. The scenery divides into a series of segments and checkpoints. My focus alternates between the road just in front of the bike and landmarks that divide the distance remaining in my suffering – a white painted fence on the right bordering a "flatter" section of the climb; a shaded area marking the halfway point; the fourth mailbox on the left identifying the top. Often pedaling over the handlebars, I notice the contrasts in the road surface and what the differences in the pavement feel like at a five-mile-per-hour pace. I watch random pebbles, insects, and other debris pass slowly by my front wheel. I hear the metal of my bike groan and creak with my efforts. My slow speed and strenuous effort reveal small details unnoticed at more comfortable efforts and faster speeds. Time expands. Laborious cranking, creeping slowly up and up and up. The distance takes forever.

As opposed to the fragmented attention to the physiological and physical qualities of climbing, descending unifies things. Descending is floating and hovering over the subtleties of the road. The feel of the road through the bike becomes a consistent electric hum. In contrast to the climbing sounds of slower, purposeful cranking, the sound of descending is the deafening howl of the wind in my ears – a sound that sometimes overpowers the increasing pitch of the free-wheel purring with greater and greater velocity. Such audible changes coupled with the tactile sensations of the wheels rolling over the road signal my need to adjust to the challenges of gravity-induced velocity.

These sounds and sensations of speed are connected to my visual gaze, and it adjusts accordingly. In contrast to climbing, as my speed increases, so does the distance of my visual gaze away from the bike. Instead of dividing the distance into short, slow, uphill segments, I look deeply into my line of travel to negotiate hazards in the road and plan for turns and braking. I dread taking even a quick peek away from my path. The world is simply rushing by too quickly. I have to stay aware of what is coming up next. My eyes dart from one potential hazard to the other – a crack in the pavement, a patch of gravel, a tree branch. My intentions are focused solely on what is ahead of me. Things passing me to the left and right mean little and those already behind me even less.

Similar to how the sights, sounds, and feels of climbing reveal to me the strenuousness of the inclines, the sensuous experiences of sight, sound, and touch in descending become fused into a specific sensation that indicates my speed. While my heart and lungs enjoy some time to recover from previous efforts, my mind enjoys no such luxury. I must constantly sort out potential lines of travel, braking strategies, and more aerodynamic positioning. It is the sensuous feels of the speed of my descent that dictate the required speed of my decision-making. Time contracts. Flowing like water rapidly seeking the downhill path of least resistance, the mountain swiftly disappears behind me.

As with many cyclists, every ride – fresh adventures to standard daily commutes – reveals to me something different about my physical relationship to my environment. Whether spinning in the flats, grinding out a climb, or streaming down a descent, an elevated sensuousness between riders and their environments is created. From these examples, it appears that the bike has consistently been a human tool that allows one to develop these sensuous experiences and develop more profoundly one's sensory potential. It arguably provides an easily accessible and widely practiced means to the sensuous life.

From the time we first attempt to ride the bike, we experience new sensations – sensations steeped in the simultaneous balance of physical forces necessary for pedaling, steering, braking, and other cycling skills. We also begin to develop a keen sense of the physicality of our environment – the up and downhill grades of roads, the consistency of road surfaces, and other feels, sights, and sounds formerly unknown to us without the use of the bike. We may even become exceedingly "physically" educated to the sensuous world through more advanced cycling challenges that change our perceptions of time, distance, and speed; heighten our physiological feels of effort and recovery; attune our psychological feels of decision and reaction; and elevate our emotional feels of challenge and success. It is an education that begins for many of us with a youthful right of passage – that day our "miracle" takes place. It is an education that all cyclists, at all levels, experience with each ride, bringing us continuously closer to realizing our potential for a sensuous life.

Finding the Words

Like others, it still remains challenging to verbally describe my continuing physical education from the saddle – especially to the non-cyclist. My words often fall short of what I have actually felt, seen, heard, tasted, or smelled during my rides. I still know more about cycling than I can say. This does not stop me from attempting to regale my friends with the characteristics of a "beautiful ride" – the smoothness and effortlessness of the experience; the organic feels of the ride fitting together from beginning to end; the dissolution between the challenges of the route and the efficiency of my efforts in the saddle; the satisfaction I feel when my resulting performance seemed to be far greater in measure than my perceived effort. But I often fail in communicating my experiences. In contrast to the fluidity of my ride, I fumble over my words. I can perform the ride. The sensuous feels of the ride are very real to me. Yet I cannot find the language to clearly describe it.

But there are clear descriptions out there. We simply need to identify and use them – to fill the void of literature that more completely describes the bike-riding experience. I recently came upon one such opportunity. While training for another century ride on my local rail-trail, I had the opportunity to existentially look back upon myself through the experiences of a 10-year-old boy – a fresh reminder of what lessons the bike has taught me over the past several years.

During my ride, a mother flagged me down and asked me if I had seen a young boy dressed in red with a red bike on my travels. I had not but assured her that if I did see him on my ride, I would send him in her direction. I came across him several miles from his parents. "Are you Timmy?" I asked. He said yes. I said, "You know, your parents are looking for you at the other end of the trail." His eyes widened. He immediately hopped back on his red BMX bike and began pedaling furiously back toward his mom opposite of my destination. I watched him go, churning out huge RPMs. He did not seem to realize that he was almost 10 miles from his parents. I turned around and pedaled up next to him. "Are you going to be all right riding back by yourself?" I asked. He said yes. Unconvinced, I asked another question. "Do you want me to ride back with you?" Holding back tears, he said yes again. Averaging five miles per hour for the next nine miles, I was asked at least 36 times, "How much farther is it?" and "Are we there yet?" Timmy clearly had no concept of distance. In fact, his physical education of distance, speed, vision, and effort from a cycling perspective – indeed, his cycling "sensuous life" – was undoubtedly underdeveloped. I hold hope for him as a future cyclist. But for now, he was simply a vision of me on that segmented sidewalk three decades ago.

NOTES

1   Paul Fournel, *Need for the Bike* (Lincoln: University of Nebraska Press, 2001), p. 26.
2   Jeffery Hammond, "Riding for Nefertiti," in *Bicycle Love: Stories of Passion, Joy, and Sweat*, ed. Garth Battista (Halcottsville, NY: Breakaway Books, 2004), p. 101.
3   Bill Strickland, ed., *The Quotable Cyclist* (New York City: Breakaway Books, 1997), pp. 172–3.
4   Scott R. Kretchmar, *Practical Philosophy of Sport and Physical Activity* (Champaign, IL: Human Kinetics, 2005), pp. 248–50.
5   Kretchmar, *Practical Philosophy*, p. 249.
6   Phenomenology is a branch of philosophy that uses careful description to capture the way things reveal themselves to us in everyday life. David Sudnow, *Ways of the Hand: The Organization of Improvised Conduct* (Cambridge, MA: Harvard University Press, 1978), p. xiii.
7   Mark Twain, "Taming the Bicycle," in *The Complete Works of Mark Twain: What is Man?* (New York: Harper, 1917), pp. 285–96.
8   Paul Pastnot, "My First Wheel," *Outing* 4/2 (1884): 138–40; Chris Wheeler, "My Initiation to the Bicycle: A Tale of the Tavern Talkers," *Outing* 10/4 (1887): 370–6.
9   Twain, "Taming the Bicycle," pp. 288–9.
10 Ernest Ingersoll, "My First Bicycle Tour: The Adventures of a Learner," *Outing* 26/3 (1895): 205–7.
11 Pastnot, "My First Wheel," p. 139.
12 Twain, "Taming the Bicycle," p. 287.
13 Pastnot, "My First Wheel," p. 138.
14 Twain, "Taming the Bicycle," p. 293.
15 Jean Porter Rudd, "My Wheel and I," *Outing* 26/2 (1895): 126.
16 Jamieson L. Hess, "Confessions of a RAGBRAI Addict." Available online at www.nordicskating.org/cycle/ragbrai.html.
17 See www.railstotrails.org/index.html for details.

CHAPTER 3

BECOMING A CYCLIST

Phenomenological Reflections on Cycling

To be human is to experience a lifelong second birth of such subtlety that its echoes can be extended to our experiences of riding and racing bikes. Almost daily, definitely in the summer time, my bike lives through its second becoming. The "delivery" – design, production, and assembly of the bicycle – is long gone, but it gets reborn under me whenever I ride it. The bike is an attractive dream on standby with an inherent ability to tempt me to leave books and computer behind, and to escape the lazy bodily standstill.

My knowledge of my bike and confidence in it are situated in my body – and my legs, arms, and thoughts are extensions of my bike, which is a part of my organism. On my bike I am capable of doing much more than I know of. For example, I do not reflect about how to keep my balance, nor do I think about how I manage to react to dangerous events in a dense pack of competitive riders. The concept of "tacit knowledge" ought to have been invented by a practicing and thinking biker.

Extended Embodiment – Cycling Thoughts

The touch of the tires on the road makes up the outer membrane of my being in the world and the handlebars are the admission to navigate intentionally and freely. It is possible to change direction, gear, and speed, to follow whims, to react upon possibilities, to break away from the beaten track, or race against everything and everyone on the road. With intensified awareness I sense every obstacle and change in the quality of the track below me. Always and prior to the presence of my conscious will I give meaning to the motto: "I pedal, therefore I am." Many things can be questioned, but one thing is beyond any doubt: in the beginning there was real motion and not just the symbolic motion of my thoughts as I carry out sedentary office work. Unimpededness is our primary state.

The scant security provided by the rubber's tiny point of contact marks the outer skinny limit of the body. The human body expands beyond its borders, it becomes more intense, amplified, and it engages in muscularly demanding, exploratory high-speed processes. But even with a 170–180 heart rate and hard pedaling the body sits quite still, possessing an energy surplus to enjoy, think, and regain power for the return to my non-biking life. The bicycle is a life-giving paradox.

The thing is mute, but humanity is talkative. *Homo sapiens* is the living species, but its being is not solely what it is by nature. Being human is to be changeable biology, equipped with a flexible and learning brain, said to be taking form according to the things we do, experience, and reflect on. In spite of different inevitabilities like the history of evolution and the law of gravity, human nature is not determined, nor is the human body simply a load. When the neuronal couplings that concern the bike are grounded and formed in the brain, the synapses are influenced by spatial interpretations, the sensual quality of rough rides, the linguistic exchanges in a group of tense riders heading towards the final sprint, the appraisal of new asphalt with no hole. This happens via the muscular conquests through which you become aware of the power you possess, the future performances, and the options to which the roads of the world might invite you. We are doomed to search for meaning. We can't help ascribing sense to things and events while we swiftly move sitting on slim gel-filled saddles, calm and stoic on steel, aluminum, or carbon frames.

New times are coming up in the Occident. The recent Danish "civilized" winter gives us the possibility to exercise on bikes in February. In the old, cold days when "real" men rode bikes, this was impossible. My silhouette paints the landscape with a 50-meter oblong, changing, and unpredictable shadow. It "interferes with" stonewalls, furrows, and bushes. The shadow cannot be fixed. And it creates droll patterns. The pictures are inscribed on the retina. They will never be exhibited in the Louisiana Art Museum in Humlebaek, Denmark, even though it is situated close to home and my riding grounds.

Campagnolo *Ti Amo* (I Love You)

My thinking ego is inseparable from my body, and the roads of the Earth are not objectively existing and materially phenomenal "out there" in the world. Through my cycling, my legs devour these roads. I ride a white and red steel Schrøder stallion, a traditional and proud bicycle brand made at Bernstoffsvej in Hellerup, north of Copenhagen. Having a 102 cm inseam I *had* to buy a custom bike. No stock frames on the WWW were big enough to fit my body.

My life is a life among and with things. I am flown and spoiled by good, solid, Italian-designed Campagnolo components. My consciousness is embedded in things and my cognition is incarnated in a restless body. My *being-in-the-world* is transformed to a *body-on-a-cycle-in-motion*, being able to do more than it knows. My identity is in a process of becoming, an "inter-being" between the bike, the experience, and an ocean of interpretations. To cycle is an extended, mind-stimulating rendezvous with and in nature. Free and age-independent joy awaits us. After a bike trip you're enriched and have become another. Our existence gets qualified via the feedback processes that our own doing brings about. Cycling offers and invites us to edifying and devotional doings: exercise and training – over and over again – exercise and training.

We whizz through a world, we belong to and have it within ourselves when we sense and grasp it. One bikes fast because one bikes fast. The will to speed is its own foundation and explanation far beyond contemporary health messages and the dominating and sickly dread of mortality. Muscle power and wellbeing become fused within the cyclist, who doesn't have to accept being forced to argue for the right to play and ride. In plain words: we ride because we ride and want to ride.

Other times I go for a cozy and silent ride along the coastline with my 7-year-old son, Albert Cornelius. The bike provides us with opportunities to engage different types of performances and ways of being together. These expressions cannot be captured or grasped by a utilitarian approach. The demon between the "useless" (leisure time, autonomy) and the "useful" (working hours, purposefulness) breaks up and vaporizes.

Frankly speaking, if you talk about cycling in utilitarian terms, you haven't understood anything at all.

The "primitive" bike technology fosters an *ecstatic-present-attentive* being. One might say that I become bigger than my own flesh (and I'm big enough at 6 ft. 7 in.!), when I fasten metal and rubber to my skin and extend my outer extremities. The racing bicycle is the extension of the body and the ultimate skin of thought and awareness. The intense presence of the winds of the world, whistling through hairy arms and legs, gets sharpened: the gaze anticipates the activation of the brake; ominous gravel and holes are sensed faintly, even before they are within eyesight; the eyes in the back of one's neck become suspicious of an overtaking elite biker in the imaginary rear-view mirror, and they can "see" a menacing car in a switchback behind me while I, in perfect balance and with no fear, I descend Mont Ventoux – the windy, white mountain – at 80 km/h. The mountain is waiting for you, but it is no laughing matter, nor is it there in order to be criticized. As the German philosopher Peter Sloterdijk proclaims in his newest book, *Du mußt dein Leben ändern*: "You don't mess with mountains, either you climb them or you leave them alone."[1] Emanating from the mountains of the world, a vertical imperative hits the horizontal human. Pull yourself together, leave the lowlands, and conquer the summit!

A Multiple Bombardment of the Senses

The senses and the parts of the bike work together while the thoughts are sent on a heavenward flight through a past that is never over and done with because they open a future that has already begun. Let me illustrate by taking you on different rides. Still on Mont Ventoux, I come to reflect upon the giant performances of bike heroes of times past on this bald mountain, and I catch a glimpse of a cross, erected to commemorate the departed, dope-laced English rider Tom Simpson. At the foot of the mountain the warm wind is felt. It rumples the blond hair on my sun-tanned legs and arms. I can sense every one of them, but it's impossible to fix on them singly: the hairs are countless small ripples in low tide above the sea bed of the skin. Trickling sensual qualities are pure invitations to reopen the multiple and often dormant sensuality "files"; then, there are the beech trees in full green flower, hyper-yellow under the firmament, full-blown, pungent white elder

STEEN NEPPER LARSEN

bushes after rain and dizzy, descending, and winding roads on the beautiful west coast of Corsica; a bewildered wasp stings you under your jersey while you ride at 65 km/h somewhere in Zealand; a dog ravages another dog in a remote spot in Sardinia; an invisible but audible skylark way up high, and the taste of an awful, half-melted, and all too greasy chocolate bar swallowed down with nearly boiling water (I swear) from the bike bottle on sub-tropic Losinj, in the northern part of Croatia's archipelago.

Sounds, tastes, odors, visions, and touches are not simple add-ons. When they are activated at the same time, the result is a kinesthetic and tactile surplus. "The tactile-kinesthetic body is a body that is always in touch, always sounding with an intimate and immediate knowledge of the world about it."[2] Imperceptible but appreciable, the gaze dwells on the sounds and the tastes. The odors become fused with the world of my ears and eyes. Just try to follow a twisting vertical path via lava-encircled roads overlooking the blue sea of the southern Mediterranean, through flocks of sheep and blossoming vineyards, all the way to the end of the road at 1,880 m. Up there, with clear skies, you can envisage the snow-covered volcano, Mount Etna. On the way to the top you pass by a small town called Linguaglossa, a marvelous double-name (both words mean "tongue"). It sounds a bit redundant, but it might be a declaration of love to language, which makes it possible for us to think, talk, and write about the refreshment cycling brings. Occasionally the Sicilian roads are insanely steep and too straight, the reason being that newer floods of lava have encroached on parts of the steep curves. On the other side of dizziness and blissfulness one can race down the mountain and celebrate a dip in the sea and a cold beer in the shade. Maybe there is only one absolute limit and one rule for racing cyclists: after 6 liters of water, a bunch of energy bars, and many a banana, the body is crying out for real food ... and a beer.

The now transforms to more than a point on a time line. I become embedded in an extended moment: time falls off its hinges and achieves fullness. To bike is to see the homogeneous, low-quality clock time vanish. Still, the bike computer and the heart-rate monitor glow with the newest figures from the fringes of my performances. No saint or purist, I am paradoxically quite calm, thrilled by a will to accelerate and an indomitable but futile lust to construct some real mountains in Denmark. Vanity, play, and the will to excel become mixed. The biker is as transparent and naked as his fellow non-cycling creatures, the baboons with the big red-purple bottoms in zoos.

Riding a bike exposes and opens you up to a never-finished exchange between the bombardment of the senses, the importance of shifting contexts and climates, your vivid bodily sensuality, and, not least, your afterthoughts.

Liberté Vélocipédique

Where there is a body on two wheels somewhere in the world, a new being comes into existence. Practice makes perfect. Surprising self-acknowledgment and knowledge of the surrounding world become possible through perpetual cyclical exercises. Don't forget the telling fact that the women's liberation movement in the twentieth century demanded the right for women to ride bicycles in trousers, with an open and curious gaze through landscapes and towns, as French anthropologist Marc Augé writes in a high-tension tribute to "l'autonomie vélocipédique" in his miniature manifesto, *Éloge de la bicyclette*.[3] The standard bike is a piece of low tech, the nearly divine epitome of sustainability, and an absolute necessity when cities have to be rethought and redesigned without the present profusion of noisy, space-hogging, energy-consuming cars. In contrast to several years of gasoline-engine monotheism and tailpipes, the cycling polytheism will open many possibilities of otherness and gliding unpredictable processes.

The trajectories and escape routes of the bike do not follow the flows of commodities, money, and capital. The mobility of the bicycle reminds us much more of the old dream of being as free as a bird in the sky than a trip on the discounted economy expressway that commodifies our experiences. The freedom of the road contains much more than the modern, "creative," self-managed workplace and is much richer than the freedom to consume. It is possible to accelerate your bike, but at full throttle it ironically contributes to a deceleration of the accelerating technologies of globalization. Cycling is an alternative version of rich global communication. Far from the Net, the PC, and the mobile phone, the life-world of the cyclist becomes saturated by the senses and overwhelmed by the physical and climatic reality "out there." No protective walls or phantom digital walls to lean on. Below the helmet one is happy to enjoy what other people might consider to be empty and dead commuting time to be traveled at the speed of light, while moving from destination A to destination B. The biker knows that the road taken is more important than the

STEEN NEPPER LARSEN

end goal. It's no fun getting there if the getting there is deprived of quality and lacks adventures. The Germans have an expression for this fertile *time-in-between*: *Zwischenzeit*.

In the autumn of 1991 my wife and I cycled 4,000 km from Denmark to Sicily, loaded with a heavy waterproof trailer bursting with luggage, down through Germany and over the Alps. My part of the caravan weighed 90 kg, including my almost 2-year-old daughter Olivia. The journey lasted three months. With the most comfortable gearing – 32 teeth, both front and rear – we managed to "go" 5 km/h – the minimum climbing speed before overturning – over Julier Pass (2,284 m) in southeast Switzerland. My wife Ida, with her old overloaded black Centurion racer, passed the summit with a clenched fist raised against the sky and a triumphant expression on her face. Today Olivia is taller than Ida, and has long since left behind her wagon and self-invented safety belt, but I'll never forget her mom's proud and relieved gaze that day in Ober Engadin.

Eudaimonia, or profound wellbeing, is an opportunity within reach of the cyclist. Adventurous bike trips and amateur bicycling can be interpreted as a collective and mutual rejection of telereality, and concurrently an attempt to overtake and wave farewell to the scandalous doping "culture" in professional cycling. But devoted bikers are no longer minimalists. Cycling is not just a modest form of transportation for people of limited means, but often a demanding, high-tech, and expensive affair. The "seepage" of quality from the professional upper-class biker and inventive designers to the "people" apparently happens faster than ever, and the bicycle has become an upgraded, individualized, customized, and personal investment phenomenon. Really, one is liable to "go berserk" if the bicycle is damaged or stolen, because one is damned close to losing a precious limb – maybe worse for some.

Settling of Accounts – In the Long Run It Is Impossible to Cheat

First, you have to do your best when you climb a hill or race against the wind. Then you are able to harvest the benefits while you descend or welcome the subsequent breeze. When you bike there is an intimate relationship between becoming and doing. In the long run it is impossible to cheat on a saddle. Theologians have a phrase for that: deed of justice. Very seldom is there a direct and balanced 1:1 rate of exchange between the advantages and disadvantages while you bike. Neither roads nor weather respect democratic claims to equilibrium. The immediate, unmotorized, and unmediated relationship to the world makes the cyclist an unprotected guest in the landscape, exposed to wind, climate, and topography. Once, in northern Slovenia, I felt cheated and disappointed. After a long climb in the high mountains, the way down from the top was a nightmare: every single switchback became a layer of broken cobblestones, transforming what was supposed to be a pleasant ride downhill into a horrible brake festival.

Of course it is possible to cheat, arranging for comfort-giving circumventions. Your loved one can take the car and let you off at the peak of Col du Galibier so you can fly 50 km down the mountain to Bourg d'Oissans, in the lowland at the foot of the legendary Alpe d'Huez. It is possible to sit on the wheel and benefit from the invisible protective windshield formed by your fellow riders all day long, overtaking them in the sprint just over the line. You can choose to ride only in sunshine or with tail winds – or you can take a rest along the route, stopping at a store or a restaurant to eat and drink till the end of the day. In the end, bike riding has a fair amount of ups and downs over a cyclist's lifetime, with hints of grace, the hard claims of the landscape, and shifts in the weather oscillating unpredictably.

Cycle Speech

The social speech patterns of bicycle communication are primarily audible or gesticulatory. One shouts to the group: "gravel," "pass inside," "look up, right," "car" – and when you utter "hole" or "grating" you point at the road, so everyone behind you can see the dangerous spot. Wildly parked cars, unexpected opening of car doors, alarmed horses, wild dogs, pedestrians, joggers, abruptly stopping vehicles, or trucks coming from side roads foster mutual hand signals – if unsignaled, such dangers result in panicked chain reactions throughovut the group. One communicates using silent elbows and raw muscle power. Not without foundation, neuroscientists label humans as the animal that possesses "we-intentions," and the "bike-we" is intensely preoccupied with the security of everyone in the group. Ruthless riders are criticized in no uncertain terms, and new riders who happen to move carelessly, even

STEEN NEPPER LARSEN

though they don't intend any harm, are patiently but firmly inaugurated into the unwritten rules of bicycling.

When not on a "social ride," it happens once in a while, before the start of a race or after an interval in a training ride, that riders do enjoy exchanging real sentences. In the hilly, sunny, and friendly Tuscany landscape I joined the Empoli bike team, riding a whole Sunday in 2002 with 30 unknown and talkative Italians. In 2006 we were two Danes who lined up with a local group of riders from Millau – a bike mechanic, a banker, and a butcher – and they showed us "hidden" bike roads in the gorgeous and mountainous landscape around the River Tarn in southern France. The basic cycle semiotics opens for richer forms of communication. Sundays are great days for cultural bike exchanges – you just have to check out where meeting points are situated for unknown yet soon-to-become friends (in small towns, just ask some young sporty chap). Over the years you come to practice the capacity to speak bike-Italian and bike-French: *piano* for take it easy, *salida* for a tough climb, or *à bloc* for going all out. After a brief introduction you join the rhythm of the team and take your leads – then you are welcome across national borders, gender, and age. Exercise is open for everyone, happiness cannot be excluded from an open system, but the access comes at a price: you have to maintain your speed!

A Trembling Experience

To cycle is to open the landscape with your own force, such as on the Spanish island of Mallorca in the spring. Already on the climb to the small town of Caimari the first raindrops fall, but the asphalt is so miserable that it forces us to find and avoid potholes and rocks. On top of that, there's no risk of getting cold spinning at a reasonable cadence, least of all when a flock of accelerating Germans comes from behind and you try to catch on to the last two fast and shapely female riders. But from Lluc towards the tough mountain lakes and further up through the dark, nasty, and fridge-like tunnels to Puig Major the rain intensifies.

Per, Jens Ove, and yours truly, devoted members of Kronborg Bicycle Club (Elsinore), continue undaunted. If we turn back now, we are very faaaaaar from the pleasant shower at the hotel and the rich and fata morgana-like evening supper.

The advice imparted at lunch break fades out of sight – the other fellow riders were much better weathermen than we are. They anticipated that the clouds over the mountains in the northwest would be filled to the edge with fountains of water. They were right. But we repressed their intuitive experience with grandiosity. Now reality bites, and we are more alive than alive, we fight like dogs, sense ourselves, every muscle fiber is tightened. Every cell in our bodies freezes and longs for home.

An aging triad of a combined 170 summers has chosen to set out for this lunatic ride in these wet elements, deliberately and voluntarily. One wonders – perhaps *you* don't wonder. These existential hardships and profound questions do not seem to bother us, because the end result is this: you have to pedal, you have to trample hard!

It's pouring down, the roads become far too slippery, and our bike shoes are filled with water. A well-known feeling arrives: the toes are transformed to imprisoned and cold aquarium fish. These outer extremities might still be a part of my body, but they go through a metamorphosis and become alien elements. The glasses ought to have wipers, but unfortunately they don't. Three times on different summits in the asphalt landscape I wait 10 minutes for my noble followers.

The trio is far away from home and convenient urban civilization, while the cold, this uninvited and powerful opponent, dominates the otherwise smiling and calm spring day. We are frozen to the marrow. The dramatic existential transformation is not just a pleasant narrative – it is damned real and unquestionable.

A Descent – Living Up to Its Reputation

We feel as if the descent consumes more time than the ascent. Not really a big surprise as we have to use the brakes all the way to prevent skids and falls. Gradually the field of vision is occupied and overrun by fierce and violent rivers. We ride softly through the curves, the velocity is ridiculous. My right eye stings, it is damned close to being completely closed, and my ungovernable hands shiver so much that I start to imagine the front fork or even the bike frame has broken, just like my old winter bike broke recently in a remote and very inconvenient spot in Denmark after it had served me well for 50,000 km.

I have been transformed to a 2-meter-long preposterous icicle, out of place and out of time.

In vain I try to change gears, but none of my fingers function any longer. Both hands seem to be welded to the rubber of the brake grips. Formerly unknown chemicals from my helmet enter my eyes and for a short while I have to stop and dry them off using my drenched hands and the remnants of my gloves. In the end I have to take off my glasses, which means that a half-blinded person will take the rest of the trip downhill.

Finally we are below and spot a restaurant that has a cold, oversized, and desolate-looking glass veranda attached, as if a savior dressed up in awful architecture has created a rescue plan for us. But we do not care about aesthetics; in here it is much warmer than out there. And we can order hot black tea, as well as steaming coffee!

A Collective Shiver

Next scene: I shiver so much I am unable to lift the cup without spilling it. Speechless and dumbfounded I gaze at Per and Jens Ove and to my great surprise they have exactly the same problem with their sense of balance. Weird images stick in my memory, a swathe of absurd scenarios. Three adult males have to bend their necks towards the table and try to let their slurping mouths meet the edges of the cup and the restorative fluids. We try to communicate but the assertions sound like senseless crap beyond comprehension. We witness mutual speech defects – maybe we've all got Alzheimer's like a flash from a dark and rainy sky? Have we been attacked by a collective fit of the shakes? Who knows? We just know that we are freezing cold while we acknowledge that the table becomes filled with small streams of tea and coffee – embarrassing, but there's nothing we can do about it. The table begins to resemble the streets out there in the lowland, in miniature. The streams of water are mirrored on a smaller scale. But it is warmer in here so we order another life-giving round, and slowly, very slowly, we regain our strength. Paradoxically, this incident and the regeneration made us both 10 years older and younger in record time, so the final result is that we are the same as we used to be ... just a little bit more oddly supercooled and unmistakably frisky. Through these kinds of unintended physical and metaphysical transformations, life gets challenged and enriched by cycling.

Fortunately the rain decreases, while we tear towards the last climb and the many small curves south of Soller. The cars hog the tunnel for themselves, and we prefer to try to regain the heat while we ascend the empty road heading for Palma. We succeed and when we at last can celebrate a well-earned bath at the hotel, the cyclometer proclaims that we have ridden 152 km this Thursday in April 2009. On the other hand, it doesn't tell us anything about the troubles and obstacles on the road. We have to listen to our vivid memory and create our own narratives. The work of the biking man's legs and muscles are his embodied thought.

NOTES

1   Peter Sloterdijk, *Du mußt dein Leben ändern* (Frankfurt am Main: Suhrkamp, 2009), p. 251 (my translation).
2   Maxine Sheets-Johnstone, *The Roots of Thinking* (Philadelphia: Temple University Press, 1990), p. 16.
3   Marc Augé, *Éloge de la bicyclette* (Paris: Payot, 2008), p. 29.

CHAPTER 4

UNLEASH THE BEAST

Technology and the Time Trial

Getting Out of the Gate

Of all the cycling disciplines, none are so pure in their intent than that of the time trial. There is a timeless honesty of propelling a bicycle as fast as possible. There is also is a stark yet sadistic attraction to the lactic acid-infested, hyperventilated effort required in breaking your personal best, beating your friends (or your enemies) over that fixed distance. It starts with your nerves and the word "go" and rewards you with oxygen debt and collapse.

The first time trial within the Tour de France took place in 1934 and saw its competitors using the same bicycles they had been racing on for nearly four weeks. A hundred years on and the riders currently have extremely aerodynamic machines designed to minimize air resistance, using unique wheels, riding positions, and strategies but still ultimately seeking the same goal: more speed for the result of less time.

This act, whilst simple in concept, contains a paradox. The discipline is about one sole rider against the clock, yet this is tainted by our need to manipulate our machines to help provide this result. The second we alter something technologically, the purity and subsequently the validity of the result are surely called into question. A new disc wheel, maybe a tweak of your saddle height, and then suddenly the conditions of your trial have been changed. The result may be a faster time, but was it the rider or the changes made to the setup that provided the improvement? If time trialing is really about the rider against the clock, we seem more willing to accept a consequentialist view, in that it's not the journey but purely the end result that matters.

There have been attempts to immunize this paradox from the arena of play. One of the most well known within the concept of time trialing is that of the "athlete's hour record." This is the maximum distance achieved by a sole rider over the duration of one hour. It uses a bicycle that has dropped handlebars, spoked wheels, and appears devoid of innovation in its design. This machine is defined by strict rules of the cycling's international governing body, the UCI (International Cycling Union), which define a bicycle's general technical specifications.

Up until 2000 the hour record had been broken 37 times since the turn of the nineteenth century. It had been achieved by many of the most notable champions cycle sport has ever produced. These included the Tour de France's creator Henri DeGrange through others such as Fausto Coppi in the 1940s, Eddy Merckx in the 1970s, and Miguel Induráin in the 1990s. The record had been increased from the informal record achieved in 1870 of 22.785 km (14.18 miles) up to 56.375 km (35.1 miles) in 1996. At this point, the UCI felt that a bicycle's engineering was potentially going to influence the result. In an act to preserve the purity of the endeavor, it decided to heavily define the bicycle's specification for any subsequent record attempts. This included restricting wheel spoke count (and banning discs), removing the use of aerobars, and emphasizing a strict double-diamond frame format with no unusual tube sections. The hour record evolved into the "athlete's hour" instead. The previous interpretation then became known as the "ultimate hour record" but was never endorsed or attempted again. This restrictive approach to sports technology was an attempt to isolate the physiological ability of the athlete in the saddle rather than arguably becoming an alleged race amongst engineers in the lab.

My concern is that the UCI has taken the stance that time trialing is about man against the watch rather than man *and machine*. It is argued that this definition is unclear, as riders are not assessed on their individual power output in a laboratory. Technology will always have some impact in sport. The UCI's philosophy of minimizing this impact, whilst noble, is fundamentally misguided.

Presently, as someone who leaves the soul between a start and finish click of the stopwatch (more often than he should), plus as a fan of any "toys" that make me go faster, I'll make a case that the athlete's hour record should be dropped and restored to its pre-2000 "ultimate" definition. This is based on the suggestions that the concept is unfair, has eroded interest in the discipline, and that the bicycle's identity can make a positive contribution to the sport.

Banking the Turn in Pursuit of Fairness

The UCI does have responsibilities that extend far wider than our needs to remain interested in the record. An interesting sport should also fundamentally be a fair one. Without this, imbalances are created, meaning some riders are disadvantaged and that any record is meaningless and irrelevant. There's no pleasure in a rigged game whereby only some can have access to resources or equipment that others simply don't or can't have. Parity between athletes in sport is ultimately about the "level playing field." Sports philosopher Andrew Holowchak has attempted to explore the implications of performance enhancement when using sports technology.[1] Holowchak argued whether assistive technology actually contributes anything extra of value to a sport. For example, have the use of belts in weightlifting (which assist with the stability of the lift) actually provided anything more of interest? Yes, the weight attained has increased, but with every athlete using them, the competition's philosophy effectively remains the same. This suggests that all things being equal, the adoption of new technology is of no significant value. I argue, though, that just because a playing field in its core sense remains level, raising this to a different point can create increased excitement for both its participants and its spectators. If this were not the case, road cycling technology would not have seen the acceptance of gears, lighter wheels, and dual pivot brakes. All of these have allowed riders to climb higher or more severe ascents faster, providing exciting spectacles within road racing.

The use of performance-enhancing drugs is a useful analogy for bicycle mechanical enhancement. Drug type is determined as illegal under the World Anti-Doping Code if it violates two of three philosophical and scientific criteria. These are whether a drug is *performance enhancing*, is *dangerous to an athlete's health*, or *violates the "spirit of the sport."* Using the outlawed Lotus bicycle ridden in 1996 as an example, although the machine personifies a bull-charging aesthetic of speed that scythes time, the health of the cyclist is not actually violated any more than with any other design. The question is therefore whether the Lotus technology is against the spirit of the sport and ultimately unfair. The World Anti-Doping Code does offer some suggestions when considering chemical enhancements as to what violates the "spirit of a sport." These include a list of values such as honesty, health, excellence in performance, character, joy, commitment, courage, respect for rules, and community. If any new technology is transparent in its nature and contribution to a sport is fair (both in terms of cost of and access by a rider), none of these values is infringed. As a result, the spirit of time trialing would have remained in place under its "ultimate" format. It would only have infringed one of the criteria using the World Anti-Doping Code framework, in that it enhances performance.

If issues such as cost and access are integral to discussions relating to fairness, it is prudent to understand what this fairness is being judged by. The UCI's default for the athlete's hour has been suggested (although not in writing) as Eddy Merckx's 1972 hour record ride. But actually, this is not as fair as it first appears. Merckx's record was actually performed at high altitude in Mexico, and he had prepared over six weeks using an oxygen chamber. As a result, he would have benefited from lower air resistance when he rode plus specific preparation in the runup to the attempt. None of this came cheap, which means that any rider trying to best Merckx would either have to come up with the dough or start at a big disadvantage before he'd even swung his leg over the saddle. Both Chris Boardman's and Graeme Obree's later attempts in the 1990s were performed at sea level. I strongly suggest that ethical debate should not only be applied to the bicycle's design, but ultimately also be expanded to the entire nature of the attempt. The 1972 record obtained by Merckx was not performed under the same conditions as the majority of the athletes who have tried since that point. As a result, the UCI athlete's hour legislation either needs to be tightened up considerably or is fundamentally unfair. In fact, it seems to be merely cosmetic, restricting only the more aesthetic aspects of the athlete's hour record.

Athletes seek every performance advantage allowable within the rules. Merckx sought his advantage by optimizing geography and climate, and subsequent athletes have adopted a similar mentality. Boardman in his 2000 record was sprayed in alcohol to help keep him cool, on top of having his helmet modified with closed vents to help smooth its airflow. Ondřej Sosenka in his 2005 attempt allegedly used flyweights within the wheels to help maintain momentum once he was up to the desired speed. Michael Hutchinson in his documented failed hour record attempt was allowed to use wheels that had bladed spoke sections. Boardman stated

🚲 BRYCE T. J. DYER

within the video documentary *The Final Hour* that he was unconcerned about whether the UCI would ratify his equipment or not.[2] If that were truly the case, then his helmet's more aerodynamic design over that used by Merckx was of no relevance, yet he still chose to use it anyway. Why else would he have done so if not to get any advantage he could over Merckx's mark within the rules? Obree, around the same time, literally had officials running onto the track to stonewall his charge for technological progress (although he was not deterred enough to warrant both running them through and then subsequently creating several more innovations). The UCI's interpretation of the hour record, then, fundamentally goes against the nature of athletes: we are supposed to go faster, longer, harder, or higher, but then the UCI takes away our ability to express this.

Philosophically speaking, the concept of the athlete's hour record seeks to limit the variables other than those differences created by the athlete's natural ability. The problem is that some riders have constraints not determined by choice. Physically, all of us are different. Chris Boardman was approximately 5 ft. 8 in. tall whereas Sosenka was around 6 ft. 3 in., thereby being considerably taller. Both riders would need different handlebar widths and crank lengths. This would affect and change both the ergonomics and the aerodynamics of their attempts. A technological and physiological inequity is evident with every athlete who races a bicycle – it is just a question of how much it is tolerated. The UCI didn't really want the aerodynamic drag being manipulated; however, this comes with the turf – I've done enough races to see riders half my width come sailing through. This is a factor of any machine in motion – mechanical or biological. According to aerodynamist Chester Kyle, Induráin had to produce around 10 percent more power to beat Obree, mainly because he was just bigger in stature and had limitations as a result to just how aerodynamic he could get on a bicycle. The record therefore should not be based on the pursuit of athletic primacy – it can't be – but rather should evaluate what benefits this technological pursuit brings to the sport. The concept of intergenerational comparison between riders is difficult to implement short of fixing the location and the bicycle used. This is not possible. This level of restriction would satisfy the record's aims, but in the end it shows how ethical decisions are easier to implement in offices, on paper, than in the real world, where one has to push on those pedals.

New technology is inherently expensive, limited in supply, and expertly informed, which to some could be unobtainable or unfair (if it is unobtainable, it is not a matter of being "seen"). Holowchak suggested that unfairness is a fact of life. As a result, the UCI's attempt to simplify the bicycle seems justified to limit as many of the contributing variables as possible to the record. If we accept variety and a degree of unfairness with ourselves biologically, what is the point in our bicycles being allowed to be immune to this? The wider interest in the technology should not be at the expense of the attempt's credibility. However, this need based on the equity of both cost and access to any technology is not as straightforward as it appears. The record attempt requires two bicycles present, so every athlete has to finance two identical bicycles for any attempt (one of which probably sees no service whatsoever). All of the post-1996 attempts have still involved unique, expensive, and not commercially available machines. Interestingly, more elaborate time trial designs are commercially accessible, and arguably affordable. Ironically, I propose that a bicycle has become exotic equipment in itself due to the continued technological evolution since 1972.

Counting Down the Laps in Pursuit of Happiness

I would like to pursue not just how technology is viewed generally *per se*, but also what technology embodies to us as users. Stephen Bayley, in his book on "product," would suggest that any product we use creates identity, character, and therefore interest.[3] While the UCI's philosophy is honorable in its defense of fairness, has its restriction of technology effectively made us – the fans – lose interest in the record because we are not allowed to be interested in the products we use? Boardman's Lotus bicycle used in the 1992 Olympics and later in the 1996 hour record is arguably as famous in many respects as its rider. It completely redefined what a bicycle was in appearance and tradition. It changed what were the accepted norms in frame design, and instead focused entirely on its needs – speed. Likewise, Obree's unconventional approach to aerodynamics led to the creation of an unusual riding position on two separate occasions. This created interest and ultimately an iconic design. His "Old Faithful" bicycle caused controversy yet created romance within the record. Obree steadfastly refused to conform to the conventional, creating record-breaking machines using parts from old washing machines whilst the UCI repeatedly banned his innovations. He came up with increasingly radical solutions to generate greater speeds as the UCI came up with increasingly complex rules to stop him.

The problem is that the UCI, by focusing on the rider and then stringently defining the bicycle, has made the hour record lose its identity. Knobbly tires in mountain biking or the drop handlebar in road cycling had provided their respective disciplines with a defined character. The inception of disc wheels and aerobars during the 1980s had achieved much the same with time trialing in the hour record. Take the technology away and you then become solely reliant on the identity of the rider. In a sport less popular than, say, football, this will diminish interest – not enhance it. The bicycles used by the athletes can become icons, such as Obree's "Old Faithful" fabricated by his own hands, Boardman's wind tunnel-refined "Lotus," and Miguel Induráin's resplendent "Sword."

To deny the role of technology is to deny the evolution of the bicycle in the first place. When Baron Von Drais developed his predecessor to the modern bicycle in 1817, this was to solve a particular need, in this case more efficient transportation. In effect, his creation was either a solution to a design need or an application of invention. As time has gone on, the bicycle developed key characteristics such as increased performance, comfort, and the ability to traverse a wider range of terrain and topography. The racing bicycle, which has more recently diversified into a specific time trial bicycle, has taken its form based on the concept of the pursuit of *speed*. The UCI, by restricting the use of the racing bicycle, undermines this concept. The identity of the bicycle is suppressed and then lost when both the evolution and innovation of the technology are restricted or ignored.

The bicycle is a functional product but its use has wider-reaching possible applications. Sports footwear has demonstrated the ability for utility-led products both to transcend their intended market and to enter the public psyche. Denim jeans (originally invented by Levi Strauss as an effective hard-wearing garment for ranchers) demonstrated the ability to transcend their origins by moving into everyday fashion. Within cycling, mountain biking and BMXing demonstrated that allowing a product-based identity to develop creates social cultures and movements. This in turn will expand interest and bring new athletes to the sport. It's a tall order for time trialing to have sex appeal: can you picture a 1970s-style bicycle being ridden around a circular track alone capturing the public's imagination? Taking the example of mountain biking, its challenge is the ability to traverse difficult terrain. The technology and aesthetics of its equipment fulfill this accordingly. Time trialing, while originating as a solitary endeavor, evolved as a tandem of human *and* machine against the watch. This type of cycle sport should reflect the aims and values proper to its discipline, such as speed and aerodynamic efficiency, not be isolated from them. If Formula One officials were like their UCI counterparts, the F1 guys would still be doing laps of Monaco using horses, carts, and whips.

What I am defending here is that the time trial bicycle is not a feat of engineering. To do so denounces the humanistic influences on products when we use them. I would argue, therefore, that the modern bicycle is a feat of *design*. Design is driven by a need but is also the balance of both the humanistic and technological factors. It is not whether bicycle X is more aerodynamic than bicycle Y, but how the rider engages with that bicycle's innovations. Design innovation can provide pleasure, even happiness, but also discomfort and unsettlement. As a result, you'd better have a backup plan (or a very comfortable saddle) to deal with this.

Emotive effects in product design can be connected to what technologist Ernest Braun referred to as "the pursuit of happiness."[4] Braun emphasized that worthwhile technology should reduce pain or anxiety to the user. Braun also stated that new technology should be driven by progress and that this technological progression effectively then leads to user happiness. On this premise, acknowledging that an interaction between user and product takes place, the UCI's attempts to withhold technological progress ultimately withholds a promotion of happiness. I suggest that this may help understand why the athlete's hour has waned in interest with only a handful of attempts since Boardman's in 2000. The lack of any interesting toys to play with by the riders throws the focus onto the riders' personalities themselves. With respect to the riders who have attempted it since this point, none will be remembered as icons of the sport. In fact, the majority of the most successful cyclists of the past decade have not pursued it. In the 1990s there were well over a dozen attempts, including world champions and Tour de France winners. Ethically, it may not be prudent to acknowledge the bicycle's role in the record, but it does provide a greater potential for interest. A utilitarian view is therefore proposed. If reviewing the legislation creates greater interest, or as a result more of us get out there in the saddle or watch the sport on TV, then for the good of cycling surely this must be encouraged.

The act of design provides its own challenges to the hour record, which can involve emotive responses like happiness. It is not merely a question of a new technology being introduced to an athlete but whether the interaction of that technology (be it ergonomic or psychological) engages with the individual. In 1993, Obree's hour record attempt obtained an unlikely feat of athletic excellence. This achievement took the unusual occurrence of two attempts within 24 hours. During his first attempt, he used a refined evolution of his original bicycle design, which had been built by the Lotus bicycle conceptualist Mike Burrows. Obree undertook his hour record attempt, failed, only to return the next morning. He then attempted the record again, this time using his original prototype. On this occasion, despite having exerted himself less than 24 hours beforehand (and using arguably a technologically more inferior product), he broke the record. Granted, that's a hardcore, painful way to pursue happiness.

In his book *Designing Pleasurable Products*, Patrick Jordan defines four pleasures as a framework for people – product relationships.[5] These are:

1. Physio-pleasure: the feeling from the senses such as touch, taste, and smell.
2. Socio-pleasure: products that facilitate social interaction.
3. Psycho-pleasure: an emotional reaction to a product's use.
4. Ideo-pleasure: the values created through use of the product.

Use of a product or technology generates either a positive or a negative response from its user. In Obree's case the emotive result of using his own bicycle contributed positively to his attempt. Taking Jordan's framework, this would have been the tactile feel of using his own machine (physio-pleasure), and both his reassurance of using his own bicycle (psycho-pleasure) with the reinforcement of its use (ideo-pleasure). This effect is unique to the athlete and therefore entirely relevant to the concept of the hour record being the athlete's individuality. At the end of the day, Obree went back out and tried again using his original bike. He could have tried again using the newer one, yet opted not to. This to me suggests a very personal connection to "Old Faithful" that stretched beyond one of just technological innovation.

There is a risk, however: does acknowledging the need for happiness and then granting increased freedom in product design become harmful to competitive cycling? Bioethicist Andy Miah referred to one of the implications of doing so as *deskilling* and *reskilling* a sport.[6] In some cases, new sports technology innovations have provided an advantage over the sport itself. In essence, this is a new equipments introduction allowing a sport to become easier to perform because of the technology rather than because of the athlete's actual ability. *Polara* golf balls changed the conventional dimple pattern on the surface, which then reduced the likelihood of slicing or hooking. "Spaghetti strung" tennis rackets in the late 1970s increased the size of the "sweet spot," making it easier to return the ball. However, a time trial bicycle does not power itself. It is not a technology that assists us to make the act of cycling easier. With deskilling Miah suggested that a technology's impact reduces the skill of a sport. In this case, did aerodynamic aids such as disc wheels or the aerobars in the hour record reduce the skill required? Absolutely not. Riding the bike was still performed by the same use of a fixed wheel and the same physiological action. The only change is that the speed achieved in a successful attempt is marginally greater. With reskilling, Miah's suggestion was that a technology's introduction would allow a sporting act to be achieved more easily. Again, with the bicycle this is not the case. The definition of the time trial is a maximum effort undertaken over a distance or duration. As a result of this, the very nature of time trialing has not changed in its premise: having been seen at several roadsides searching for what remains of my lungs after a time trial, I can assure you that *maximum* effort is still *maximum* effort. Therefore, returning the hour record to the ultimate format is fundamentally acceptable.

The UCI is concerned with the implications of equipment innovation evident in other technologically influenced sports such as motor racing. In this case engineers and team finances are significant to the eventual result. However, this doesn't advocate the need for banning it outright in cycling, but rather the need for continual vigilance. It's a question of balance. What we need is to make technological innovation possible *à la* Graeme Obree, and to keep this ability viable to all of us. This would prevent the recent situation with the Great Britain track cycling team, whose bicycles were not commercially available and whose skinsuits were shredded after the 2008 Olympics to stop competitors from obtaining the same advantage – which, by the way (ironically), the UCI failed to prevent.

The Bell Lap

Presently, I have focused on the argument that the interest generated by embracing technology is worth more to the sport than the maintenance of a concept that was fundamentally unfair in the first place. We cannot go back to a baseline set in 1972 short of making all riders use the same location, the same machine, and the same unappealing outfits – for goodness' sake. Even then, training methods have also continued to change. Progression is inevitable. Setting fairness based on the more aesthetic values of what a bicycle should look like rather than what it actually does is no more ethical or fairer in principle than any technological innovations that have arisen over the last four decades.

The UCI has seen the role of technology as something that diminishes the achievements of the athlete. The contribution of the technology is still offset by the requirement of turning the cranks to provide forward motion. A bike may be ultimately more aerodynamic than another, but this is merely a fraction of what is required to break the hour record. Chris Boardman demonstrated that it eventually boils down to the man when he claimed the ultimate hour record in 1996 and then took the athlete's hour in 2000. Cream will ultimately rise to the top.

Technology offers something more to a sport. It provides an identity that helps image, brand, and character. Design provides both interest and happiness for those who participate in or are spectators of bicycling in all of its forms. Some bikes have become icons in their own right as their innovation and form are celebrated. These technological "celebrities" transcend their context into the wider sports community, providing interest and excitement.

Ultimately, to achieve the UCI's ethos of the athlete's hour, a record should be a rider's own application of power to the pedals. Despite this, no record is judged on the raw power output of the athlete in a laboratory. With this in mind, debating or denouncing sports technology is meaningless. To ignore its influence within the athlete's hour record is both futile and flawed in concept. Time trialing isn't about a person against the clock; it's about the pursuit of speed. In other words, loosen the legislation and let us unleash the beast.[7]

NOTES

1 M. Andrew Holowchak, "Ergogenic Aids and the Limits of Human Performance in Sport: Ethical Issues, Aesthetic Considerations," *Journal of the Philosophy of Sport* 29 (2002): 75–86.
2 *The Final Hour: Chris Boardman's Quest for the Hour Record*. DVD. Bromley Video, 2003.
3 Stephen Bayley, *Taste: The Secret Meaning of Things* (London: Faber & Faber, 1991).
4 Ernest Braun, *Futile Progress: Technology's Empty Progress* (London: Earthscan, 1995).

5 Patrick Jordan, *Designing Pleasurable Products* (London: Taylor & Francis, 2000).
6 Andy Miah, "New Balls Please: Tennis, Technology, and the Changing Game," in *Tennis, Science, and Technology*, ed. S. Haake and A. Coe (Oxford: Blackwell Science, 2000), pp. 285–92.
7 See www.atisbos.com/cyclingandphilosophy for further reading suggestions.

VELO VIRTUES

CHAPTER 5

WARM UP

A Test of One's Mettle

The first lightning strike shakes my pots and casts shadows through the open end of my tent. Leaves become tentacles, branches become arms. The spark bounces off my crankset like an angry eye and I blink, as though that might save me.

I'm alone in the campground, my tent pitched not 20 feet from the Lochsa River in northern Idaho. The evening had been cloudless, hot and still, but the night has no such attitude. I just want to sleep. After 115 miles in the saddle with a touring load, a sad dinner of potatoes and apples and nuts – too much white food, give me a peach, or a leaf of spinach – I just want to sleep. I worry over little things, like the $30 in my wallet and the small roll of food stamps that needs to last me another 400 miles.

I don't know what time it is, other than the night, sometime after sunset and before sunrise. Sweating on top of my sleeping bag. Mosquito bitten, but too hot to slip inside. The lightning isn't helping. Between strikes there is only the rush of water and the absolutely black night. The metallic scent of the light's arc. I wait – for sleep, for its interruption. Another strike, this one nearly on top of me, the crack rippling over my tent. I'm on my elbows now, watching the show, trying not to blink. I wait for things to move, but all I get is the shimmering afterburn of images: my orange panniers, my bicycle leaning against the scarred bark of a tree, wild berries, skeletal branches, and the purple edge of my tent. I don't know why I expected a world of black and white. Maybe

I wanted the reprise of old movies I had watched as a child, the comfort of imagination.

The first rustle of brush surprises me. The wind? Raindrops? A wet snort punctuates the darkness, my tentflap bends and presses against my shoulder. I don't feel alone anymore. This isn't the show I want. My heart refuses to find its rhythm. The next strike finds me ogling a bear's tongue as he tosses his head and slaps my bicycle with his paw. Is this the circus? The thunder is more in my chest than the sky. I can't hear anything past the thump-thump that fills my tent. The bear is 10 feet away, sniffing at my panniers.

I run the inventory in my head. I don't have any food packed away. Maybe a candy bar. Maybe the scent of yesterday's hotdog stuck to my handkerchief. Some dirty clothes that even I don't want.

The sky quiets. No light. Just his sounds, scrounging, scuffing the dirt, slapping my chain. Make noise, I think. With what? My pots are outside, at the firepit. I have a belt. What am I supposed to beat the buckle on? My head? Light a match. A match? That's so stupid I almost laugh, but I'm voiceless. I know, because I test my mouth, try to whisper, and all I get is a pathetic croak.

My bicycle scrapes down the tree. The chain rattles against the frame. Another bolt of lightning. I watch a claw catch my left pannier, strip the bag off its rack, and heave it toward the water. My bicycle flips onto its front wheel. Stands there, as the light flickers off. Blackness, but for the blue afterburn on my eyes. The bear gets bigger when I can't see him, and I allow that, because something has to justify the thump in my chest.

I can smell him now. Hear him nosing through my pots. Then nothing. Not a sound. A few big drops thrum on the tent, in the stiff brush near the shore. The river. The dim roll of the storm, slipping away down the valley. Blackness.

I just want to sleep, or I want the sunrise, but I'm not going to get either. I lie awake, listening harder than I ever have. I don't know how long until first light. I don't know what I'm supposed to do, so I continue to lie as still as possible. An hour. Two. I don't have a watch. Damn my romantic streak, foregoing time. I think I can make out the ridge on the other side of the river. Is that light in the sky? Color seeps into the landscape. First color. I can rise. I will myself to sit up. Wipe the sweat off my chest. I just want to be on the road.

My bicycle is splattered with mud. One pannier is gone. I peek around the tentflap. I'm alone. I feel alone. The trail to the water is a narrow dirt track. I need to rinse off. I have to move. The light gives me courage. I step from my tent and make my way to the water. I kneel on the shore, cup the cold water in my hands. I find my pannier, lying atop the brush, fully intact. I smile at my fortune. I search, but see no sign of the bear … except for the paw print at my knee. I decide to eat my breakfast on the road.

CHAPTER 6

LANCE ARMSTRONG AND TRUE SUCCESS

 Is Lance Armstrong a "success"? The question may seem absurd. After all, Lance has won the Tour de France a record-breaking seven consecutive years, been named the Associated Press Male Athlete of the Year four times, survived cancer against long odds, helped and inspired millions through his Lance Armstrong Foundation and Livestrong website, and in the process achieved fame and fortune. As we'll see, however, Lance would arguably *not* be a success on many classic philosophical accounts of success and human achievement. What lessons should we draw from this apparent clash? Should we reject the philosophical theories, or rethink our view of Lance? What is "success"? What counts as a truly successful human life? In this chapter we'll explore these questions by looking at both classical and contemporary theories of success. The best account of success, we'll argue, is what contemporary philosopher Tom Morris calls the 3-D Approach to Life. On this view, Lance Armstrong is a remarkably successful individual.

Classical Theories of Success

Ancient and medieval philosophers didn't speak of "success" in exactly the way we use the term today, but they did explore certain closely related ideas. For instance, Greek philosophers from Plato to the beginning of the Dark Ages endlessly debated what *eudaimonia*, or ideal human flourishing, consists in. Similarly, Roman and medieval philosophers discoursed at length about what they called the *summum bonum*, the "highest good" or "final goal of life" that human beings could pursue and achieve. Neither of these concepts is exactly the same as our present-day idea of success. In particular, both *eudaimonia* and the *summum bonum* imply a kind of ideal or exemplary level of achievement that isn't connoted by our idea of success. (A gambler can be "successful" if he wins only slightly more than he loses. Not so with a Russian Roulette player, obviously.) But with suitable modifications, we can certainly ask what classical and medieval philosophers saw as a "successful" human life.

In ancient and medieval times, the five most influential theories of success were offered by Plato, Aristotle, Epicurus, the Greek and Roman Stoics, and Christian philosophers such as Augustine and Thomas Aquinas. Plato taught that people "flourish" – are ideally or supremely successful – when they achieve wisdom and virtue, and live as spiritual and god-like a life as is humanly possible.[1] Aristotle believed that humans flourish when they maximize their human potential, particularly their capacity for purely intellectual contemplation, which Aristotle saw as the highest human capacity.[2] Epicurus believed that pleasure is the only good in life and that some pleasures are qualitatively better than others. He thus maintained that a successful human life is one that involves as much high-quality pleasure and as little pain and anxiety as possible.[3] Stoic philosophers such as Seneca and Epictetus taught that virtue is the only good and believed that people flourish when they lead lives of stern and self-reliant moral excellence.[4] Finally, Christian thinkers such as Augustine, Boethius, and Aquinas held that a completely successful human life is one that involves perfect service to God and obedience to His will on earth, followed by eternal bliss and union with God in the next life.[5]

Is Lance a notable "success" in terms of any of these theories? It would seem not. Religion plays a big role in both Plato's conception of a flourishing human life and the Christian view of the *summum bonum*, and Lance has made it clear he's not a religious person in any conventional sense.[6] Nor does Lance score well on Aristotle's intellectualist view of success. Though Lance is no dummy and in fact is a very smart athlete and businessperson, he would hardly claim high marks in contemplative theorizing.[7] How about the Stoics' ethical theory of success? Though he has plenty of good moral qualities and has done great good through his charitable activities, Lance himself admits that in ethical terms he's "not storybook material."[8] And if pleasure is the goal of life, as Epicurus believed, then professional cyclists like Lance are definitely in the wrong line of work.[9]

Clearly, none of these classical and medieval conceptions of human flourishing gels with the way most people think about success today. Some of the theories are just plain implausible. Few people would claim, for example, that only hedonistic pleasure-seekers are successful, or that only moral or intellectual paragons are. Moreover, all the theories assume a kind of one-size-fits-all view that ignores or downplays the role of individual choice and fails to recognize the *multiple* ways in which success in life can be achieved. For a more adequate and up-to-date account of success we need to turn to more recent philosophers. And no contemporary philosopher has done more to illuminate the concept of success than Tom Morris.

Morris's 3-D Approach to Life

A former award-winning philosophy professor at the University of Notre Dame, Tom Morris is today one of America's leading public philosophers and most active business speakers. In books such as *True Success: A New Philosophy of Excellence* (1994) and *The Art of Achievement* (2002), Morris offers a theory of success that we believe to be compelling. Morris calls his theory the "3-D Approach to Life." It consists of the following three principles, each of which begins with the letter "D":

- Discover your positive talents.
- Develop the most meaningful and beneficial of those talents.
- Deploy your talents into the world for the good of others as well as yourself.[10]

According to Morris, these principles lie at the core of all true success, whether in business, sports, personal relationships, or life itself. To see why, let's look more closely at the 3-D Approach and how Morris defends it.

Morris contrasts two visions of success – "outer success" and "true success." Outer success is generally measured in terms of the "four markers of

GREGORY BASSHAM AND CHRIS KRALL

public success": money, fame, power, and status. True success, by contrast, is measured in terms of "personal growth and positive contribution."[11]

The idea that money, fame, power, and status are the touchstones of success is the greatest case of mistaken identity in the modern world, Morris believes. How often have we seen the unhappy lives and self-destructive behavior of the rich and famous splashed over the tabloid pages? Two thousand years ago, the philosopher Seneca observed the same phenomenon in ancient Rome, leading him to remark that "the 'successful' are least successful."[12]

Why is the single-minded pursuit of the four markers of public success so often self-destructive? The basic problem, Morris says, is that "the concept of 'enough' can't get a grip at all" when these markers are pursued as primary aims. Morris writes:

> The dissatisfaction of acquisition feeds on itself in an almost cancerous way. The more you give in to it and try to satisfy it, the more it can grow, until it is literally out of control. ... What amount of money is enough? Everyone I know who has a little wants more. But it's even more interesting that everyone I know who has a lot wants even more. A reporter once asked John D. Rockefeller how much money it takes for a man to be happy. He replied, "A little bit more than he's got."[13]

Researchers have found that the happiest people tend to be those who have close, supportive personal relationships and believe that they are contributing to a better world.[14] As Morris notes, there is a natural human tendency to strive for excellence and to find fulfillment in intimate relationships and service to others.[15] For these reasons, success cannot consist in chasing externals such as money, fame, power, or status.

True success, Morris believes, is a process of inner growth and positive achievement. It is a lifetime process of self-examination, personal development, and active service in which we seek out our positive talents, cultivate those talents, and deploy them in the world to achieve both our own good and the good of others.

This is an attractive theory of success for a number of reasons. First, unlike the classical and medieval theories we examined earlier, it recognizes that there are many ways of living a successful life. There is no single standard – intellectual, moral, or religious – that serves as a litmus test for successful living. As Morris remarks, different "people have different talents, different skills, different experiences and different dispositions. We should also expect to have interestingly different forms of success."[16]

Second, Morris's account acknowledges that success isn't an all-or-nothing thing. Success comes in degrees. One person can be highly successful in discovering, developing, and deploying his positive talents. Another may be only moderately successful in these pursuits.

Third, Morris's 3-D Approach recognizes that humans are social animals. Humans naturally find fulfillment and shape their identities in communities. As Morris says, the "greatest fulfillment comes from our relationships to others and comes most deeply when we are living in creative, loving service to those other people."[17] Consequently, any satisfactory theory of success cannot focus simply on self-centered ends. The good of the community must also be considered.

Finally, Morris's theory correctly recognizes that success isn't entirely a matter of personal choice. There are objective as well as individual standards of success in sports, business, teaching, medicine, and in life itself. A person can achieve all of his major life goals and still not be a success. If my main goals in life are wholly trivial – like amassing the world's largest collection of Alberto Contador bobble-head figures – then I can hardly consider my life a success even if I accomplish all of those ends. Even more, if my life goals are seriously unethical – like running as many cyclists off the road as I can with my bad-ass pickup – then achieving those goals won't make me a successful person. In fact, most philosophers would agree that accomplishing unethical ends will actually make a person's life go worse.

Morris's 3-D Approach is thus a plausible and helpful way to think about success. But are there important forms of success that it fails to capture? Some people, after all, may not have much of a chance to discover their positive talents, or to develop or deploy them. A paraplegic may be fully aware of her positive talents but be unable to develop them. A potentially world-class cyclist may have discovered and developed his talents but not get a chance to use them because of his moral obligation to take care of a needy child or an elderly parent. As Seneca said,

> We are all chained to [fate]. ... All of us are in custody, the binders as well as the bound ... some are chained by office, some by wealth; some weighed down by high birth, some by low; some are subject to another's tyranny, some to their own. ... All life is bondage.[18]

Or in the words of the Roman philosopher Epictetus,

> Remember that thou art an actor in a play, of such a kind as the author may choose: if short, a short one; if long, a long one; if he wishes you to act the

🚲   GREGORY BASSHAM AND CHRIS KRALL

part of a poor man, see that you act the part naturally: if the part of a lame man, of a magistrate, of a private person (do the same). For this is your duty, to act well the part that was given to you; but to select the part belongs to another.[19]

In short, it seems, not everybody has the time, opportunity, or freedom to discover, develop, and deploy their most meaningful and beneficial talents.[20] Sometimes the best we can do is to play well the cards we've been dealt. But can't merely doing your best – whatever your life circumstances or role-responsibilities – result in significant forms of success? In fact, don't life's greatest triumphs often occur *in the face* of the greatest challenges and limitations?

Absolutely. But such cases are consistent with the 3-D Approach, Morris contends. Even a paraplegic or Downs' Syndrome child can discover his talents, such as the talent for love or for communication, develop them and deploy them, on his own personal scale. And a loving mother who gives up her promising musical career to care for an autistic child should not be seen as sacrificing "her success" for the good of her child. Rather, in these circumstances, her success is achieved and expressed through the success and well-being of her child. In asking, therefore, what a person's most "meaningful and beneficial" talents are, it's important not to think of those talents in any narrow utilitarian or self-centered way. Sometimes our 3-D duties to ourselves are overridden by particular obligations, where we are called to discover, develop, and deploy other talents, such as talents for love and service.[21] The 3-D Approach acknowledges such cases, and in fact helps us to make sense of them.

So is Lance Armstrong a success? Having rejected a number of false theories of success and identified what we think is the correct view, the 3-D Approach, we're now in a position to answer this question. Lance is a success if he has (1) discovered his positive talents, (2) developed the most meaningful and beneficial of those talents, and (3) deployed them into the world for the good of others as well as himself. Let's see how he measures up.

Lance Discovers His Positive Talents

Lance grew up in Plano, Texas, raised by his young single mother, Linda, who often struggled to make ends meet. His father, Eddie Gunderson, walked out on the family when Lance was less than 2.

In North Texas in those days the competitive sports were football and football. Lance tried football, but he wasn't very good at it. But he was determined, he said, "to find something I could succeed at."[22] So at age 11 he tried running and found it was something he *was* good at. Soon after, Lance also began swimming, and while not instantly successful, he persevered and rapidly became one of the best swimmers for his age in the state. To get back and forth to swim practice Lance rode his bike 10 miles each way, and found that this was another endurance sport he was good at. At age 12 Lance found out about a triathlon event, which he entered because "it was all the things I was good at."[23] He won that one, then another, until he was ranked nationally and earning $20,000 per year in high school. Lance's strength was the bike, and in his senior year he was invited by the US Cycling Federation to train with the junior national team.

Did winning come easy to Lance? In fact, it didn't. As we noted, Lance was not a very good swimmer when he first began. He even had to swim with the smaller kids until he learned proper technique. But he knew how much of himself he had to give and he was willing to do so, even if he looked silly or if he had to find his own way to swim practice. The same grit showed through in his early days of triathlon and club cycling. Lance had a fierce determination to win, boundless self-confidence, a positive attitude, a rare genetic ability to efficiently process lactic acid,[24] an extremely high VO_2 max, and a remarkable capacity to endure suffering. As he later said, "If it was a suffer-fest, I was good at it."[25] Before Lance finished high school, he knew he wanted to be a world-class athlete. Developing his talent was going to be up to him.

Lance Develops His Talents: Pre-Cancer

The next phase of Lance's journey began when he raced for the US national team under Chris Carmichael. Carmichael knew Armstrong had the ability, but it took Lance some time to learn that raw talent would not always be enough. In his first big race, against his coach's instructions, he built up an early lead only to get blown away at the end. Not long after, in his first pro race, he finished dead last.[26] Lance had yet to learn that race tactics and teammates were critical parts of the winning formula. Likewise, it took him some time to figure out that his brash Texas attitude was not making him many friends among his teammates and competitors. Learning and practicing these more holistic aspects of racing were part of the development process that soon enabled Lance to begin to win big races and make a name for himself.

It became clear that Lance's greatest talent was as a bicycle racer after he won the US amateur championship in 1991. He followed up with some great results in this early stage of his career, finishing second in the US Olympic time trials in 1992, winning the prestigious US Triple Crown (and a million bucks) in 1993, winning a stage of the Tour de France in the same year (the youngest man to ever do so), and topping it off with a victory in the 1993 World Road Race Championship. By most measures, Lance had a successful career now. He wasn't the best cyclist ever, or even the best in the world, but he was earning loads of money and leading the arduous but exciting life of a top road-racer. However, Lance didn't just want to be successful, he wanted, as he told Coach Carmichael, "to be the best."[27] To accomplish this goal, he realized that he would have to "find a new kind of strength, that inner strength called self-discipline."[28] He would need it for what came next. For in October 1996, Armstrong was diagnosed with a rare and usually fatal form of metastatic testicular cancer that had spread to his lungs and brain.

How did Lance face this challenge? Once he and his doctors had determined the extent of his illness, he knew it would be a battle to get to the finish and beat this opponent. From the Tour de France, he knew that the stamina required just to finish is "not unlike the stamina of people who are ill every day."[29] He faced this setback as he would preparing for a big bike race – by assessing the situation, assembling his team, laying out a game plan, and finally by enduring the suffering his aggressive treatment plan involved without losing hope or quitting. He intensively researched treatment options and learned to know what his blood markers were, and he used those numbers to motivate himself. "They were … my yellow jersey," he later wrote.[30] Each day when he heard his new counts he would envision himself on the bike, with his race director telling him how far ahead of the field he was. By the end of 1996, he was through with his brain surgery and the chemo, but the recovery process was slow, and he would not return to racing until 1998.

Lance Develops His Talents: Post-Cancer

Lance has always said that "cancer was the best thing that ever happened to"[31] him. On a purely physical level, it helped him lose 15 pounds – a huge difference on Alpine climbs. More significantly, it redoubled his determination to be the best cyclist ever, gave him a new appreciation of the fragility and preciousness of life, and sparked a powerful new sense of a "mission to serve others."[32] After surviving cancer, Lance said, "I saw my life whole. I saw the pattern and the privilege of it, and the purpose of it, too. It was simply this: I was meant for a long, hard climb."[33]

When Lance returned to racing in June 1998, he didn't fare particularly well in the one-day classics, as he had lost the swagger and anger that had propelled him to victory in these types of races in the past. But he had a new focus, and that was the Tour de France. In 1999 he skipped the spring classics (as he would continue to do) in order to focus solely on the big race. Lance's formula for preparation was not unlike his battle against cancer – he became a walking textbook of facts, calculations, and computer graphs, all designed to "get me to the finish line faster than anybody else."[34] He didn't eat without first measuring his food, so he knew exactly how many calories he needed to burn. He became, as he put it, a "geek" on the scientific aspects of training and the biological effects on his body. He also assembled his team, which included not only his US Postal Service teammates, but also his wife, Kristen. She became his support crew, which allowed him to remain 100 percent focused on preparation. Lastly he trained, putting himself through extreme punishment. "I rode, and I rode, and I rode. I rode like I have never ridden, punishing my body up and down every hill I could find."[35] He rode in all weather, typically seven hours a day, slogging through sleet and snow in the Alps when most of his Tour competitors were relaxing in the off season. By July 1999, Lance was ready to take on the world.

Lance Deploys His Talents

Lance and his US Postal Service team entered the 1999 Tour as major underdogs – almost no one expected them to win.[36] Lance won the first stage by setting a new course record, and once in the Alps built a lead he would not relinquish. He won that year's race by over seven minutes, his largest margin of victory in a Tour ever. It was a great comeback victory not only for Lance the cyclist, but also for Lance the cancer survivor and for all such survivors. "I hope it sends out a fantastic message to all survivors around the world," he said. "We can return to what we were before – and even better."[37] And return he did. When it was all over, Lance had won a record-breaking seven consecutive Tours, winning 25 individual stages and 11 time trials.

Cancer changed Lance so profoundly that he now sees it as the single most important event in his life. Before cancer, while he was successful, he admits he was not really giving his best effort. Post-cancer, Lance began to feel that he had a higher sense of purpose – that it was no longer his "role in life to be a cyclist. Maybe my role was to be a cancer survivor."[38] Through his struggles and successes, Lance hopes to convince people "to reconsider their limits,"[39] to show them that "we are much better than we know."[40] In 1997, he started the Lance Armstrong Foundation, with the goal of helping people affected with cancer. He wanted to give cancer victims hope, to help them "fight like hell, just like I did,"[41] and demonstrate that cancer can become "a route to a second life, an inner life, a better life."[42] To date, the Lance Armstrong Foundation has raised over $250 million to support cancer awareness and research.[43] As a result of his philanthropic activities, Lance has inspired and empowered millions. In fact, according to author and former professional triathlete Brad Kearns, "no athlete in history has used his celebrity to do so much good."[44] While Lance was unsuccessful in his attempt to win an unprecedented eighth Tour de France at the hoary age of 37 and a half (finishing a remarkable third behind Alberto Contador and Andy Schleck), his high-profile comeback attempt has raised new awareness and enabled his cancer foundation to hit new fundraising highs.[45] Much to his credit, when it became clear that Contador was the stronger rider, Lance subordinated his personal goals to the good of the team.[46] Without question, therefore, Lance has achieved that inner growth and outer service that marks a successful life. According to Morris's 3-D Approach to Life – or any reasonable standard of success – Lance is an extraordinarily successful human being.

NOTES

1   See, for example, Plato, *Republic*, 580; *Phaedo*, 64ff.; *Apology* 30b.
2   Aristotle, *Nicomachean Ethics*, 1177a.
3   Epicurus, *Letter to Menoeceus*, reprinted in *Greek and Roman Philosophy after Aristotle*, ed. Jason L. Saunders (New York: Free Press, 1966), pp. 51–2.
4   Cicero, *De Finibus*, Book 3, IX; Diogenes Laertius, *Lives of Eminent Philosophers*, Book 7, LIII; Seneca, Letter 76, in *The Stoic Philosophy of Seneca*, trans. Moses Hadas (New York: Anchor Books, 1958), pp. 208–15.

5 Augustine, *The Morals of the Catholic Church*, ch. 15; Boethius, *The Consolation of Philosophy*, Book III, X; Aquinas, *Summa Contra Gentiles*, Book 3, ch. 37.

6 Lance Armstrong with Sally Jenkins, *Every Second Counts* (New York: Broadway Books, 2003), pp. 96–103 (hereafter *Every Second*).

7 Lance admits that he's never been much interested in self-examination (*Every Second*, p. 25) or books (Lance Armstrong with Sally Jenkins, *It's Not about the Bike: My Journey Back to Life* [New York: Berkley Books, 2001], p. 88 [hereafter *Bike*]). For a discussion of Lance's cycling and business smarts, see Brad Kearns, *How Lance Does It: Put the Success Formula of a Champion into Everything You Do* (New York: McGraw-Hill, 2007), ch. 6.

8 *Bike*, p. 3. Lance admits, for example, to having been cocky and disrespectful in his early cycling career (*Bike*, p. 52). Nor would he claim that his love life has been pot-hole-free (*Bike*, p. 80). He strongly denies, of course, persistent doping accusations.

9 Someone once asked Lance what pleasure he got out of riding a bike for six or seven hours a day. " 'Pleasure?' I said. 'I didn't understand the question. I didn't do it for pleasure. I did it for pain" (*Bike*, p. 88).

10 Tom Morris, *Philosophy for Dummies* (Foster City, CA: IDG Books Worldwide, 1999), p. 311.

11 Tom Morris, *The Art of Achievement: Mastering the Seven Cs of Success in Business and Life* (Kansas City: Andrews McMeel, 2002), p. xxii.

12 Seneca, Letter 124, in *The Stoic Philosophy of Seneca*, p. 261.

13 Morris, *Philosophy for Dummies*, pp. 309, 308.

14 See, for example, David G. Myers, "Want a Happier Life?" Available online at davidmyers.org/Brix?pageID=46.

15 Morris, *Philosophy for Dummies*, p. 313.

16 Morris, *The Art of Achievement*, p. xxii.

17 Morris, *Philosophy for Dummies*, p. 313. Or, as the philosopher Ralph Waldo Emerson puts it, "[E]very talent has its apotheosis somewhere. … [H]eaven reserves an equal scope for every creature" (Emerson, "The Uses of Great Men," in *The Complete Writings of Ralph Waldo Emerson* [New York: William H. Wise & Co., 1929], p. 336).

18 Seneca, "On Tranquility," in *The Stoic Philosophy of Seneca*, p. 93.

19 Epictetus, *Enchiridion*, sec. 27, trans. George Long, in *The Discourses of Epictetus with the Enchiridion and Fragments* (New York: A. L. Burt, 1929).

20 Mother Teresa's oft-quoted remark, "We are called not to be successful but to be faithful," may reflect a similar insight.

21 Morris, personal communication. (On file with the authors.)

22 *Bike*, p. 21.

23 Ibid., p. 23.

24 Daniel Coyle, *Lance Armstrong's War: One Man's Battle Against Fate, Fame, Love, Death, Scandal, and a Few other Rivals on the Road to the Tour de France* (New York: Harper, 2005), p. 52.

25 *Bike*, p. 23.
26 Ibid., p. 50.
27 Ibid., p. 49.
28 Ibid., p. 64.
29 *Every Second*, p. 4.
30 *Bike*, p. 141.
31 *Every Second*, p. 7.
32 *Bike*, p. 151.
33 Ibid., p. 197.
34 Ibid., p. 219.
35 Ibid., pp. 221–2.
36 With the exception of five-time Tour de France winner Miguel Induráin, who predicted Lance would win.
37 sportsillustrated.cnn.com/cycling/1999/tour_de_france/news/1999/07/25/tour_final/.
38 *Bike*, p. 151.
39 Ibid., p. 158.
40 Ibid., p. 267.
41 Ibid., p. 152.
42 Ibid.
43 www.livestrong.org/site/apps/nlnet/content2.aspx?c=khLXK1PxHmF&b=4913573&ct=5990503.
44 Kearns, *How Lance Does It*, p. 1.
45 John Leicester, "Armstrong on Comeback: 'We Have Already Won,' " *USA Today*, July 3, 2009. Available online at www.usatoday.com/sports/cycling/tourdefrance/2009-07-03-armstrong-column_N.htm.
46 "This is a team sport," Lance commented. "I think now is the time for me to put my chances aside, and focus on the team." Quoted in "Final Climb Puts Contador in Lead," Wilkes-Barre *Times-Leader*, July 20, 2009, 2B.

CHAPTER 7

LEMOND, ARMSTRONG, AND THE NEVER-ENDING WHEEL OF FORTUNE

Perhaps the most important issue concerning the topic of heroes in contemporary American society is whether or not we still have them.
Athletes and the American Hero
Dilemma, Janet C. Harris, PhD

Heroes and Quasi-Heroes

For centuries heroes have existed as an integral part of our society representing the human potential. They are personified in mythic tales, folklore, and figures brought forth from generations past. Often maintaining traits of rugged individualism and strength of character, they have outlasted other elements of cultural evolution and influence. Heroes are created both by the desiring masses and by their own personal challenges. "But whoso is heroic," Emerson reminds us, "will always find crisis to find his edge."[1]

During the mid-twentieth century with America fresh on the heels of World War II and unprecedented economic and mass culture expansion, we endowed a certain universality to the popular hero figure. War heroes, captains of industry, politicians, and religious leaders emerged out of this period. Yet the promise of a *postwar manhood* somehow betrayed those in search of heroics. After we had defeated communism, explored outer space, and suffered through the unpopular Korean and Vietnam wars, there appeared few quests with universal appeal. The very concept of "hero" was put to question. Within half a generation society was looking for "heroic" figures in such new social movements as feminism, civil rights, environmentalism, and a generic resistance to anything status quo. During the 1960s a hero was anybody who had a cause, waved (or burned) a flag, and was on the six o'clock news. Now, in the midst of the *Information Age* where no public act goes undocumented, the definitions, roles, even the existence of heroes are subjected to close scrutiny. What has developed since is a kind of hero-identity shift. We now have *quasiheroes*, celebrities, entertainers, event-makers, and professional athletes, who rarely fit the ancient folkloric definition of a hero – that of aiding others in need, often while placing themselves in harm's way during the everyday course of life. Mostly they are noteworthy for their notoriety; famous for being famous.

It is difficult to say why we have deified athletes amongst this group of popular icons. The rational mind must not confuse contributions to humanity with great physical feats; saving a young life from saving a late-inning homerun. But we do. Perhaps professional sports exist, in a roundabout way, only to create heroes, to keep our mind off of more important things – that old Karl Marx adage about being the "opiate for the masses." Would it follow, then, that the sporting game has replaced other platforms of hero and myth-making? In the increasing secularity, fragmentation of the family, and general malaise concerning failed *leaders of men*, are we driven to the celebrity athlete simply because we lack hero-options? Is modern professional sport the best way to produce myth as described by mythologist Joseph Campbell as "the secret opening through which the inexhaustible energies of the cosmos pour into human cultural manifestation"?[2] Or can we look toward a simulacrum where the tail (tale) is now wagging the dog and heroes are made under our own noses because, lacking true leaders from established social institutions, all we have left is ESPN 2?

I first met Lance Edward Armstrong in June of 1986. It was at the President's Triathlon near Dallas, Texas, and his mother, Linda Mooneyham, had taken him out of his Plano High School class early on a Friday afternoon to attend the event.

"Do you mind keeping an eye on my boy for me?" I vaguely remember her asking a group of us older athletes. "This is his first race against you all professionals." We looked at each other as Mooneyham went off to register her 15-year-old son for the race while the young

Armstrong sat confidently adjusting his goggles or his derailleur or the way he held himself up against the world. Lance was brash, talented, and unaffected in the presence of some of the best endurance athletes in the world. I liked him immediately.

I had won my second Ironman World Championship in Hawaii the year before and was voted Triathlete of the Year. The title and resultant accolades, however, I wore like a misanthropic crown of thorns, never feeling comfortable in the role of champion. Lance Armstrong, as a cocky junior ditching his afternoon Woodshop class, seemed early-destined to embrace the rights, privileges, work, and duties inherent to the hero's role. Without a driver's license the kid carried himself as if he owned a fleet of dealerships. There was nothing pseudo or quasi about the teenager. With Lance, there was never ambivalence – you either understood him or you didn't, like him or didn't. The astute could see that he had something very old and wise inside of a very young body.

Quasi-heroes are created in large part by what German-born sociologist and philosopher Theodor Adorno labeled the *culture industry*. Capitalist industry manufactures and produces iconic figures for their own purposes. A new young star will simply supplement our notions of immortality while the aging athlete's lost luster in declining performance reminds us that we too shall someday pass. To see a 40-year-old center-fielder drop a fly ball is to witness ourselves at 80, out of breath, and struggling from a short flight of stairs. This is the tyranny of fame.

Still, we cannot summarily dismiss quasi-heroes as history has proven not only our need and desire for heroes, but also the import of their social function. From royalty to Robin Hood, heroes serve a purpose for social organization, politics, and individuals' creations of meaning. Heroes help us to know better who we are and where we stand in relation to others and the world around us.

Two-Wheeled Heroes

During the late twentieth century, elite bicycle racing produced several heroes of note. In the absence of Eastern bloc teams during the 1984 Los Angeles Olympic boycott, the US Cycling Team won nine medals, including four gold. Between 1983 and 1990, a charismatic blonde kid with a Huck Fin grin and the perfectly Anglo-French name of Greg LeMond won two World Championships and three Tour de France titles, two of which occurred after a 1987 hunting accident nearly took his life and left 37 shotgun pellets permanently embedded in his tissue. His come-from-behind-8-second victory over Frenchman Lauren Fignon in the final day time trial into Paris during the 1989 Tour is touted by many as one of the most thrilling moments in the history of modern bike racing. Then in 1999 Lance Armstrong won the first of his record seven consecutive Tours de France.

But even earlier in the late nineteenth century, bike racing, along with other rugged individual sports such as boxing and horse racing, had spawned some of America's first sport heroes. Based on the rising popularity of cycling as a form of recreation and new-found freedom, bike racing produced famous figures such as Chicago's German immigrant, Charlie Miller, who excelled at the famed six-day races; A. A. "Zimmy" Zimmerman, the first star of American cycling to reach international attention; and Marshall "Major" Taylor, an African American who won one of the country's first "world championships" within modern sport. Taylor had a near 90 percent rate victory in European racing, but he couldn't sit at a lunch counter in Birmingham, Alabama, or race in many American cities.

Illusions and Disposable Heroes

But where our society has made great advancement in racial equality, it seems our confusion of the terms *hero* and *celebrity* has caused us to see greatness as a kind of polysemic illusion where it is difficult to discern those who are *known for their wellknownness* from those who are heroes for being heroic. The primary suspect for this illusion is mass media. The world of sport, it seemed, was passing through the filter of the culture industry. And cycling's heroes were not immune to the test. Was LeMond's victory an ornamental twist to some unfolding puzzle of modern heroes?

Our desire for immediacy in all things has prevented the slow distillation of the hero that folklore and oral tradition offered. After LeMond's first Tour de France victory we wanted more. Just to be sure that it wasn't a fluke, we told ourselves. And after the second we invested in him as something and someone beyond quasi, the possibility of a ... legend.

The passage of time which might establish a truer hero as they sustain their role would also deny the celebrity hero as they burn too hot and then implode. If we invest in someone, we used to think, they owe us something in return. But fame is fleeting, as the cliché goes, and the concept of *disposable heroes* gains traction. Cycling fans hoped that LeMond's reign would become a Second Coming even as they looked for ways not to like a very likable guy.

But in the wings was the cocky kid from Plano, Texas.

Training and racing with a young Lance Armstrong was a study in directed intent – he knew what he wanted and seemed only to be testing the ways of achieving it; feeling his edges to find his center. Among the rank and file professional triathletes his reputation lay somewhere between cocky kid and gentleman phenom; much of it depending on if he liked you or respected you. For some reason, perhaps because I was older and had a young child, I understood him. But I also knew that as smart as I thought I might be, Lance was a very quick study and knew, in the words of the actor Gene Hackman, that "The difference between a hero and a coward is one step sideways."

Cycling's Identity Crisis

Between 1900 and 1984, American bike racing wallowed in relative obscurity. The Springfield, Missouri, native, John Howard, is better known for his 1981 Hawaiian Ironman Triathlon victory and his world land speed record on a bike (152 mph) than his participation in the 1968, 1972, and 1976 Olympic Games as a member of the US Cycling Team. Jonathan (Jacques) Boyer, the first American cyclist to compete in the Tour de France (1981), is better known for winning the Race Across America (RAAM) endurance cycling event (1985 and 2006) and for a guilty plea on a charge of child molestation. Yet, these cycling pioneers, unrecognized as they might have been, can now be counted along with other mythic and flawed heroes because we need human sacrifice and lines of athletic genealogy to connect the dots when we constitute our own paint-by-number past.

I remember when Lance decided to leave triathlon to try his hand at professional cycling. I tried to be ambivalent but there was a sense of loss; not like a child going off to make his way in the world but something more selfish as if his way of carrying himself in the world was something I had yet to learn from him. Both of us shared a kind of Camus-type metaphysical rebellion, steeped in early patriarchal tragedies. I felt an unspoken kinship to Lance on the basis of lost fatherhood. Lance's biological father had left his mother when he was 2 and he's called the man who subsequently adopted him and from whom he takes his superhero name "deceitful." My own father – the greatest hero in my life – died of cancer when I was 15, leaving seven children and a young widow to fend for ourselves. I didn't know it then but like twin stars on separate trajectories, we would be connected by the pathology of the evil crab constellation, Cancer.

The summer after our initial meeting in Dallas, Lance and a high school pal drove a barely legal Pontiac GTO out to Southern California and pulled the oil-leaking beast onto my perfect driveway.

"Get that piece of shit off my new driveway, Junior," I told him. Nonplussed, I think he took off a sweaty t-shirt and tossed it under the car before asking to meet our 6-month-old daughter, Torrie. "Where you living?" I asked him and his muted bud. "Right over there." He was pointing to an apartment complex 300 yards away. "Wanna be close to the epicenter if I'm gonna own this sport."

Heroes in the Midst – Too Many Choices

At 16 years old Lance Armstrong could never have known the circumstances that would come to shape his life and those he would in turn influence. Triathlon and cycling were just vehicles for him to achieve something, to make a mark, to deal with his own unique Oedipus. Endurance sport was, for Armstrong, an extension of his immutable will.

When Armstrong conquered testicular cancer to win one of the most difficult sporting events in the world, the foundational definition of folkloric heroes returned. Armstrong had slain the cancer beast and for everyone who has seen its evil up close, they now had a popular hero. If some kid from Texas could beat cancer and then win the Tour de France, we thought, then damn … we can slay our own dragons and be back at work on Monday. Skeptic philosopher David Hume suggests "the same principles naturally deify mortals, superior in power, courage or understanding and produce hero-worship."[3]

But what of our other cycling hero, Greg LeMond? Wasn't his return from a hunting accident to win the Tour also significant? There is conjecture as to why LeMond's fame never reached that of his younger successor. Perhaps it was a comparison of tragedies as if somehow a "hunting accident" is a less noble tragedy than *metastasized nonseminomatous testicular cancer*. Perhaps LeMond's earthy, Midwest approach to life was somehow considered less righteous than Armstrong's *Don't Mess with Texas*. Perhaps it was LeMond's Jamesian pragmatism set against Armstrong's Nietzschean *überman*. Some have suggested that where LeMond was surprised by his resultant mass popularity, Armstrong was not. LeMond lived in Minnesota, not exactly a hero-laden state. Texas had Davy Crockett and the Alamo and manly oil rigs. Minnesota had an NFL team named after a Norwegian country's settlers. But to hair-split the tyranny of fame is to ask, What is the end result? What difference will it make? LeMond's return from tragedy must be as personally significant as Armstrong's. The difference, perhaps, is that at the time, it did not represent (and then sustain) the same shared meaning as Armstrong's. Even though LeMond was the first American to win the Tour de France, how many of us can remember the first American luger to win a gold medal at the Winter Olympics?

> I remember when Greg LeMond came to San Diego for a bike show and there was a small dinner gathering for him. Instead of holding court or regaling in his then-lofty role, Greg sat in a corner and talked with a local shoe cobbler who was working on new materials for cycling cleats. Greg was at times gregarious, engaging, and goofy. He was the guy next door who made you laugh and was always working on some new idea or invention, some brilliant, some not so much. If I picked up the phone to call LeMond he'd call back in an hour and have some off-color joke to tell. It was almost as if he was too approachable to be thought of as heroic.

The Need for Heroes in this Postmodern Age of Reason

The story of the hero is often the story of the Individual, one of the key narrative themes in American history. Armstrong endowed that rugged yet refined aura like his fellow statesman and recreational cyclist, George Bush, Jr. But an emerging content-hungry New Media has turned iconic figures into celebrity stereotypes, causing a deep division in our national ideology. Can elite athletes who live insular lives from their young teens, who are coddled by a cadre of handlers, and compensated like kings, be considered "individuals?" Armstrong was the Outsider, working the fringe, doing it his way and up-ending a long-time love – hate relationship that American cycling had with the French cycling community. To an extent so was LeMond. But the lead from the pellets got him first.

When the Hero Faces Death

When heroes are discussed in the literature, often they are "conceived in a relativistic or idealistic fashion."[4] LeMond and Armstrong are, no doubt, both victors and victims of their situations. Campbell suggests that a hero must eventually make his return to society and assume his anointed role. But there is a price to be paid for living in that hallowed place. And how that fine is paid nearly defines mythic figures and men alike. Icarus' fate for flying too close to the sun still reminds us that though naïve, his act informed others of the dangers of hubris.

Within medical and sports circles there has been discussion on whether Armstrong's cancer survival (let alone his athletic success) was the result of his omnipotent will to power, fate, or arguably the best oncology team ever assembled. His autodidact quest to know his enemy and therefore destroy it has established his health and perhaps unfairly associated him with the dark rumors of performance-enhancing drugs. But as a result, Armstrong lives.

> I remember when we heard about Lance's diagnosis. He was a budding star in the cycling world by then and I was closer to my own competitive grave than cradle. Armstrong was living in Europe, speaking French, making a salary that was many times that of a professional triathlete's best years. He wasn't easy to get to. I followed his treatment through various connections in the sporting community and sent him notes and video from time to time. I'd seen real and deep cancer up close, felt its halted and indiscriminate breath. My own sophomoric skin cancers had taken more chunks out of my face than if I had fallen into a wood chipper. But cancer hadn't killed me like it had my dad. So I cheered for Lance, rooted for him because he was going to beat it the way that he'd done everything in his short life – by asking it to step aside. And if it didn't, he'd run right the hell over it.

Armstrong was John Wayne, a cowboy remolding a "foreign" sport to make it uniquely his. And uniquely American.

We are fascinated by the hero, such that heroes seem real enough or valuable to us and remain with the passing of war heroes and religious leaders and political figures. Higgs in referring to sport heroes suggests that the sports world disproves such assertions, and reminds us that "here the hero is alive and well. It is not a question of whether ... but what *type* of hero is popular at any particular time in history."[5] Sport heroes (or quasi-heroes) may offer us a popular vehicle in which to connect gods with mortal men. Moreover, popular athlete heroes offer us a personal reference. To hold the hero up to the light of social examination is to turn the lamp on ourselves. As we create and talk about heroes, they tell *us* who we are.

But Lance Armstrong wasn't simply telling us about ourselves. His message was one of the mortality of men. As with most things Armstrong, there was both his passion for success and strategy of knowing and control, a Foucauldian power/knowledge trip. Cycling pundits have argued that this trait, this need to control, is what grounds Armstrong, what connects him to many of us who want to regain agency in our lives as they spin out of our grasp. Lance was always the informed team captain calling the strategic plays.

LeMond, on the other hand, the boy-next-door, appeared to have seen the vicissitudes of a post-professional sports life get the better of him. Continued struggles with his health as a result of the shooting, a boom and bust ride with the fate of his LeMond Bicycle Company, rumored challenges to his marriage, his weight control, other failed business ventures, Armstrong played Percival to LeMond's Fisher King.

This wasn't medieval, though; this was what Anderson calls Philosophy Americana;[6] the love of wisdom bound for glory as folk musician Woody Guthrie might take us. So where LeMond had won and lost his Grail, Armstrong's former generalissimo-style was now tilting at a new-found humility. Was this post-cancer Lance the real man, we'd ask. The one that *needs* to succeed but never forgets that the battle goes on?

LeMond's struggle with holding his place in the genealogy of bike racing was the constant but indeterminate infection set against Armstrong's seven-year Tour *blitzkrieg*. Armstrong's cancer was in remission but few wanted to ask LeMond about the pellets bleeding lead into his system. Armstrong was hosting awards shows and LeMond was dropping his kids off at school. The two bristled and barbed in the press over seemingly small details.

After Lance started winning the Tour de France, it was hard to get to him. The man/kid was rich, famous, and busy. He was an A-List celeb hanging out with U2's Bono and the hyperkinetic comedian Robin Williams. But what Armstrong did to sustain his own *parmi les dieux* beyond the level of other athletes-as-quasi heroes was to keep on winning. And keep on talking about beating cancer. Thus, during this *Information Age* where other athletes might have been summarily disposed of after having fulfilled the consumer's need, Armstrong's feats had time to simmer, to sit naturally among the hyperbole of *sound-bite* journalism and *need-it-now* consumption. Any *naturalization* requires mythologies, a series of myths over time. After Lance had won the Tour five times, it all seemed so natural for him. His denial of death had become both living metaphor and link to the past, a history that somehow skipped LeMond and landed in some place more mythical than Minnesota.

And Lance was still battling the Cancer beast, however real or imagined.

All Too Human but Still Heroes?

Emerson tells us that all mythology opens with demigods.[7] And if the modern demigods have taken on the form of entertainers and athletes, perhaps, as Oriard asserts in *Dreaming of Heroes*, "the star athlete may be a 'diminished hero' but remains our only link with heroes of earlier myth, the Adonises and Galahads."[8]

> I had a good friend and triathlete develop Hodgkin's lymphoma. He needed a bone marrow transplant; 30 days in isolation. Not a fun way to spend a month. Mike Caudill was a huge fan of Lance; posters on the wall of his hospital cell and all. I sent several unreturned messages to him. "Junior," I pleaded, "I rarely ask you for anything but I'd like you call Mikey in the hospital and wish him well." Two days later, Caudill wrote me and said that Lance had called a couple of times. Left him gracious and buoying messages. Forget about the bike or the high-profile dating, when the duty of cancer called upon Armstrong, he would answer. If you looked for ways not to like him, they were there. But it was mostly the cynic, the frustrated competitor, and the unaffected who sought chinks in Armstrong's armor.

There is a tension between the inherent stages and actions found within the arc of Armstrong's life that help create the meaning of the hero myth in a quasi-hero's world. Myths are no longer understood as the random constructions of an over-simplified and backward mentality. Armstrong was the unlikely hero who, when reconsidered through his life story, seemed the perfect candidate. What catalyzed his ascension to hero was fate, that random assignment of disease that you carry around as both conquered scalp and crucifix. Still, some hero scholars will contend that there is an underlying order that serves to help us understand myth and the fundamental structures of the unconscious and collective mind.

For some myth is used to naturalize and universalize that which is political, primarily class, gender, and racial or ethnic differences. US bike racing in the 1960s and 1970s was associated with another fringe, Ivy League-styled sports such as lacrosse and rowing. Yet this was not the case in Europe where it was a working-class outlet, an everyday place for domestiques to aspire towards. People who raced "ten-speeds" in the US were not part of the mainstream youth or collegiate sports grouping. When I was a kid, we rode bikes to the beach before we could afford VW Bugs. The guys who had racing bikes with gears and a leather seat stayed inside, shaved their legs, and learned Italian. Most of them came from wealthy or at least *petit bourgeois* families. Lance Armstrong, the kid, was not rich and was mostly raised by his single, working mother. During the seven years of Armstrong's Tour wins, both the interest in bike racing and recreational cycling increased many times and many zeros were added to bike companies' bottom lines. And then subsequently fell away after his retirement from cycling.

What's It All Mean, Anyway?

Athlete heroes, quasi as they may be, might contribute more than given credit under what might be called the stories about the wisdom of life. Perhaps there is an innate need in the human species to aspire toward something beyond what we are capable of. Realizing the unique and challenging intersections between the psychological, the social, and physical, we must realize that the hero exists within each of us and it is up to us to access that individual through actions, deeds, or by simply living our lives in a certain heroic style.

Sport as a popular social institution has given us ample opportunities to find and embellish heroes. And certainly cycling has done its part in providing the stories that offer us some guidance if not wisdom on how to live a life. Perhaps one of the most profound and resilient cycling myths is centered around the death of one British cyclist, Tom Simpson, who died while racing up Mont Ventoux in the 1967 Tour de France. The cause of death was listed as heat exhaustion but was certainly complicated by his use of amphetamines and alcohol. Grainy video footage shows Simpson weaving wildly across the road before falling and then asking spectators to put him back on the bike where he nearly reached the summit before collapsing again. When he was finally attended to, they found him clipped to his pedals, dead. What mythologizes Simpson's fate is an amalgamation of man versus nature, man versus man, and man versus himself. Mont Ventoux has been climbed 14 times in the Tour since 1951 and has often been the scene of deplorable weather conditions, courageous performances, and allegations of pharmaceutical use. Such is the power and draw of myth that athlete heroes will risk all to embed themselves in the folklore.

The myths of Greg LeMond and Lance Armstrong are the myths of war – the wounded veteran healed and back on the front lines, fighting the good fight for all that is righteous and just. Thus, even as we abhor the notion of war we are still in a perpetual dance with heroes. We don't always like contextual heroes in our midst because they make us ask ourselves, "What can I identify with in my life that illustrates principle, courage, and some kind of righteousness?" And yet we exalt them. Our use of heroes, whether personal or social, is varied, dependant, and fluid.

Athlete heroes, while *celebritized* as they are, must be closer to authentic heroics than game show hosts or pop diva singers. "What sport stars do," Mandlebaum reminds us in *The Meaning of Sports*, "is real and spontaneous rather than contrived and predetermined … the sports figure fills a role that responds to yet another need that religion once monopolized. Sports … supplies heroes."[9] Perhaps one of professional sports' great attractions is that it may be the last form of popular entertainment where the outcome remains unknown. It requires a degree of *faith* but we are sometimes rewarded for having invested in it.

Postscript

In 2009, Lance Armstrong returned to bike racing and the Tour de France. One television commentator, Craig Hummer, in reflecting on Armstrong's comment that he was competing again to bring awareness to LAF (the cancer-fighting Lance Armstrong Foundation), said, "I wonder if Lance is sacrificing his body to fight cancer."[10]

NOTES

1 Ralph Waldo Emerson, "Heroism," in *The Complete Works of Ralph Waldo Emerson*, ed. Edward Waldo Emerson (Boston: Houghton Mifflin, 1903), p. 205.
2 Joseph Campbell, *The Hero with a Thousand Faces* (New York: MJF Books, 1949), p. 3.
3 Thomas Carlyle, *Heroes, Hero Worship and the Heroic in History* (New York: A. L. Burt Company, 1840), p. 328.
4 Janet C. Harris, *Athletes and the American Hero Dilemma* (Champaign, IL: Human Kinetics, 1994), p. 3.
5 Robert J. Higgs, *Sports: A Reference Guide* (Westport, CT: Greenwood Press, 1982). See Sidney Hook, *The Hero in History* (New York: Qualitone Press, 1943), p. 137.
6 Douglass Anderson, *Philosophy Americana: Making Philosophy at Home in American Culture* (New York: Fordham University Press, 2006).
7 Emerson, "Heroism," p. 12.
8 Michael Oriard, *Dreaming of Heroes: American Sport Fiction, 1868–1980* (Chicago: Nelson-Hall, 1982). See Higgs, *Sports*, p. 146.
9 Michael Mandelbaum, *The Meaning of Sports* (New York: Public Affairs, 2004), p. 211.
10 See www.atisbos.com/cyclingandphilosophy for further reading suggestions.

CATHERINE A. WOMACK AND PATA SUYEMOTO[1]

CHAPTER 8

RIDING LIKE A GIRL

The Start Line

Women face an uphill battle in cycling – in more ways than one. In addition to having less lean muscle mass and a higher percentage of body fat than men, women have had to contend with long-standing social barriers that discourage them from becoming athletes. Problems of access and funding for women's sports, social pressure not to be physically active, and lack of role models are just a few of the many issues that keep girls and women from sports participation in greater numbers. One Victorian writer described cycling as "an indolent and indecent practice that could even transport girls to prostitution."[2] One wonders if he was worried that a bike would get them there faster than walking. In fact, the bicycle played an important role in the women's liberation movement, providing means of independent movement, introducing less restrictive clothing, and even influencing bike design.

However, there is no doubt that many women are joining the ranks of recreational, commuter, and competitive cyclists. With all of this change, a couple of questions come to mind: how does this influx of women on wheels affect cycling – as a sport, as a pastime, as a way of life? And how does cycling change the ways that women think about themselves – as athletes, teammates, club members, authorities, and even as women?

We explore some of these questions by taking a look at what feminist ethicists say about how women can and have changed the face of all sorts of human activities. We will see numerous effects on cycling, from what counts as a cyclist to the norms and values by which cyclists abide. We will also see how cycling affects the women who participate in it. We provide some stories from race reports to show some of the differences in the ways women and men view cycling, and also how some of the values endorsed by women and men differ. We conclude with an explanation of how cycling can change to be more in accord with so-called "feminine" values.

Lap One, Where Cycling Practice Meets Feminist Ethics

Cycling, like any other sport, has its share of ethical dilemmas. Debates about doping in professional cycling have been highly publicized, but there are many sorts of life questions that cyclists face in their lives: balancing training time with family time, weighing obligations to volunteer for biking organizations, team loyalty, personality conflicts, even choices about how much of one's disposable income to spend on bikes.

Before we can decide what to do in some of these situations, we have to decide how to decide. That is, we have to figure out what rules we think we should follow in order to do the right thing. Ethics is the study of exactly that – the kinds of features of actions that make them right or wrong (or neutral). In Western philosophy, there are three main approaches to ethics: consequentialism, deontologism, and virtue ethics. Let's take a look at these three theories, and then we will look at how feminist ethics differs from these views. Finally we will see how the feminist ethical principles apply to cycling.

Consequentialist ethics places the moral value of an action in its consequences or states of affairs that come about as a result of that action.[3] In cycling, many of the rules we observe, such as saying "on your left" when passing someone or not crossing the yellow line during road races, follow this consequentialist lead. They are designed to protect against harm, a moral evil, or promote wellbeing, a moral good. If I cross the yellow line and a car has to swerve to avoid hitting me, then my action potentially causes harm to others. Raising money or doing a century ride for charity is considered a good action because it benefits others (and is also personally satisfying). Consequentialism identifies something very

CATHERINE A. WOMACK AND PATA SUYEMOTO

basic about what we value in life – the actual ground-level states of our existence. If actions or policies cause us pain or privation, we tend to avoid them or rank them as undesirable, even to blame those who brought them about.

There are, however, aspects to morality that consequentialism overlooks. A deontologist identifies the moral value of actions in the reasons or principles underlying them.[4] Using the yellow line example, deontologism holds that it is morally wrong because it violates general principles that make road racing possible; deliberately breaking these rules is considered always wrong for everyone at all times. Even if the action might bring about other benefits (like bridging up to a teammate who can use our help later), it is considered wrong because it is a violation of a universal law against intentionally breaking the boundaries of the field of play. In the case of volunteering for charity rides, the reason why it is considered a good action is based on principles about duty toward the less fortunate (remember the Golden Rule – do unto others as you would have them do unto you). Deontologism works well to explain the differences between cases of intentional and unintentional actions; if I get bumped by another rider in the peloton across the yellow line, the official will not penalize me (if she sees the bump), as it was not the result of my actions or intentions. However, if I sign up for a charity ride just to meet cute fast guys on road bikes, my action is not considered morally valuable because I am not doing it for the right reason (my duty to help others when I can).

Virtue ethics offers a different take on the nature of morality; it shifts the issue to us – what makes a person good or bad?[5] The answer lies in the notion of virtue. The good person embodies virtues, or good moral character. The person who engages in charitable giving is striving to be benevolent and compassionate. Similarly, if a person is striving to be honest, that person will avoid cheating, stealing, and many other morally defective activities. The cyclist who regularly cuts people off in the corners, wheel-sucks instead of taking pulls, or tries to drop others on group recovery rides reflects the presence of vice (the opposite of virtue): selfishness, lack of compassion, or pride, to name a few examples. Rules for good sportsmanship and paceline etiquette are designed to help cyclists be considerate, safe, competent, and trustworthy. When clubs require riders to carry repair kits and know how to use them, they are encouraging development of the virtues of self-sufficiency and knowledgeability.

Shifting to virtue as an important element of morality lets us look not just at individual actions, but at social practices that develop over time.

Much of what we do is not a disconnected set of decisions to "do this, don't do that"; in fact, it is a set of habits, patterns, traditions, and customs that we engage in with others. Traditional virtue ethics values virtues like independence, autonomy, intellect, will, and courage. This allows us to see how individuals like generals, world leaders, or Tour de France cyclists embody virtue. But what about mothers, teachers, or recreational cyclists? They clearly embody virtues, but different ones, like interdependence, community, connection, sharing, emotion, and trust. Feminist ethicists argue that these latter virtues have been overlooked or undervalued. These latter values are also crucial to maintaining stable social groups.

One version of feminist ethics – the ethics of care – emphasizes the importance of caring as a primary feature of morality.[6] Virtues that stress the importance of relationships, rather than individualistic virtues, form the foundation of this theory. Proceeding from the experiences and practices of women such as mothering, nursing, teaching, and community-building, the ethics of care takes into account the complexities of the situations in which we find ourselves, and their proposed resolutions of moral conflicts are sometimes at odds with those of the traditional views. For instance, most moral theories place great importance on justice and fairness, enforcing impartial treatment of others. However, care ethics emphasizes the importance of special relationships (like parent, friend, nurse, teacher, teammate) and the special obligations we have to those with whom we share close emotional connections. Even though cycling is in some ways an individual activity and sport, its practice and flourishing require significant community participation and reliance on others. From race planning to training to bike maintenance and commuter advocacy, application of care ethics principles would, we will argue, dictate different paths than those endorsed by traditional moral theories. We will offer some examples of transformations of cycling culture in Lap Three.

According to feminist ethicists, not only have feminine virtues been devalued, but the way a practice gets defined (for instance, what counts as a proper cyclist) seems to be governed by male values. Catharine MacKinnon argues that this is a pervasive phenomenon across all aspects of modern society:

Men's physiology defines most sports, their health needs largely define insurance coverage, their socially designed biographies define workplace expectations and successful career patterns, their perspectives and concerns

CATHERINE A. WOMACK AND PATA SUYEMOTO

define quality in scholarship, their presence defines family, their inability to get along with each other – their wars and rulerships – define history, their image defines god, and their genitals define sex.[7]

To the unassuming cyclist reader of this volume, MacKinnon's words may seem threatening and confusing. However, her words suggest to us that it is worth taking a look at the cycling world to see which aspects of cycling reflect traditional male virtues and which reflect traditional female virtues. In fact, many women's cycling practices often illustrate feminine virtues at work, and can help transform mainstream cycling to improve it in ways that benefit cyclists at every level. Let's now move onto some stories from race reports to see what men and women cyclists have to say about what they do and how they see themselves.

Lap Two, Words from Our Teammates or The Dirt Documentaries

It is common practice for amateur cycling teams to send out email race reports to their club or team mailing lists. We have gathered some examples of these reports, along with some reflections on how this information illustrates distinctions between traditional male and female cycling identities and values.

For mountain bike racing, we had the advantage of mixed team reports, with individual contributions from men and women. Most racers had clear goals for their race; the women's goals seemed more modest (finish, don't get hurt) than the men's (beat personal best, earn a podium spot). Most of the women's reports finish on an upbeat note, pointing out what they learned, how well other teammates did, and how much fun it is, despite the obvious pain of racing, and the residual scratches and scrapes of mountain biking. There were many encouraging email responses to women's race reports from other women, especially from more experienced racers, relating their own crashes or technical problems and how they overcame them. They praised "newbie" racers for meeting their goals and for participating, implicitly validating their shared identity as bike racers, regardless of where they finished.

In one report sent by two beginner women, the first one, whom we'll call Ann, reported a second lap endo that left her a bit dazed, but still determined to finish the race.[8] Her finishing time was five minutes behind her goal, but she reported being satisfied with the race, as she overcame some obstacles (literally) and finished. The other woman – she can be Barbara – set her sights on finishing ahead of another competitor (called "Hammer Girl"), detailing the difficulties she faced (including a knee-slamming crash) and how she kept going, concluding with a first place finish.

In one response, a female expert racer wrote, "Well done!! Excellent competitive spirit from both of you – Ann for getting up and finishing after your [endo] and Barbara for the killer instinct to stay ahead of Hammer Girl!" In another report, a woman who was having a bad race nonetheless pointed out positive news: "I did manage to pass two of the older male sport riders. Gotta count the little victories." She concluded, "Third lap was all about survival and just finishing. Which I did. First sport XC race completed. Compared to my performance last year, my skills have really improved. No falls, rode everything. Never dabbed once. For me, that's an accomplishment."

The men's race reports we examined include much more structured details about the course as well as their position among the racers. We found that the women tend to write about the course and race in a personal narrative, emphasizing what is hard or easy, fun or scary. Consider the kinds of detail in these expert racers' reports; the man's is first:

> Our wave started with 13 guys and I settled into 5th position on the narrow path leading out to the dirt road. There was some jockeying for position ... we all knew the single track was just ahead. Bob put in a last minute attack and went into the single track in 1st position.
>
> I was sitting somewhere around 7th until we started to hit some up hills. I was able to see a group of 4 ... I thought they could be the lead group. I was able to rejoin with a few good efforts on the short undulating hills. There was a lead guy who I'd connect with on the technical sections but he'd pull far away from us and had a minute ahead in other spots.
>
> I knew the race was almost over so I kept the pace up until the end, finishing 5th in my class and breaking into the top 10 overall. I was psyched!

Here is the woman's report:

> I did not take the hole shot, but was perfectly happy to tail three of my competitors up the opening climb. I then proceeded to crash hard over a pipe. I lost enough time getting untangled from another rider and shaking off the crash that by the time we hit the second extended climb, I could see the leaders ahead still ... but quite away ahead. I had also been skeptical

CATHERINE A. WOMACK AND PATA SUYEMOTO

about being able to ride the long downhill as fast as others in my field, and I think that proved to be the case. Think you are slow, you are slow. So, the first lap was a bona fide disaster ... suffering and feeling downright sorry for myself.

For the final lap, I decided to try to get over being so pitiful and salvage some small victories. I regained the requisite aggression to ride the lower course singletrack clean and well. I finally saw another woman riding ahead, tracked her down and pass her on the final big climb. Then I rode the long downhill well enough to stay ahead of the rider I had just passed. I ended up 7th of 9 in the combined field and 5th of 6th amongst the experts (2nd of 2 in my age group). Not spectacular, but I learned a bit about what to expect physically on these ski area courses and the mental toughness that is required to excel in XC racing (where I've got a ways to go).

Many of the winning women's reports seem to be a little conflicted about the competitiveness of racing, despite their actions. We did not find this attitude in the male race reports. One female racer who finished first in her category expressed ambivalence about taking advantage of an opponent's fall: "She followed me into Lap 2, but fell crossing the first log. With that, I kicked some to take advantage (cold and heartless!), and built a gap."

In that same race, an Expert Category male, who also finished first, reported using a variety of race tactics, including intentionally irritating idle chatter, offering to work with other riders in order to recover, and planning his getaway on a section where he knew his abilities were superior:

I complimented them in my most collected but bubbly voice, on how fast they were going and how badly they were crushing me. Then I mentioned how we should work together to sew the race up. I was, of course, bluffing but hoped they would buy it and I could escape with enough gap that they would eventually give up ... We shared another rotation ... and then I took over for a tight twisty singletrack section ... When I came back out I had a decent gap and decided it was time. I kicked it up and kept moving solo.

We found men's race reports to be more individualistic, describing other racers as obstacles to get around, sources of danger, or motivating but impersonal goals. They report working with others, but only inasmuch as it helps individual performance. Women' reports were more personal, describing events as they remember them happening, commenting on their reactions and feelings about aspects of the race. They often comment on opponents' performance in terms of lessons or goals for themselves. Both groups report positive connections to team members and friends, but in the women's reports there seems to be a theme of greater connectedness to the group of racers as a whole.

Compare the following two reports on the same race – ladies first:

> This course had just enough technical stuff for me to get schooled by the race winner ... we entered the definitive rock garden and she flitted through it effortlessly as I bounced off everything in sight, and then watched her disappear when the inevitable dismount-inducing bobble occurred. Alas. One zen-like lesson of the day ... was "clean riding is faster riding, even if it means slowing things down a bit."

Here is the man's report:

> From there we were hammering. Joe joined up ... and we traded spots a couple times. During one bermed turn into a hill he really had a bad shift, ha what a roadie! I got away for a little bit until my seat hit me ... and tilted back. No not this, not now! ... Suffering for a mile ... I decided it was time to pull over and make the adjustment. There goes spots 1-2-and-3, have at it guys! Here comes Jim, damn he's going fast today. As I remounted he was just up and gone, absolutely disappeared right in front of me on a straight away!

From these reports, we found some suggestive patterns. The men's accounts reveal their pursuit of individualistic virtues: courage, strength, expertise, and competitiveness. They seem to view themselves either in isolation from or in opposition to other riders (for instance, by keeping their heads down and working as hard as possible, or by fixing on an opponent they want to catch or to drop). Also, their characterizations seem to be localized to the race at hand, focusing on details of the course or their performance at that time. While they do mention development, the emphasis seems to be on an absolute pronouncement of how they did – they talk about their race as satisfactory, or disappointing, or successful, or fun.

The women's reports paint a different picture of identity and goals. First, they stress relational virtues: growth and development as riders over time (both locally within the race and in the long term), education (lessons learned from others are important), and connections with others – both their opponents and their teammates. Their reports emphasize the

CATHERINE A. WOMACK AND PATA SUYEMOTO

emotional and experiential features of racing and riding rather than an analytical account of the event and course. They are upbeat about overcoming obstacles and finding victory independent of performance. In summary, relational feminine virtues seem more present in the women cyclists' accounts.

Lap Three, Different Lines, Same Course

We have seen how feminine virtues, the basis of an ethics of care, are in many ways embodied in the practices of some female cyclists' reports we examined. Is it possible to embed relational virtues in the sport itself – the way it is organized, implemented, and taught? Some feminist scholars of sports say yes. In a report on women and sports by the Feminist Majority Foundation, experts endorse what they call a "partnership" model of sports: "partnership models of sports emphasize health, cooperation, and enjoyment over the 'winning at all costs' philosophy that has caused so many athletic injuries, even among children."[9] Glover and Anderson describe the model this way: "teammates, coaches, and even opposing players view each other as comrades rather than enemies. Players with disparate ability levels are respected as peers rather than ranked in a hierarchy, and athletes care for each other and their own bodies."[10]

Research on the subjective experience of girls and women in sport offers suggestions about how sport relations might be restructured to support an ethics of care; alternative models of sports designed both to encourage female participation and to expand the boundaries of sports are found in the scholarly literature. In cycling, there are many programs already in place that emphasize development, mentoring, team building, and community. Many clubs offer women's rides and women's race clinics. Promoters are sponsoring more women's fields in road and cross races, including some entry-level or first-timers races solely for women.

Talbot contrasts two different models of sports organizations, one centered on strategic planning and another on community development, the latter of which she argues promotes greater gender equity.[11] Strategic planning is characterized by top-down decision-making, governed by rationality and tidiness, and the agendas tend to be set by major stakeholders in the organization. The main concern is outcomes that justify the investment of time and money in carefully prescribed plans. Clubs and race organizations that focus on grooming select members to compete at top amateur and pro-level events tend to fall into this category. The meters for success are often very narrow and quantitative – how many top-ten finishes, how many primes won, which sponsors are signed up, and so on.

The community development model shifts the emphasis away from a small number of elite athletes, events, or sponsors, and works bottom-up to help people build capacities, leadership skills, and improve the quality of participation in the sport. Creating an environment in which people can trust each other and themselves, are tolerant of diversity, irrationality, and passion, and are empowered rather than directed are some of the key goals of this view. The Boston organization Bike Rides for Ordinary People is an example of this model in action: it plans rides for those who are enthusiastic about cycling and for whom spandex and Dura Ace components are strictly optional; it is open to all, free, and its rides include snack breaks, photo ops, and social chat.

Recalling our introduction to ethics, the first model is individualistic, rule-based, focused on valuation of outcomes, and designed for uniformity of procedure across all aspects of the organization. The second model prioritizes the development of relationships, which are meant to share the burdens of governing through consensus-building, incorporation of diverse points of view, and a less hierarchical structure of leadership. Which model is more successful in practice is an empirical question – it has to be implemented in the real world in order to be tested. However, the second model clearly reflects care ethics virtues in its relational and emotional approach. Donovan describes how this model can work in general in society:

> A caring ethic requires an awareness of contingencies of a situation. Power differentials – differences rooted in class, race, sexuality, and ethnicity – as well as personal histories are not ignored … Rather they are factored into the ethical/political decision-making process and given appropriate weight.[12]

Enacting these sorts of structural changes allows for the development of women's agency in sports, and, in this case, cycling. When we move away from a model of cycling that is top-down and externally driven by the agendas of teams and sponsors to win, toward a model that works to empower individuals and value their experiences, we create a space for women, people of color, and those who have not been part of the old boys club. When women participate in sports that are traditionally male

CATHERINE A. WOMACK AND PATA SUYEMOTO

dominated and bring to them different values and ethics and then enact those values in their practices, they create change in the sport. Even the act of writing a different sort of race report represents a departure from the traditional definitions of what it means to be a cyclist. They are, in effect, creating an alternative model for the cycling community, one in which riding like a girl is celebrated.

Last Lap, How Women Cyclists Transform Cycling

Women are participating in all aspects of cycling – on the road, on the dirt, on the track, and around town. However, according to a survey done on the general population in the United States, men travel on bikes more than twice as much as women do. Anecdotal reports from women cyclists all report that the ratio of male to female club cyclists and racers is easily more than 10 to 1.[13] And yet, women are making their way into almost all the echelons of cycling. Along with this influx have come some different practices and values – more clubs are developing their teams by encouraging entry-level racers (of both sexes); junior females are being mentored, coached, and supported; women's race fields are increasing in size, competitiveness, and quality; and there are women-only rides and events.

The result of this influx is not merely more participation, but a creation of an alternate discourse about what it means to be a cyclist. The feminine virtues and the ethics of caring push against traditional male values in cycling, and we argue that this changes, albeit slowly, the nature of the sport. However, it is not a one-way street, where women change the sport yet are unchanged themselves. As women create a place for themselves in cycling, they also negotiate the established norms and values, all of which results in a transformation of sport and self. For instance, women can develop strength and power as athletes, while working to promote collaborative structures that nurture teams and community.

We close with a story of how one woman describes this type of transformation – Selene Yeager, the Fit Chick from *Bicycling Magazine*, has this to say:

> It was the day of the Monkey Knife Fight, in which riders challenge each other to the top of the wickedest climbs in the area. The route would be 70 miles, including 13 "rounds" of lung-popping, leg-searing madness.

I felt strong on some rounds; empty on others. In the end, I managed to win a stage, take a second in another and stay within reach of the top riders every round.... I scooped up the last podium spot.

Afterward, ... over beer and pizza, [someone] made a crack about "riding like a girl." I playfully slapped him upside the head. "No really," he said. "You've redefined that phrase for me. Now I think, 'I was hanging pretty tough, but then you started riding like a girl and dropped my sorry ass.'"

That summed it up. Sometimes I cry. Sometimes I'm riddled with the shrapnel of self-doubt. Sometimes I feel invincible. Some days I know all too well that I'm not. I do ride like a girl, in all that that means.[14]

NOTES

1 Catherine would like to thank Northeast Bike Club for their support, mentoring, companionship, and coercion – all important tools for creating good cyclists and racers. She thanks Rachel Brown for getting her into this business in the first place. Finally, many thanks to her coach, Steve Weller, of Bell Lap Coaching, for his expertise, encouragement, and unbridled enthusiasm for life on two wheels. Pata would like to thank her partner David for giving her the gift of "bici," and her daughter Niko for loving her even if she embarrasses her by wearing spandex.

2 Cited in S. Scraton and A. Flintoff, eds., *Gender and Sport: A Reader* (London: Routledge, 2002), p. 58.

3 See Jeremy Bentham, *An Introduction to the Principles of Morals and Legislation* (Oxford: Clarendon Press, 1907); and John Stuart Mill, *Utilitarianism*, ed. Roger Crisp (Oxford: Oxford University Press, 1998).

4 For one of the classic philosophical texts, see Immanuel Kant, *Groundwork of the Metaphysic of Morals*, ed. H. J. Paton (New York: Harper and Row, 1964).

5 Aristotle, *Nicomachean Ethics*, Books II–IV, trans. with an introduction and commentary by C. Taylor (Oxford: Oxford University Press, 2006).

6 See, for classic accounts, Nel Noddings, *Caring: A Feminine Approach to Ethics and Moral Education* (Berkeley: University of California Press, 1984); Carol Gilligan, *In a Different Voice: Psychological Theory and Women's Development* (Cambridge, MA: Harvard University Press, 1993).

7 Catharine MacKinnon, *Feminism Unmodified: Discourses on Life and Law* (Cambridge, MA: Harvard University Press, 1994), p. 36.

8 All names have been changed to protect the cyclists ... and the authors, too. But we promise that they are real race reports.

9 Feminist Majority Foundation, "Empowering Women in Sports," *The Empowering Women Series*, 4, 1995. Available online at feminist.org/research/sports/sports8a.html.

10 D. Glover and L. Anderson, *Character Education: 43 Fitness Activities for Community Building* (Champaign, IL: Human Kinetics, 2003), p. 18.
11 M. Talbot, "Playing with Patriarchy: The Gendered Dynamics of Sports Organizations," in *Gender and Sport*, ed. Scraton and Flintoff, p. 279.
12 J. Donovan, *Feminist Theory: The Intellectual Traditions* (New York: Continuum, 2000), p. 10.
13 J. Pucher and J. Renne, "Socioeconomics of Urban Travel: Evidence from the 2001 NHTS," *Transportation Quarterly* 57 (2003): 49–78.
14 Selene Yeager, "Hanging Tough," *Bicycling Magazine*. Available online at bicycling.com/article/0,6610,s-4-404-19640-1,00.html.

CHAPTER 9

BICYCLING AND THE SIMPLE LIFE

Simple (or Hard) Decisions

Today was not the best of mornings to ride my bike to work. It was humid and overcast, cool enough that I chose not to wear shorts (my usual commuting wear during the summer months), but still humid enough that my jeans were sticking to my legs by the time I arrived at Friends University, my destination, about 25 minutes later. It could have been worse, of course; it could have been raining. In some ways, I actually prefer the rain when I'm riding in the warm, creeping dampness that you so often experience on cloudy days. A real downpour can make navigating city streets and sidewalks a little tricky, but a good clean, moderate rainfall has never caused me any serious navigation trouble. Besides, the coolness it can bring is refreshing, especially in contrast to those days when the moisture in the air seems to surround you with a stale stillness, no matter how fast you're moving. Still, I rode my bike, as I do most days when there isn't ice on the streets or I don't have an appointment that requires me to travel to the other side of Wichita. I was happy to do so.

On the best days – and much as I like autumn, my favorites are hot, cloudless, blue-skied summer ones in July, bright days where the horizon on all sides of you lays revealed – my ride to work and home again is a quiet delight, a stream of reminders from my senses with every rotation of my wheel of the world of nature and human deeds (good and bad) around me. But even on not so good days – like this morning – I mount my Trek 7100 to make my six-mile journey and don't give it much of another thought. It has become habitual for me. There is no *need* to give it much thought, because the half-hour I have to myself, pretty much every morning and evening during the work week, is the time I get to keep my thoughts completely to myself. I am not thinking about refilling the gas tank, I am not thinking about changing the oil, I am not thinking about how the jerk in front of me is slowing down just when I need to change lanes so that I don't miss my exit; on the contrary, I am thinking about whatever strikes my fancy, or about nothing memorable at all, because my bicycle – my relatively simple locomotion machine – is capable of getting me to where I need to be without obliging me to deal with complex realities. It is slower than commuting by car, of course, but that slowness itself gives me the opportunity to let my mind wander over the day ahead of me or the day just past, let my eyes wander over the world around me – both its busy parts and the parts which remain still – without having lost anything in the meantime. Issues of efficiency need not plague me. After all, I've already unplugged myself from the oil economy more than most people in Wichita: I'm riding a bike.

Is this all too simplistic a picture? To those for whom the idea of being responsible for physically powering one's own commute, a commute that takes place in all sorts of weather, and which includes no Internet connection or a cell phone or any means of getting any work done at all during those precious minutes you're pedaling away, it may not sound simplistic so much as pathetic. But seeing as how you're reading a copy of a book titled *Cycling – Philosophy for Everyone*, that probably doesn't describe you, at least not entirely. Still, my commuting anecdotes may beg more than a few crucial questions: is it really *that* simple? Forget the fact that anyone who commutes to work via bicycle obviously *does* have to mind the complex interactions around them: speeding automobiles, changing lights, oddly parked cars, unobservant pedestrians, and all the rest.[1] Beyond that, isn't achieving a life situation wherein any of this kind of "simplicity" is even possible itself a rather complex feat? And the answer is, of course, yes. For my family and for myself, it was the result of a series of decisions regarding what kind of career I hoped to have, where we wanted to buy a home, what activities we would commit ourselves and our children to, and more, all of which have had multiple ongoing implications, always needing to be attended to and adjusted as time goes by.

The decision to live a "simple life" can often be, and historically has usually been, attached to relatively uncomplicated acts of downward mobility: a counter-culture drive to drop out and retreat from the ever-enlisting pressures and expectations that come from living in an age of modern technology, mass production, and capitalist consumption. The iconic model for this sort of passive, rejectionist approach to simplicity is Henry David Thoreau, with his call to "simplify, simplify" being inelimi-nably tied to his retreat to Walden Pond and his abandonment of city life. But for the majority of residents of modern, market-oriented, complex states like ourselves, simplicity is actually, well, rather complex to achieve. It is not so simple as hopping on one's bike (though, of course, everyone *should* do that, and regularly, completely aside from any philosophical or lifestyle concerns). Rather, to be able to see the bike as part of a larger, theoretical extension of the freedom to travel and work and live at a slower pace is to acknowledge that achieving simplicity can be a rather complicated project to pull off.

Simplicity and Complexity

The modern world – at least the incarnation of it so familiar to those who live in the societies of Western Europe and North America – is premised upon fluidity, calculation, specialization, transformation, and speed. That's how we have framed the acquisition of knowledge, economic transactions, social organization, and the development of the person for a few centuries now at least.[2] That such speeding means many good things may be lost by the wayside is a commonplace and mostly uncontro-versial. What *is* controversial is believing that controlling our pace is within our collective power, and amounts to more than easy, cranky con-demnations. Of course, attacks on modernity are legion, have been around since Rousseau (the original modern crank, perhaps) and the Romantics at least, and have only been made easier by apologists for globalization who see some new kind of human emerging from Thomas Friedman's Golden Straightjacket.[3] But just because there are lots of anti-modern posers out there doesn't mean the problem is real, and isn't painful.

To stick with Friedman, consider the core of the case "simplicity" makes against globalization and modernity: a great many people around the world really *don't* want to live their whole lives under olive trees, but they'd also prefer that their olive trees not be mowed down by Lexuses. To insist that the only remaining route to simplicity, to preserving the olive groves, is to live there and never move again is to engage in a longing for homogeneous and traditional communities which invariably privileges the perspective of educated (and usually wealthy) elites who feel themselves in possession of some custom or tradition with inherent, superior value. Many of the intellectuals you find flirting with anti-modern arguments often seem to be oblivious to the limited and ordinary lives of actual families, their pleasures and labors and hopes and fears. Actually living out the traditions, customs, and ways of life which constitute "simplicity" requires work, memory, openness to change, and a chastened sense of possibility. (Not to mention a willingness to contemplate the changes that riding one's bike to work might require.) It may also sometimes mean somewhat *less* respect for the particular content of said customs and traditions. Attacking the technological diversification, and resulting alienation, which our acquisition-focused modern economy thrusts upon us demands sacrifices that many people without adequate political, economic, social, or cultural resources may not be able to make, at least not without causing themselves and possibly others (in particular their children) potentially serious harms. Far better, then, to focus on the people who desire simplicity, and the stratagems by which they attempt to secure it, than the "pure" idea of simplicity itself. (Real people ride bikes, not ideals.)

Some years ago, Timothy Burke wrote a stimulating essay[4] defending the complexity and fragmentary nature of the modern world, with all its "dizzy, glorious excesses." The made stuff of the world is all good, in his view. Well, that stuff is stuff that the people want, surely, and borderline socialist though I may be, I hardly think the whole modern marketplace is a matter of false consciousness. So Burke is right when he condemns "those who want less not just for themselves but all the world, who want only their own vision of what is refined and elegant to propagate, who so fear the authentic popularity of global popular culture that they imagine its successes to be impossible save by conspiracy, subversion and subjugation." But he goes too far, I think, when he claims:

> [I]t's true that those forms of expressive practice which are fundamentally antagonistic to a cultural marketplace – the equivalent of usufruct ownership of land, the kinds of cultural practices that are unowned and unownable, collective and communal, and that require a protected relation to power, are threatened by the explosive force of market-driven popular

culture. My feeling about that is the same feeling I have about [community] in general: good riddance.... All that is lost [through the marketplace] are the forms of social power that reserved particular cultural forms as the source of social distinction or hierarchy, all that is lost are the old instrumentalities of texts, performances, rituals. The achievement of liberty loses nothing save the small privileges of intimate tyrannies. Culture, even in the premodern world, is ceaselessly in motion and yet also steady as a rock. In getting more and more of it for more and more people, we lose little along the way.

A strong argument, perhaps persuasive to many who read this essay. But what does it have to do with simplicity, much less bicycling? Well, let me start by defining my terms.

What's the point of trying to live simply, if it doesn't involve a rejection of technology and a return to subsistence farming? I would say the point is to exist in an environment which isn't likely to multiply out of one's control, making one simultaneously dependent upon and divorced from those complex forces, actors, and decisions that shape one's options. That is, a world where one can see clear through from basic personal choices to more or less dependable results, both personal and public. Of course, the world is never *really* going to be like that: human life is an often random, frequently tragic, always unpredictable existence. (Long-distance bicyclists and bicycle commuters alike are sure to be aware of this!) But nonetheless, some environments lend themselves to being *enclosed* more easily than others, and enclosure doesn't just mean retreating from reality: sometimes it means cultivating the better parts of it.

For example, look at your bicycle. It is, to be sure, an impressive and demanding piece of technology, with brakes and sprockets and derailleurs all needing to be properly tended to. But that finite number of parts is available in open sight, requiring but also readily responding to simple, everyday, basic acts of maintenance. Compare that to the kind of complex, often hidden mechanisms that lay buried, sometimes inaccessible, under the hood of a car, requiring expert (and expensive) work to keep in running order. Moreover, said work often runs on and on, with one system's breakdown causing another's. This is not to say that the mechanics of the internal combustion engine cannot be "enclosed," to a degree mastered, and thus made reliably responsive to the engagement of any given driver; cars, too, can be made "simple." But it is much more difficult, and thus much more unlikely, that the typical driver will be able to reach that point. With bicycles, simplicity, the ability to see a project through from beginning to end, is much more in reach.

RUSSELL ARBEN FOX

Of course, the danger of imposing an authoritative content upon one's – and others' – acts of cultivation which Burke makes mention of is real. The number of hippies who just wanted to drop out of modern life and tune in to their communes who ended up embracing Maoism and talked of purges in their bean rows was probably pretty small, historically speaking, but that doesn't mean such a slippery slope should be ignored. The bicycle fascist, the rider who claims to have found a public answer to all modern problems through his ancient Schwinn and is determined to make sure everyone else enjoys it just as much as he, is no more appealing than any other kind. Burke surely wasn't kidding when he spoke of "intimate tyrannies." But not all intimacies are tyrannical, and he is, I think, perhaps less attendant than he should be to how much that rock of culture he speaks of can be shattered by the roar of Lexuses driving by. John Stuart Mill scratched his head over the "half-savage relics" who choose to "sulk on their rocks" rather than embrace the liberty of (English) civilization;[5] there is just the barest hint of a similar condescension in Burke's assumption that wanting to hold onto the rough and rocky soil in which "social distinctions" and olive trees take root is likely about "hierarchy" and holding dominion over others. Maybe, instead, wanting to enclose off certain areas of life, to set at least a few aspects of one's life into a "protected relation to power," is about wishing to exercise dominion over *one's place in the world* – which is at least part of what is meant by "self-government," after all.

Globalization, Coffee, and Sweden

Consider something even more prosaic than bicycle riding: coffee. (I'm not a coffee-drinker myself, but surely the stereotype is that urban bicycle commuters are all about their Starbucks lattes, right? Or at least so I've heard, biking along the semi-rural streets of Wichita. And don't worry; we'll be back on our bikes here soon.) The story here is a fairly familiar one. The transformation of coffee into a status marker, via Starbucks and others, has increased the demand for certain kinds of coffee. This pulls the world market towards ever greater specialized production, as patterns of work and prices shift in order to maximize profits and keep costs down, thereby making coffee cheap enough that its consumer base will continue to grow. In short, coffee becomes – as most manufacturing in our globalized world has become – part of the "pull economy," where power is no longer in the hands of producers and laborers but in the hands of retailers and marketers. Buy coffee, and you're buying a good that's been hurriedly yanked away from one place and out of one form then put into another, and then yet another, and then finely delivered to you, nice and hot.

A few years ago, Daniel Brook wrote an interesting article about Sweden in *Dissent*.[6] This highly egalitarian country, where more than one-half of the total GDP goes to the government in the form of taxes, has weathered the storms of globalization with its high standard of living, generous welfare state, and low wage differentials mostly intact, despite the fact that, strictly speaking, Sweden is poorer than every American state except West Virginia and Mississippi. This is an interesting story, but what I found most intriguing about it was how it explained what it means to provide and serve coffee in a country of "capitalism without capitalists":

> [C]all it the $3 cup of coffee debate. One of the most striking things for foreigners about Sweden is the high price of consumer goods. A simple cup of coffee at a café in Stockholm costs nearly $3. The main reason a cup of coffee in Sweden costs two to three times what it costs in the United States is the labor costs in the café. Pouring coffee is a minimum wage job the world over, but in Sweden the lowest wage is much higher than in the United States, and the employer is responsible for more social benefits. On top of that, a 25 percent value-added tax is paid by the consumer. I would gladly have paid $1.25 for a cup of coffee in Sweden, but ... consider what my $3 bought. The added cost made sure that the person who poured my coffee lived in decent housing, enjoyed health care coverage, and could send her kids to college if they could get in. Swedish society had decided that coffee would cost more than anywhere else in the world in exchange for these public goods. Weren't they worth the money?

It's not that Swedish society is wholly admirable; there is much to complain about in regards to the choices they have collectively made. But Sweden has determined, in at least a few key areas, to resist the Golden Straightjacket of the globalizers, and instead to impose some rules and controls of their own, directing (though some would say warping) the local coffee market so that it became a part of their own larger, egalitarian enclosure. There's nothing about "simplicity" in Brook's article; and indeed, one might argue that they've been able to "buy off" the frustration which must inevitably arise from controls such as these by making sure numerous cultural and social outlets remain unobstructed, open-ended, diverse, and complex. Still, the basic point remains: this is a society that has undertaken the work to construct an environment wherein a certain simplicity, a certain socioeconomic humility, abides. Coffee is not native to Sweden; if they want to drink it, it has to be grown and processed and shipped from somewhere else. The Swedes, in effect, decided that if they want coffee to be part of their environment, they need to pay the price for it, and they need to *put that price to work* in sustaining what they already have.

The application of this "Swedish lesson" in the structuring of transactions and choices in Sweden to debates over paying for building bike lanes on busy streets, constructing more extensive bike parking options, and adjusting work schedules and expectations should be fairly obvious. Not that the needs which such projects would serve are necessarily vital to the achievement of a simpler society, anymore than it was vital for the Swedes to express their egalitarianism through coffee prices. But the fact that they don't leave such a prosaic good out of their considerations ought to be suggestive to those who might balk at broad, public actions being taken in the name of making the movement of people a simpler, more reliable affair.

Are there costs to all this? Of course. Creating an environment where even comparatively simple goods – like the time used up in biking instead of driving, or the expense of a cup of coffee – are socialized, to prevent costs from falling solely on singular individuals who choose to buck the trends of complexity, narrows the margins of invention. It always partially *encloses* things, places and plans them, in the same way that a frugal person might think hard about her every purchase, reflecting on the space which the item bought or used may take up and the waste which will likely result. Only in such a way can her footsteps be light and her personal ecology resist being swept away by the lure of complexly produced, low-cost, high-impact goods. No, Sweden is not a place for mad, brilliant, disruptive entrepreneurs – but it is a place for working citizens and families, most of whom prefer to exercise a little control over the vicissitudes of existence, and preserve a place for a reliable, secure, and more simple everyday world. Few people would describe Sweden as a conservative country, yet compared to the US there is a sense that they "conserve" far better than we do. As with many other social democratic countries, in the Swedes' analysis of their own situation you can see evidence that socialists and egalitarians of many (if not all) different stripes share an intellectual preoccupation with agrarians and others: the "conservative" concern with tending to what one has, and a willingness to structure life so that one's tending isn't made moot by realities that *ought* to be subject to the will of the people. Karl Marx and Edmund Burke aren't necessarily that far off from each other, at least not at their roots.[7]

Simple (or Hard) Gifts

So, fine. Perhaps you, dear reader, are persuaded – or at least intrigued – by the claim that "simplicity," if it does not just mean a rejection of modern life, may necessarily involve an element of intentional, restrictive, enclosing, and thus expensive action: a social restructuring (maybe to a radical degree) in order to conserve the ability of ordinary men and women to exercise real control over, have a real connection to, and feel a real identity with the choices they make and their forms of life. Simplicity, then, isn't so simple; the experience of it may be, but the achievement and maintenance of it is not. So I return to the beginning of my reflections: could bicycling be part of that structured simplicity, in the same way the Swedes have made their cup of coffee part of a system of dependability? To which I say: no *can* about it; it absolutely is.

A few years back, my brother-in-law, a physics professor, expressed to me his discontent with the high technology and science that surrounded us all. In an email he asked:

> Have we become slaves to our machines already? If we live too far from work and have to drive to work, then are we slaves to our cars? If we can't grow our own food, are we slaves to the trucks that drive in the food and to the machinery that plants and harvests and processes our food? I have often thought of our trips to the gas station as a type of worship service – we go to pay homage to the gods of petroleum – the gods that dictate how we live our lives and to whom we must pay our tribute.

Americans today have no excuse to not be well versed by now in the obvious expenses generated by our national dependence upon oil; that trade deficits, labor costs, foreign policy, interest rates, job openings, working conditions, and so much more depend to a discomforting degree on the price of a barrel of oil is not easily disputable. Perhaps even more important, however, are the less obvious, even hidden, costs that shape the basic infrastructure of our lives. For example, a huge amount of the congestion on the roads in American cities is a function of the crowded

RUSSELL ARBEN FOX

spaces which automobiles occupy while moving from one point to another: in other words, the crowded nature of our roads. Why are they crowded? Ironically and to a surprising extent, because so much land has to be used to place those cars when they *aren't* being used. The amount of parking space which our nation's automobiles necessitate equals in size the state of Connecticut, and the cost of maintaining those "free" spaces (mall parking lots and street-side parking, to name a couple) in the face of competition over real estate (not to mention roads!) amounts to subsidies to drivers of over $220 billion per year.[8] This is not to argue that such expenditures aren't warranted, or just. Rather, it is simply to point out the hidden as well as the open costs that shape and control our available decisions in a complex society. Leaving aside the car the next time you commute – or planning one's work choices so that one *can* leave aside the car – is thus a powerful blow for personal control over one's choices, and hence for "simplicity."

"I really felt the bicycle could be for the world's cities what the spinning wheel was for Gandhi," was how John Dowlin, a 1970s-era bicycling activist, put it.[9] Gandhi's vision of restructuring India's economy around self-sufficient means of production – that is, spinning its own cloth – was hardly a simple undertaking, but its goal was a society which could extract itself from the complex dependencies of Great Britain's imperial economic order ... and along the way, it became a symbol of independence, local reliance, and, yes, simplicity.[10] The bicycle – and, more specifically, the bicycle commuter – could be, and should be, the same.

That is not to ride over the difficulty and sacrifice that may be involved in shifting gears in our pattern of existence away from an automobile-centric one to a bicycle-centered one. In my family's case, upon moving to Wichita, KS, deciding where we would live required above all a determination of the routes I would take to work, and the limits within which we would look for a home (this meant no more than 9 miles from campus). Given that we wished to pass along our commitment to bicycling to our children, that choice was also affected by where our kids would go to school, and how they would get there.[11] And then, of course, there follow issues of extra-curricular activities and after-work responsibilities: how many can we accept, and how many must we turn down, if we are committed to having only one car and relying on walking or the bicycle for everything else? It obliges us to turn local, and turn down our level of programmed commitments in order to keep our lives simple *and* sane.

The sometimes hard – but invariably pleasing – choice of the bicycle *structures* our lives, in the same way the supposedly liberating powers of free market competition structure the shopping, schooling, and commuting of millions of drivers. In seeking a different structure, we find ourselves becoming rebels, living lives less noisy with organized demands, and more responsive to needs and choices that are more organically our own. Of course, there are still demands: I leave a little earlier for work than I might have to otherwise, and there are opportunities for building relationships and impressing friends and colleagues that my family and I no doubt miss out on. On the other side of the road, there are also meaningless distractions that our slower, simpler structure of life enables us to avoid (my co-workers have more than once expressed jealousy at the fact that I am excused from late-running faculty meetings, since I have to bike home). And then there are other compensations, my intimate familiarity with all the variations in Wichita's weather being one.

The old Shaker hymn, "Simple Gifts," is deceptive. It speaks of the gift of simplicity and freedom, yet it connects such gifts with turning and bowing and bending "till we come round right." Simplicity ain't easy. In modern, fragmented, fast-moving, overtime-working, traffic-stressing, coffee-gulping, oil-guzzling America, that's doubly true. The decision to ride a bike to work won't make simplicity suddenly easy – on the contrary, especially at the beginning, investing one's time, money, and energy into a rethinking of one's conception of daily life will probably be hard; it will involve no small amount of bowing and bending, to see the way through to a freedom from the complex dependencies we all carry with us. But in the end it will come round, like the wheels of your reliable, muscle-powered, two-wheeled transportation machine. The same logic holds for any attempt at public restructuring. Building and maintaining resources for bicycle commuters and families who want to use that humble form of transportation for their daily routines will face great obstacles, though perhaps becoming slightly less so as more people hop on saddles after recognizing the hidden costs of a complex market that broadly structures our lives without much input from us. However achieved, it will be a gift. A small gift, perhaps. But a gift all the same. It may be one that will not be appreciated at first; maybe it won't be fully appreciated until you've experienced plenty of both hot and rainy days on your bike. But then, the weather, like many other things, is a gift that those who never step out of their automobiles rarely know.

NOTES

1 There is something particularly American about this "obviously," though: American bicycle commuters have come to recognize themselves as, and have fought to *be* recognized as, vehicles with as much right to streets as cars – which means American bicyclists have to think about traffic constantly. This is not so much the case in many parts of Western Europe, where the bicycle as a primary mode of ordinary transportation has been long accepted, with the result that more peacefully ordered and extensive bike lanes, with their own norms and patterns, are plentiful. Contrast the descriptions of Amsterdam bicycle commuters and American ones in Jeff Mapes, *Pedaling Revolution: How Cyclists are Changing American Cities* (Corvallis: Oregon State University Press, 2009), pp. 75–6; and Robert Hurst, *The Cyclist's Manifesto: The Case for Riding on Two Wheels Instead of Four* (Guilford: The Globe Pequot Press, 2009), pp. 133–7.

2 This account of the modern Western world is indebted to many authors, but probably none more so than Charles Taylor. See his *Sources of the Self: The Making of the Modern Identity* (Cambridge, MA: Harvard University Press, 1989); and *Modern Social Imaginaries* (Durham, NC: Duke University Press, 2004).

3 Thomas L. Friedman, *The Lexus and the Olive Tree* (New York: Farrar, Straus, and Giroux, 1999), ch. 6. The "Golden Straightjacket" refers to the idea that adapting one's society, economy, and patterns of personal behavior to the norms and expectations of the wealthy, expanding, trade-hungry capitalist states of the West is difficult, with results that many cultures experience as confining and homogenizing. The material benefits, in terms of medicine, jobs, technology, education, and consumer goods, however, are undeniable.

4 Timothy Burke, "They Call Me Dr. Pangloss." Available online at www.swarthmore.edu/SocSci/tburke1/perma101204.html (accessed September 9, 2009).

5 Mill, *Considerations on Representative Government*, ch. 16, "On Nationality," in *On Liberty and Other Essays*, ed. John Gray (Oxford: Oxford University Press, 1991).

6 Daniel Brook, "How Sweden Tweaked the Washington Consensus," *Dissent*, Fall 2004.

7 For more on this theme, consider my essay, "How Germany Made us 'Conservative.'" Available online at www.frontporchrepublic.com/?p=3018 (accessed September 10, 2009).

8 Donald Shoup, *The High Cost of Free Parking* (Chicago: APA Planners Press, 2005).

9 Dowlin cited in Mapes, *Pedaling Revolution*, p. 37.

10 For more on this argument, see Rebecca Brown's forthcoming *Gandhi's Spinning Wheel and the Making of India* (London: Routledge, 2010).

11 I say more about this in my essay, "Walking to School, Slackerdom, and Other Revolutionary Acts." Available online at www.frontporchrepublic.com/?p=2807 (accessed September 8, 2009).

RE-CYCLING

CHAPTER 10

WARM UP

When Two Wheels Meet Four

 I heard the words every father wants to hear from his son who lives 700 miles away.

"First of all, I'm okay."

"Okay. Anything else?"

"I was really stupid."

Three years ago my son, Tony, was entering his last year at St. Mary's College of California. True to the family genetic code, he found release from the general angst of becoming an adult by disappearing for hours on his bicycle. Steepest climb for a hundred miles around? He's there with a smile. No matter that he would have to wrestle the traffic of Oakland or Walnut Creek. He's a savvy rider. He should be. I screamed him through his cycling coming of age on the roads and trails of Oregon's Yamhill County. That doesn't mean I wasn't terrified of letting him ride off on his own.

Tony was just playing that day, on a long ride to Mt. Diablo. Cruising along the bicycle path west of Walnut Creek at 20 miles per hour. Traffic streaming past, halting and jerking at every intersection; 65 degrees already and the scent of eucalyptus. He imagined torturing his father with that when he called to tell him about his ride, knowing that Yamhill County was soggy and cold, and if I was riding at all, I was on my rollers. He accelerated from the stop sign, keeping up with the traffic, playing a game of beating them off the mark.

That Jaguar that just passed him? A little burst of speed and he'd catch it. That would be fun. Mt. Diablo already heating up in the late morning sun to the east. Having to squint even through his sunglasses. A ribbon of sweat running off his cheek. Feeling pretty much invincible, as every 22-year-old should.

The traffic kicked up to 25 miles per hour. Just as Tony pulled even with the Jaguar, the driver, without signaling, decided on another course than the one straight ahead. Right turn. The vehicle swung toward a narrow side road, overlapping my son's path. Without even time to touch his brakes, Tony leapt upward – pure instinct – pulling his bicycle with him. The Jaguar was now broadside to him, still rolling obliviously through the bike lane.

Bicycle and rider rose even with the front end of the car. Tony's back wheel clipped the Jaguar's fender; his shoulder and hip slammed onto the hood. His pedal dug into the waxed paint of the Jaguar, etching his signature there. He tumbled off the car, striking his shoulder and helmet on the pavement. His body skidded into the traffic lane.

Fortunately, the vehicle following the Jaguar had seen the entire event develop. The driver stopped, fully aware of the stunned cyclist and his continued vulnerability. Two lanes of traffic halted. From his wheel-level view, Tony asked himself the questions every cyclist does after a fall: Is this the ground? How did I get here? Where does it hurt?

The driver of the Jaguar rolled down her window. "Are you okay?"

"Yeah. I'm all right." Spoken from the pavement.

Tony rolled to his feet. He checked for blood. Not even a road rash, except a little rawness he felt on his shoulder. He noted the huge scar on the hood of the Jaguar. The woman smiled at him and said, "I'm glad you're okay." Then she quickly drove away.

Tony pulled his bike off the roadway, exchanged a "Wow!" glance with the driver who had stopped, and took a deep breath. As the son of bicycle shop owners, he knew to check his bicycle for any damage. Not a scratch. Then, as the traffic accelerated past, he thought to sit down. The first words he said to himself: "Man, that was stupid." He wasn't talking about the driver of the Jaguar.

My son was in the right of way. He was riding legally, properly, and had every right to be where he was. He was very lucky. His mistake was the assumption that a motorist would see him when he was on her right. His mistake was an unwillingness to give up the right of way to a heavier and much more deadly vehicle.

This past winter two cyclists were killed in Portland while exercising their right of way. One was passing on the right in a bike lane at an intersection. Both of these deaths involved trucks turning right, completely unaware of the cyclists rolling beside them. Both deaths were tragically unnecessary. The truck drivers were unaware of their surroundings, and the cyclists violated one of my personal cardinal rules: rarely pass a vehicle on the right, and never in an intersection.

For some of us, cycling is function, transportation. For others, revelation. Maybe we just want to get to where we're going, or maybe we want to challenge our lungs and our spirit. But we must be ever vigilant. We must follow the same rules as motorists, but we must be ready to yield at every instance. Shouting doesn't make us heard. Waving our arms in the air doesn't make us seen. I have witnessed overly aggressive cyclists as well as nearly unconscious drivers. Both are a danger, and both must make a greater effort to contribute to each other's safety on the road.

"First of all, I'm okay."

I can live with that.

"I was really stupid."

Yup. I can live with that, too – the fact that he's able to say it.

CHAPTER 11

PHILOSOPHICAL LESSONS FROM CYCLING IN TOWN AND COUNTRY

Here I describe three lessons I have learned directly or indirectly from cycling in town and country. The first concerns the art of arguing and explains why I started commuting by bike; the second outlines what I think I have learned by using this mode of transportation; and the scene of the third lesson is the interior highland of Iceland. Although the lessons are personal and closely tied to Iceland, they may likely apply to other persons and to a wider context. That's why I have been so bold as to call them *philosophical* lessons from cycling.

When to Start Cycling

It is the job of philosophers to argue, not to cycle, but they can, of course, argue about cycling. That's what I found myself doing a few years ago. My line of argument, which I tested on colleagues at the lunch cantina, was that cycling could be seen not only as a possible but even as an ideal mode of commuting in Reykjavik, home to 120,000 hardy souls. My interlocutors, a group of friendly scientists, engineers, and scholars, were not easily convinced. On the contrary, they were quick to reject my arguments, often with disbelief, sometimes mockery. I stubbornly stood my ground as it was pointed out to me that the weather in Iceland was highly unsuitable for bikers, bike lanes were few, poorly maintained and rarely serviced, the traffic heavy and the particle pollution considerable, greater than in most cities of a similar size.

These objections, which I have encountered from all quarters in Iceland, often take the form of a most unfavorable comparison of Iceland to Denmark, the home of our former monarch, now a well-known biker paradise. In our old capital, Copenhagen, bike lanes run almost endlessly through flat surfaces, the climate seems designed for bikers, the traffic is light, bikes relatively cheap, and bike-stands accessible almost everywhere. Compare this to the winds, rain, snow, sleet, hail, and hills in Reykjavik and you'll understand why the Danes have set themselves a short-term goal to have bike trips be more than 40 percent of all trips to and from work by 2012, whereas policymakers in Reykjavik have reluctantly set their sights on 6 percent as a long-term goal to be reached by 2024.

My opponents sometimes cited impressive data on wind speed and precipitation to support their case. But apparently commuting by bike is not only inconvenient and hazardous, it also interferes, I learned, with parental responsibilities. You needed a car, I was told, to pick up the kids from school, drive them to doctor's appointments, soccer games, and piano lessons. While you are biking your wife will have to do those chores, I was told by one interlocutor, while another informed me that I couldn't do my shopping by bike. Most agreed that I lived too far from the university to bike to work. Add to this a seemingly endless list of minor obstacles to commuting by bike, such as being late to classes, stinking at meetings, the bike breaking down, not to mention the much advertised possibility of accidents and injuries. I, however, never conceded a point to my opponents. I was convinced that my arguments were sound, and I still am. But my ego was frequently bruised.

I remember riding home on the bus one Friday afternoon after taking an unusually heavy beating at the cantina, licking my wounds, carefully going over arguments in my mind, reassuring myself that mine were airtight. But this time the uneasiness that lingers after a hard debate didn't go away. Something was missing. I couldn't put the issue to rest. It took me days to realize that what was missing was not an argument but a bike. I myself didn't commute by bike after moving to the suburbs. Neither I nor my opponents had seen *that* as a serious flaw in my arguments. Reflecting on this, I'm reminded of a joke I once heard about a lady who solicited Gandhi's assistance to wean her son off sugar and sweets. Gandhi agreed to help but kindly asked the lady to bring the boy back the following week. When she did the spiritual leader reportedly shouted at the boy: *Stop eating sugar*. As the lady thanked Gandhi, she said she was curious to know why he had waited a week to deliver this forceful but simple message. Why could it not have been delivered last week? Because, he answered, at that time I was eating sugar myself.

Although the Gandhi story is probably false, it points to a question that some philosophers have come to see as pressing: When should you test your arguments by personal experience, back your claims by your own experiments in living? It's terribly convenient when you are teaching philosophy in a classroom to do without such experiments, to omit consulting your own experiences. But the price of the convenience can be an academic philosophy haunted by the suspicion that it is out of touch with the mundane problems of everyday life and with the deep philosophical problems that many aspiring students of philosophy find individually gripping in their own lives. Thoreau captured and fueled both suspicions with his pithy statement: "There are nowadays professors of philosophy, but not philosophers." But Thoreau's famous statement is followed by a lesser known claim that "it is admirable to profess because it was once admirable to live." "To be a philosopher," Thoreau writes, "is not merely to have subtle thoughts … but … to solve some of the problems of life, not only theoretically, but practically."[1] The subtlety of Thoreau's position is easily lost on us. It speaks simultaneously to the active and theoretical side of our nature. It calls for the ability to reason and argue as well as the good sense to know when to stop arguing.

An Experiment in Living

Four years ago I stopped arguing about cycling and bought a bicycle. I had learned my first lesson about cycling. My resolve now was to test the counter-arguments by riding a bike to work every day of the year, regardless of the weather or road conditions. The street bike I bought was sturdier than the cheap supermarket bikes I had owned before and I learned how to fix it, which turned out to be a pleasant form of recollection. Often enough I just had to relax a little, tool in hand, and from my boyhood days it would come to me how to change a tire or fix a chain. As I got more into biking, I bought a mountain bike and eventually treated myself to an expensive cyclo-cross bike which made my best Thoreauvian friend raise his eyebrows. My daily route, a 14-mile round trip, takes me

ROBERT H. HARALDSSON

through three towns, including Reykjavik. In winter I rely, consequently, on workers from three municipalities to keep my path clear of snow. It's a scenic route, half of which runs along the seaside. If I have time to round the peninsulas, which I often do, I can easily ride by the sea nearly the whole distance.

I have now entered the fourth year of my experiment and it is a long time since I realized that almost everything they say about commuting by bike is wrong. It's often no more than a prejudice. Let's consider briefly some of the claims of the discouraging voices. Reykjavik, so runs the first objection, is a poor city for bikers. While it is true that the city has been designed around the needs of motorists – Icelanders, like North Americans, are often said to have voted with their purse and chosen the private car – Reykjavik is not a bad city for cyclists. Bike lanes run through and around most of its neighborhoods, especially the newer ones. And they are being improved even after Iceland's economic downturn. Neither is it fair to say that our bike lanes are poorly serviced. In the first 525 days of commuting by bike I only twice experienced difficulties with snow on bike lanes that forced me to step off the bike: on account of piles of crystalline water ice, I once had to carry my bike on the shoulder, and had to take a long detour the other time. When I started my little experiment, I needed to ride on a busy highway some distance to cross a river but now a sturdy bridge for bikers has been built next to the highway. Our *main* problem in Reykjavik is not poor facilities for bikers but rather poor use of the facilities that actually do exist. Often people simply don't know of the possibilities. Many who see icy roads as prohibitive for biking are, for example, surprised when they see you cycle around on ice spikes in winter.

Time, or the lack of it, is usually cited as a major objection to commuting by bike. The car is faster and more comfortable. So is riding the bus. I must admit that I've come to love the slow pace as much if not more than the fast pace. Still, I have to point out that this objection, like so many self-evident truths, is based on a simplification. It takes me 23 to 50 minutes to ride my bike to work depending on the conditions and my own mood. The same numbers for the car, again based on my experience, are 14 to 45 minutes depending on the traffic, for the bus, 15 to 35 minutes. It has happened on more than one occasion that I have used less time on transportation than motorists living in the same town and attending the same morning meeting.

Needless to say, you are never stuck in traffic when riding a bike or held up for half an hour because some unlucky, and perhaps stressed out, motorist has had an accident. Only once have I been in real danger of arriving late to my own lecture because of a flat tire. I used to have punctures fairly often when I was running cheap tires, but I rather enjoyed fixing the tubes. Eventually I got fed up with it and bought better tires. Since then I have never had a puncture riding to work. And I can't say that car rides are comfortable anymore. I miss the free flow of oxygen and experience stress and uneasiness, especially when hitting a traffic jam. On the bike you are in control. Barring some unforeseeable disaster, I know I can be at work in 30 minutes regardless of the conditions if motivated. A motorist in a modern city cannot say the same. At any rate, I have never been late to class since I started commuting by bike.

Another objection to biking in Reykjavik is that "it's downright dangerous," to quote a fine fellow I talked to yesterday. But that has not been my experience. I have never had an accident involving a car or another bike. When it comes to horseback riding – once a necessity but now a popular past-time in Iceland – the story is altogether different. Whereas I have never met a cyclist who has seriously injured him- or herself on a bike, I've never met a horseman in Iceland who has not been injured riding a horse. Indeed, it is not unusual to read about horsemen being killed or maimed in Iceland. But no one commutes by horse – the horse does not compete with the private car – and no one warns you that it is dangerous to ride a horse. Looking at accident statistics, I see that cycling ranks low compared to other modes of transportation and most other sports. One list I have looked at in Iceland ranks cycling with golf in this respect. But even the good people who care most about air pollution have helped to maintain the prejudice that biking in Iceland is dangerous. It is a well-advertised fact about Reykjavik that particle pollution, caused mainly by ice spikes on car tires, is unusually high for a city of its size. Although it is good to keep this fact in mind – it may have convinced some strong supporters of the private car that *something* must be done about the heavy traffic – this concern helps to foster the belief that it is dangerous to ride a bike in Reykjavik. But it's not. Even on calm and sunny winter days, when particle pollution peaks, the thinning area of the pollution is relatively small: 10 meters according to one study done at the University of Iceland.

I have not yet faced the strongest and for many the conclusive objection to commuting by bike in Reykjavik. For most people, just mentioning the weather suffices and they will never give another thought to commuting by bike. This is a difficult objection in part because people's criteria for good cycling weather varies, depending, for example, on

ROBERT H. HARALDSSON

whether they are themselves bikers or not. Let's begin by accepting the criterion of the objectors. It is fairly straightforward: rain and wind are bad for bikers; calm, clear days are good for them. The only complication we encounter here has to do with whether we should settle the debate by relying on our own experiences or on hard meteorological data. I suggest we should rely on both. A heavy reliance on the former may leave us without external standards and without a possibility to convince others except perhaps those who already are inclined to agree with us. Whereas an exclusive dependence on science, just as relying overly on philosophical arguments, may keep all individualizing peculiarities of the weather sedulously out of view. The weather, after all, is a much more interesting and more peculiar phenomenon than you'd think by simply listening to meteorologists.

My own experience as a biker is that for every rainy or windy day in Reykjavik, you'll have five days when it is relatively calm and clear. For every day when it is difficult to cycle to work, given the usual criterion, there are seven days when it's a pure pleasure. For every day that I've been slowed down by a storm or excessive rain, there have been ten when I have slowed down because of good weather and the scenery. I had all but forgotten how beautiful winter days are, especially in the early morning hours.

It is not difficult to guess why non-bikers might think that the weather in Reykjavik is unfavorable for bikers. If they notice bad weather during any period of the day, or even at night, they will write the day off as a bad day for cycling. But the problem with this inference is, of course, that no one commutes by bike all day long. Even when the weather is terrible, again given the usual criterion, you can often escape the worst of it. The Reykjavik winter of 2006–7 is a case in point. From early November to the end of January, low-pressure systems moved in over Iceland from the west with frightful consistency, hitting Reykjavik with wind speed of 55–65 mph, sometimes gusting up to 90–100 mph. Anyone who didn't consult his own experience during this period would have judged it to be a most horrific time for a biker. But as it turned out, I only ran into difficulties one morning during this period. Only once was the storm at its strongest precisely at the time I was pedaling to work, but, as luck would have it, I had the winds on my back. For most of these winter days I had an easy time riding my bike to work. After four years of commuting by bike, I can state with confidence that cases when you have to fight heavy rain and strong winds the whole way are rare. And as far as I have been able to ascertain, the meteorological data support my case. The average precipitation in Reykjavik during, for example, August is 62.5 mm (but 64 mm in Copenhagen), in September it is 67 mm compared to 60 mm in Copenhagen, and the hours of sunshine in these two cities in August are comparable.[2] The winter in Reykjavik is much milder than most people have to put up with in northern USA or Scandinavia.

But we don't even have to accept the objector's criterion of good weather for bikers. It is not unpleasant to cycle in the rain or on icy roads facing the storm. If you have the right gear – on yourself and on your bike – and if you have become accustomed to put it to good use, it can be a pure pleasure to ride a bike in any weather. Fighting a rain or snow storm can even be delightful if you want all your muscles to participate in the feast of living. As much as I like calm and sunny days, I have come to appreciate even more the fresh air when it's blown with some gusto straight from the vast North Atlantic Ocean across my path. And a little precipitation usually adds to the pleasure as it brings out the smells of the soil. These are obvious truths that tend to be forgotten indoors.

Well, my main conclusion concerning the weather is that one's criterion (for good weather) undergoes a subtle change as one becomes more used to commuting by bike. It is not only, or mainly, that you get used to "bad" weather. Rather, your criterion becomes more responsive to reality. You come to appreciate all the different shades that lie between what is usually called good and what is usually called bad weather; and, also, how incredibly changeable the weather is, at least in Reykjavik. I am ashamed of the evaluative criterion I applied to the weather during my motorist days, and even of my very concept of weather, how naïve and simplistic it was compared to the concept I implicitly relied on as a young boy. Once you are in possession of a richer weather concept, it's easier to appreciate and enjoy all the variety without depreciating what people usually call good weather. But if you have gotten yourself into a situation where you consider only one type of weather as good for you it is probably because you have become inert and inactive.

Philosophical Tailwinds

I have said nothing so far about the benefits one derives from commuting by bike. Some are fairly obvious once the prejudices have been dispelled. Biking is a cheap mode of transportation. My books show that I didn't have to cough up a penny for my transportation from September 2008 to

February of 2009 as I had spare parts and oil left over from my summer trips through the highland of Iceland. Commuting by bike has also proven to be a fine way of integrating workouts into everyday life. In my first year of biking, I lost 36 pounds and got back into shape. I have not had the seasonal flu since I started commuting by bike; I have even stayed clear of the common cold.

I have also discovered that biking is suitable to my line of work, teaching and writing philosophy. Riding the bike in the morning often helps me to clarify and simplify my thoughts; the small stuff and petty worries drop out somewhere along the way. I have come to appreciate Nietzsche's advice: "Give no credence to any thought that was not born outdoors while one moved about freely – in which the muscles are not celebrating a feast, too."[3] I almost always arrive at work a more clear-headed, not to say a braver-minded man after riding my bike in the morning. On the way home, I'm able to relax and unwind if my day has been a stressful one. But what I have come to like most about commuting by bike, along with the resourcefulness it brings, is simply the time it gives you to spend outdoors, facing the elements. I had all but forgotten how much time I spent outdoors as a boy and how slowly and almost imperceptibly I was changing into an indoor creature, a sedentary man, furniture of a sort. I have at long last restarted my one-sided conversations with the stars and the ocean, and I have come to recognize again that I share this earth, or my little stretch of it, with other living creatures, especially insects but also birds and an occasional seal that looks at me from a safe distance. It is silly to forget such things but one does; just as one forgets how changeable and multifarious the weather is. If the sedentary life makes you an absolutist or a dogmatist, biking turns you into a pragmatist. That at any rate has been my experience.

To sum up, the second lesson I have learned from cycling in town turns out to be an old-fashioned one taught by philosophers from Socrates to Henry David Thoreau. It goes something like this: Do not believe what others say, test things for yourself. Received truths often turn out to be mere prejudices. What everyone accepts is often something no one has tested. What other men call bad, you'll often discover to be good. What is commonly seen as impossible you might find easy and natural. Two years into my own little experiment, I was asked to read a paper at a conference on air pollution and sustainable modes of transportation in Reykjavik. After I gave my little talk, a PhD student from geography responded to my plea for cycling, saying that his extensive research had shown that it would be impossible to get us Icelanders to commute by bike, we simply didn't want to bike. Instead, he claimed, we should look to cars fueled by hydrogen or electricity. That's where the road to our green future lay. I remember answering that we were not forced to choose between these options, that we could aim for environmentally friendly cars *and* commuting by bike. Only much later did I realize that he had overstepped his boundaries as a scientist. No scientist can, as a scientist, tell us what is possible and what is impossible when it comes to the practical matters of our everyday life. When a scientist tries to do so, he is often doing no more than airing his own private opinions. But that may be hard to see when you are dealing with revered figures like a scientist in our times or a priest in former times.

Voluntary Poverty

I have mentioned two lessons I learned from cycling in town. My point has been that a philosophy of the kind cultivated by thinkers from Socrates to Thoreau can help you to see past the prejudices that may have stopped you from so much as considering the option of commuting by bike. At the same time I have claimed that biking can give you that openness of mind – openness to reality, that is – which William James used to see as the core of pragmatism. But I have learned a lesson from free cycling in the country which I have found harder to articulate clearly. In particular, I have found it difficult to explain why I have been drawn to the barren and desolate interior highland of Iceland. Indeed, it was not until I consulted the philosophical tradition that light began to dawn on me in this area. Again, Thoreau provides a helpful starting point. He prefaces the passage quoted earlier regarding professors and philosophers with the following opaque comment: "None can be an impartial or wise observer of human life but from the vantage ground of what *we* should call voluntary poverty."[4] One can almost sense the tension between the last two words of the quotation. Voluntary poverty! Poverty is not something people usually accept voluntarily. Like most mortals, Thoreau was aware of the destructive power of poverty – that is, the inability to satisfy one's basic needs – and his philosophy taught him a method to avoid that kind of poverty. But one of his central insights was that there exists a more severe form of poverty that is masked by riches. His *Walden* is addressed to "that seemingly wealthy, but most terribly impoverished class of all, who have accumulated dross, but know not how to use it, or get rid of it, and thus have forged their own golden or silver fetters."[5] For people in this condition, the solution is not to add more stuff, accumulate more dross, but rather to take away things and simplify life. But it is not something you can force people to do; it's *voluntary* poverty.

Riding your bike through the interior highland of Iceland is like taking an intensive course on voluntary poverty. As you elevate to 500 or 900 meters, depending on where you enter the highland, vegetation recedes and thins out until you are left with endless fields of gray sand and rocks, surrounded by gray mountains, grayish-white glaciers, and often a gray sky. I have cycled alone across Iceland through the gray desert and when I have reemerged on the other side after days I've always been overwhelmed by the beauty of our world. But I do not appreciate our gray desert only for the part it can play in a gigantic sensory deprivation experiment. I don't see why it should not be as conducive to spiritual life as its famous counterparts in Egypt or Palestine. Something is stirred up from deep within your mind when you cycle alone for days in the gray desert. As things are taken away and your worldly possessions are out of reach, you are thrown back on yourself and your own resources. Cycling becomes a form of recollection. Should you be an amateur in living like myself, you might even find yourself saying silly things like: "Now I remember why human beings eat." At any rate, you are likely to lose all interest in food and drink except as forms of nourishment; but that is still showing a lot of interest in these items. And when you meet other human beings, other cyclists, you'll rediscover what a pleasure a stranger can be and how quickly you can strike up a friendship with a foreigner.

Thoreau's thoughts on voluntary poverty are not new to the history of Western philosophy. He rediscovers an old theme of classical philosophy and adopts it to life in a new world that promised, and ultimately delivered, more earthly riches and wealth than human beings had ever known before. Socrates' essential insight, for example, was that before a student could start the process of learning something had to be taken away from him or her. He came to characterize this something as the pretense of knowledge. Human beings, Socrates discovered, pretend to know all sorts of things they know, in fact, nothing about. His students would, consequently, experience their first steps toward wisdom as a bewildering process of impoverishment, a loss of intellectual comforts. Socrates' most enthusiastic follower in Copenhagen, Søren Kierkegaard, relates a similar insight by drawing an analogy between eating and knowing. "When a man has filled his mouth so full of food that for this reason he cannot eat and it must end with his dying of hunger," Kierkegaard ponders, "does giving food to him consist in stuffing his mouth even more or, instead, in taking a little away so that he can eat?"[6] My philosophical lessons have concerned the art of taking away some of the comforts of the intellect and the automobile. This may appear mean as the car and the intellect are faster and more efficient than the body and the bike. A disembodied brain in a car – which seems to be the modern ideal – can cover more mental and physical distance than (some) body on a bike. But the latter's world, I have learned, is more meaningful and also more bewildering in an agreeable sort of way.

NOTES

1   Henry David Thoreau, *Walden – or, Life in the Woods* (various editions), paragraph 19.
2   Statistics from the Reykjavik Department of Environment and Transport.
3   Friedrich Nietzsche, *On the Genealogy of Morals* and *Ecce Homo*, ed. Walter Kaufmann (New York: Vintage Books, 1969), pp. 239–40.
4   Thoreau, *Walden*, paragraph 19, emphasis in the original.
5   Ibid., paragraph 21.
6   Søren Kierkegaard, *Concluding Unscientific Postscript to Philosophical Fragments*, vol. 1, trans. Howard V. Hong and Edna H. Hong (Princeton, NJ: Princeton University Press, 1992), p. 275n.

CHAPTER 12

THE COMMUTIST MANIFESTO

All it took for me to start commuting by bike was one disastrous day with my car. My car failed a state emissions test, not because it was spewing black smoke, but because I had a small chip in a piece of plastic near the rear tail light. Slightly annoyed, I took my car to work and began calling around to find a replacement part. The more parts stores and junkyards I called, the more I came to realize that this part was rather rare. At one point a particularly helpful woman at a local junkyard, after searching a parts database, told me, "That part doesn't exist in the state of Texas." At the end of my day I walked out to my car, still uncertain about what I would do about the chipped plastic, and I discovered that one of my tires was flat. At this point I was seething, but I calmed myself, removed all the sundry items in the rear of my car, got out my spare, and changed my tire. It was only when I lowered my car off the jack that I realized that my spare was flat as well. I got the tire inflated and drove home. The next morning I just couldn't face spending any more time on my car. I got my bike out and rode to work. After riding to work for a few weeks, I couldn't find a good answer to the lingering question: Why didn't I use my bike for transportation more often?

I would like to discuss this question. I think most of us should use our bikes for transportation, and not because it will make us healthier, or smarter, or richer, or even better looking, but because we owe it to each other. The more I've thought about it, the more I've become convinced that we have a moral obligation to ride our bikes for transportation. I hope to convince you to ride your bike more often and drive your car less. Unlike me you shouldn't do this because your car is causing you vast amounts of frustration – though I must admit, that's a helpful motivator – but rather you should do it because morality requires you to do it.

An Environmental Ethic for Non-Tree Huggers

There are quite a few problems in moral philosophy that boil down to the problem of moral standing. Moral standing, as I will use it here, is the feature or set of features of something that makes it deserving of moral consideration. For example, imagine that one day I were to go to mow my lawn (this is fantasy, as my wife will attest, I hate to mow the lawn). Presumably, we would think it absurd if Greenpeace were to set up on my sidewalk protesting my mistreatment of those individual blades of grass. The grass has no moral standing – it does not deserve moral consideration. Imagine now that, while I was mowing the lawn, my cat, Cal, came outside, and upon seeing him in the lawn, suppose that I decide to run him over with the lawnmower. In this circumstance I think one would be right to find fault with what I've done. There is something different about Cal, something that the grass lacks, that makes mowing over Cal wrong. Determining what it is that gives some things moral standing is a difficult task, but if that problem can be solved we can go a long way towards solving some difficult moral conundrums. That is to say, once we get clear about what has moral standing, then we are in a better position to alter our behavior in light of this. For example, I now know that I may mow my lawn with impunity, but I may not mow Cal. Progress has already been made in my household, and getting clear about this issue may allow us to make progress elsewhere. For instance, many believe the moral permissibility of abortion is resolved by solving the problem of moral standing of the fetus, that is, once we know when a fetus has moral standing (from the moment of conception? At some later date?), we know when, if ever, abortion is morally permissible. Further, we may think that the moral permissibility of euthanasia, eating meat, animal testing and vivisection, stem cell research, use and abuse of the environment (where the bike has a role to play), and perhaps even capital punishment may all be resolved, or partially resolved, by gaining clarity on the issue of moral standing.

Ultimately this is about cycling and the environment. But I think something must be said about moral standing in order for us to be clear about what reasons we may have to protect or preserve the environment. There are a wide variety of arguments that attempt to explain the moral standing of the environment. On one end of the spectrum we find anthropocentrism.[1] According to this view, the environment has no moral standing at all, and if we are obligated to do anything for the environment it is because, by doing so, we promote the interests or wellbeing of humans. Ultimately, according to anthropocentrism, the only things that matter morally are human beings. On the other end of the spectrum we find ecocentrism. According to ecocentrism, the environment or ecosystems themselves have moral standing. So, on this view, we owe moral consideration to an entire rainforest or reef. Between these two extremes we find biocentrism. According to biocentrism, moral standing is restricted to the living because of some feature possessed by those living creatures, such as sentience, rationality, consciousness, or language. Thus, biocentrism is not as inclusive as ecocentrism, which grants moral standing to non-living things, but is more inclusive than anthropocentrism, which only grants moral standing to human beings.

Fortunately for us both, dear reader, I do not need to determine which theory is correct in order for me to convince you to ride your bike more. This is fortunate for you because solving the problem of moral standing is extraordinarily difficult and would take this essay deep into the morass of contemporary moral theory. This is fortunate for me because the problem of moral standing is the Alp d'Huez of moral philosophy, and that mountain may prove too difficult for me to conquer in this chapter. Instead I suggest that we take a minimalist approach to this topic and accept anthropocentrism as our working theory. Why call this a minimalist approach? Well, most of us are inclined to think that humans must be given moral standing. Any theory that does not attribute to most[2] humans moral standing should be rejected because it's implausible. Thus, anthropocentrism is minimalist because it commits us to a moral position most of us already accept. If you don't think we must give other human beings moral consideration, then don't take it up with me, take it up with the person who wrote the next chapter in this book.[3] Accepting anthropocentrism is crucial because it stacks the deck against me. Notice, if we were to adopt a moral theory that asks us to give moral standing to humans *and* to house cats, more actions become impermissible. Namely, mowing over spouses *and* cats. Whereas if we accept only anthropocentrism, then when I mow the lawn, I must avoid my wife, but cats (at least the slow ones) are in serious trouble. On an anthropocentrist view I must avoid harming humans, but cats, dogs, birds, forests, and tundras be damned. Adopting a minimalist approach is important because if I can show that we ought to ride our bikes for anthropocentric reasons, then even if we come to accept a more inclusive theory, one that perhaps grants moral standing to animals, then this won't reduce the reasons to ride our bikes. Rather, we'll find that the more individuals harmed by our actions, the stronger our obligations become.

It would be unfair, however, to suggest that anthropocentrism values humans to the detriment of everything else. Rather, what anthropocentrism tells us is that humans are the only things to be valued in and of themselves. So, if we were to imagine a person whose life contributes nothing good to society, whose work is useless, and who typically makes those around him unhappy (let's call people like these "philosophers"), we may not kill such a person. The person is valuable in and of himself, regardless of how productive he is or what he means to others. We may be a bit disappointed to discover this. We may have really wanted to kill that philosopher, but we also know that philosophers love their books. Perhaps, just to annoy the philosopher, we should destroy his books? Books are not humans, so they do not deserve moral consideration on the anthropocentrist view. It appears we are free to burn away. However, by burning the books, we harm the philosopher. Anthropocentrism tells us we should not harm the philosopher; thus we may not burn the books. In this case the books have derivative value. They are not valuable in themselves but because of what they mean to a person. What we can see, then, is that we are not free to damage or destroy all that is non-human, because in certain cases, when we damage or destroy a non-human thing, we harm a human as a result.

We can now see how even an anthropocentrist must be concerned about the wellbeing of the environment. If we pollute our rivers, cut down our forests, release excessive toxins into the atmosphere, and so on, then we will eventually come to harm humans on a massive scale. So while damaging the environment itself would mean little to the anthropocentrist, when damaging the environment results in harm to humans, the anthropocentrist would be quite concerned with this. Thus, the environment does have value, but its value is indirect. It is valuable, and ought to be protected, not because it is valuable in its own right, but because it is valuable to the wellbeing of humans.

Considering the Environment by Riding a Bike

We can see now that even the minimalism of the anthropocentrist's position requires that we be concerned with the environment to some degree. What we must also determine is whether or not that may lead us to abandon our cars in favor of our bikes. There are at least two reasons to think that cars should be swapped for bikes: climate change and air quality. One may be inclined to think that climate change is simply a type of air quality issue, and that may be correct, but I will treat them as separate issues. The reason for this is because there are some who deny the science associated with climate change, and while I think such naysaying is misguided, it is a bit too ambitious a project to hope to resolve the climate change debate within the pages of this chapter. So, for those of you who accept the science surrounding climate change, you have reason to commute more by bike. For those of you who do not accept the science surrounding climate change, as long as you accept the idea that air quality can affect one's physical health, then you too should hop on the saddle. If you do not believe that air quality affects one's physical health, well, now's your chance to take up smoking.

Cycles of Climate Change

During its long history the Earth's climate has undergone numerous changes. The fact that we may be at the beginning of another instance of climate change is, by itself, nothing special. Why climate change is worthy of our attention currently is because of the role that we humans play this time around. There are numerous factors that are at work when the Earth's climate changes. What is interesting in the present case of climate change are greenhouse gases and how humans contribute to these. Greenhouse gases trap the Sun's radiation in the Earth's atmosphere, and higher concentrations of greenhouse gases result in more of the Sun's radiation being trapped in the Earth's atmosphere. Certain greenhouse gases are long-lived, which means they are chemically stable and remain within the atmosphere for a "decade to centuries or longer."[4] Recent history has seen a dramatic increase in carbon dioxide (CO_2), one of these long-lived greenhouse gases. As a matter of fact, there has been a 31 percent increase in CO_2 concentrations in the atmosphere over the past 200 years, and current concentrations of CO_2 have not been exceeded in 420,000 years.[5] So, there has been a rapid, unprecedented increase in CO_2, a long-lived greenhouse gas, over the past 200 years.

There are various sources of CO_2 that we find in our atmosphere, but roughly 10–14 percent comes from automobiles. As a US citizen I am embarrassed to report that despite the fact that the United States makes up only 5 percent of the world's population, we are responsible for 45 percent of the CO_2 that comes from automobiles.[6] What we find then is that automobiles make a significant contribution to overall CO_2 levels in the atmosphere, and when we take all the other pollutants emitted by motor vehicles we find that they "cause more air pollution than any other single human activity."[7] If climate change is a serious issue, then humans, and especially citizens of the United States, should be concerned about our contributions to the problem.

So, is climate change a serious issue? To a certain degree this is the source of much of the controversy surrounding climate change. As I have already mentioned, the amount of greenhouse gases we find in the atmosphere is unprecedented, and for that reason we are uncertain about what to expect. I am a philosopher, not a climatologist, so I will not pretend to be able to tell you what will happen as a result of the high levels of CO_2 in the atmosphere. However, if climate change proceeds as some scientists expect it to, we may find an increase of droughts in drought-ridden areas, we may find millions more will be victims of flooding and related deaths, we may find there will be increases in malnutrition and related deaths, and we may find increased deaths due to heat waves, storms, and fires.[8] Even with the minimal moral commitments of anthropocentrism we should be extremely concerned with climate change, and despite the fact that the dangers of climate change are uncertain, we must remember that it is not Monopoly money that we are gambling with. Rather, we are gambling with our lives and the lives of millions of other human beings. With these significant dangers associated with climate change, we must do all that we can to mitigate the dangers that present themselves, and one important contribution we can make is to significantly reduce the CO_2 we individually add to the atmosphere. Beside the potential for preventing human suffering, it's hard to believe that cycling, or anything else for that matter, will be much fun in a vast, fiery, apocalyptical dystopia. But that's just my opinion.

JOHN RICHARD HARRIS

Pollution

Suppose, however, that the science surrounding climate change is all wrong. Even if this extraordinarily unlikely possibility is correct, we still have very good reasons to reduce our use of automobiles. Cars produce numerous pollutants, and those pollutants are not limited to greenhouse gases. One particularly hazardous pollutant that cars produce is ozone. In the upper levels of our atmosphere ozone serves to protect us from harmful ultraviolet radiation from the Sun. However, when it is closer to the ground, ozone proves to be particularly harmful. Ozone causes damage to lung tissue and long-term exposure can cause permanent damage. The damage can be so serious that, according to one recent study, an increase in ten parts per billion of ozone in the air can be connected to nearly 4,000 deaths in the United States every year.[9] Even if ozone does not kill you, it may still harm you. Ozone has been linked to shortness of breath, asthma attacks, and reduced lung capacity, and may compromise the immune system's ability to fight off infection in the respiratory tract. If one is persistently exposed to ozone, the damage to one's lungs may become permanent.

Of course, ozone is but one of the pollutants caused by motor vehicles, but what we find is that ozone represents a significant health risk to humans. While I have focused on the ozone problems that are faced by citizens in the United States, there is no reason to think it is a problem limited to just the US or North America. There are significant levels of ozone worldwide, and we should be looking for ways to reduce those levels. One important way to do that is to drive less, and to ride your bike more.

The Cycling Solution

Regardless of whether one is concerned with climate change, pollution, or (hopefully) both, we have good reason to act to limit their impact on our lives. The reason that we ought to limit their effect is rather simple, and follows directly from the minimal moral commitments of anthropocentrism. Climate change and air pollution threaten the lives and well-being of human beings on a large scale. Given that we are morally obligated to be concerned with how our actions affect the lives of other human beings, we should seek to limit the ways that our actions adversely affect others. As it turns out, widespread automobile use threatens the lives and wellbeing of other humans, and as a result we must look to significantly reduce our use of motor vehicles. Bicycles offer one of the best alternatives to automobile use. Commuting by bike offers not only a way to improve the life of the cyclist, but also a means to reduce the harms inflicted on other human beings.

A bicycle's use of energy is extraordinarily efficient, and it may have no equal that we know of. Cars require a great deal of energy to move them, but not so with bikes. The energy required to pedal a bike isn't much more than the energy required to keep your body warm while watching television.[10] If we compared the energy that is used by a car and the energy used by a cyclist, we find that the cyclist's use of energy is vastly more efficient. The Toyota Prius, a car that has one of the best miles-per-gallon ratings of any car available in the United States, gets roughly 49 miles to the gallon (on a good day, with lenient EPA officials, and a tail wind). Converting the energy expended by an average cyclist traveling 12 miles per hour we find that the cyclist gets the equivalent of 1,000 miles per gallon.[11] Interestingly enough, cycling is even more energy efficient than walking. The bike's extraordinarily effective use of energy makes it an ideal mode of transportation.

Of course, when I first began to think about trading my car for my bike, the very idea seemed absurd, and this was in part because my wife and I like to take occasional road trips to places like Austin, Texas. Commuting by bike and even biking recreationally have gotten me into pretty good shape, but the idea of making the 190-mile trip from Fort Worth to Austin by bike is daunting to say the least. If you are anything like me you will think, "Sure, it would be great to bike more, but until I'm ready to ride in the Tour de France, riding 190 miles just isn't in the cards for me." Well, put down the EPO my friend because even if the bike cannot replace all of your trips by car, it can replace many of them. According to a study done by the National Household Travel Survey (NHTS) in 2001, 41 percent of all trips by car traveled distances of less than two miles and 28 percent traveled distances of less than one mile.[12] Surely you can bike two miles! According to the same study, 50 percent of all workers commute less than five miles to work. Even my cat, Cal (who has had more than his fair share of catnip), can see that if a large number of people began biking those five miles to work instead of driving, we would begin to make a big difference in the automobile's contribution to climate change and air pollution.

It seems that we could reduce toxic emissions by 41 percent if people in the United States were to bike whenever they travel two miles or less from their home. It's worth mentioning that the news is slightly better than that. Most cars are equipped with a catalytic converter. What the catalytic converter does (here's the good news) is remove highly toxic carbon monoxide from car emissions by (here's the bad news) converting it into carbon dioxide. Carbon monoxide is a major contributor in the formation of ground-level ozone. Catalytic converters remove about 97 percent of carbon monoxide from auto emissions.[13] However, catalytic converters, to be fully effective, must warm up to about 482 degrees Fahrenheit. Even in Texas, where, I believe, the ambient temperature during the summer is 280 degrees Fahrenheit, the catalytic converter does not reach effective temperature within the first few miles of driving. What this means is that all those car trips of two miles or less are done without the benefit of the car's catalytic converter. Thus, by eliminating or even significantly reducing car trips of two miles or less, we could make major inroads to reducing ozone pollution. So, biking instead of driving for short distances is an especially effective way to reduce dangerous pollutants.

The End of a (Subaru) Legacy

After two months of commuting by bike I decided that I had to fix my car. It pained me, and I figured I would have to pay more than I liked, but I called a local dealership to see how much it would cost to buy the replacement part. The comical conclusion to my story: my mechanic was wrong. The car can pass state inspections with a broken part like mine. The reason the part was so rare is that it is merely cosmetic. I must admit that I was relieved to find this out, but I can't say I wasn't just a little upset with my mechanic. I won't ever go to see him again, but not because I'm angry. It's just I've figured out how to make commuting by bike work for me. I keep a few pairs of shoes in my office (ride to the office a few times with shoes in your bag and you'll come to see that it's just not worth carrying all that weight), I've got deodorant, a towel, and some wet wipes to clean up with once I get to work. The biggest hurdle was the terribly hot Texas summers. Once I realized I could survive those – leave for work early before it gets too hot, leave for home once it starts to cool down – I realized that commuting by bike was something I could do on a daily basis. So, my wife and I are finally in the process of fixing my car. We are going to get the car inspected, we're going to get my tire (and the spare) fixed, and then we're going to sell my car (farewell, Blue Thunder!). Commuting by bike is much easier than you think. If you do it, even for those short trips near your home, you'll improve your health, and more importantly you may be helping to save your fellow humans. The benefits of cycling are enormous, the costs are few.

Cyclists of the world, unite. We have nothing to lose but our chains.

NOTES

1   For an excellent discussion of anthropocentrism and how it relates to the environment, see Onora O'Neill, "Environmental Values, Anthropocentrism and Speciesism," *Environmental Values* 6 (1997): 127–42.

2   I say "most" here rather than "all" to avoid certain controversies. Anthropocentrists may consistently believe that only humans deserve moral consideration, but not all humans do. For example, an anthropocentrist may argue that human cognition is so unique and special that all humans that have this deserve moral standing, but those humans that do not have this level of cognition (e.g., those who have suffered massive head trauma, fetuses in early stages of pregnancy) do not have moral standing because they lack the requisite cognitive capabilities.

3   I think I heard him saying bad things about your mother ...

4   *Climate Change 2007: The Physical Science Basis. Contribution of Working Group I to the Fourth Assessment Report of the Intergovernmental Panel on Climate Change*, ed. Susan Solomon et al. (Cambridge: Cambridge University Press, 2007), pp. 23–4.

5   Daniel Albritton et al., "Technical Summary," in *Climate Change 2001: The Scientific Basis*, ed. J. T. Houghton et al. (Cambridge: Cambridge University Press, 2001), p. 7.

6   John DeCicco and Freda Fung, *Global Warming on the Road: The Climate Impact of America's Automobiles* (Washington, DC: Environmental Defense, 2006), p. iv. Available online at www.edf.org/documents/5301_ Globalwarmingontheroad.pdf.

7   Asif Faiz et al., "Automotive Air Pollution: Issues and Options for Developing Countries," Working Paper WPS 492 (Washington, DC: World Bank), cited in Ambuj D. Sagar, "Automobiles and Global Warming: Alternative Fuels and Other Options for Carbon Dioxide Emission Reduction," *Environmental Impact Assessment Review* 15, 3 (1995): 242.

8 Neil Adger et al., "Summary for Policy-Makers," in *Climate Change 2007: Impacts, Adaptation and Vulnerability. Contributions of Working Group II to the Fourth Assessment Report of the Intergovernmental Panel on Climate Change,* ed. M. L. Parry et al. (Cambridge: Cambridge University Press, 2007), p. 8.

9 Michelle L. Bell et al., "Ozone and Short-Term Mortality in 95 US Urban Communities, 1987–2000," *Journal of the American Medical Association* 292, 19 (2004): 2376. Available online at jama.ama-assn.org/cgi/content/full/292/19/2372.

10 Robert Hurst, *The Cyclist's Manifesto* (Guilford: The Globe Pequot Press, 2009), p. 176.

11 David Gordon Wilson, *Bicycling Science* (Cambridge: MIT Press, 2004), p. 160.

12 Joh Pucher and Lewis Dijkstra, "Promoting Safe Walking and Cycling to Improve Public Health: Lessons From the Netherlands and Germany," *American Journal of Public Health* 93, 9 (2003): 1509. Available online at policy.rutgers.edu/faculty/pucher/AJPHfromJacobsen.pdf.

13 Steven D. Burch, Thomas F. Potter, and Matthew A. Keyser, "Reducing Cold-Start Emissions by Catalytic Converter Thermal Management," October 1994. Available online at www.nrel.gov/vehiclesandfuels/energystorage/pdfs/reducing_emissions.pdf. Thanks to Darren Flusche of the League of American Bicyclists (www.bikeleague.org) for providing me with this information.

CHAPTER 13

CRITICAL MASS RIDES AGAINST CAR CULTURE

We're Not Blocking Traffic...

In 1992, bike riders in San Francisco began to converge at rush hour on the last Friday of every month to celebrate bicycling, express their collective solidarity, and send a public message through a group ride: "We are not blocking traffic, we *are* traffic!" Conceived as a mobile party and a leaderless demonstration, the event known as Critical Mass has since energized legions of cyclists, caused incredible controversy, and helped to transform people's imaginations about bicycle transportation in hundreds of cities throughout the world.[1]

Uniquely, this monthly event turned global phenomenon draws much needed attention to urban bicycle transportation while it gives cyclists the rare treat of doing something they are (technically) not supposed to do: take over the street and bike in the middle of the road with friends and strangers alike. By allowing bicyclists to experiment with spontaneity, playfulness, and dominant uses of public spaces, Critical Mass is a critical practice that, for better or worse, sparks a necessary dialogue about the role of the bicycle in a world increasingly dominated by cars.

Background and (Dis)organization

Critical Mass emerged from the collaborative efforts of cyclists in the San Francisco Bay area who were involved with the San Francisco Bike Coalition, social movement activism, and the largely underground bike messenger culture that flourished throughout the 1980s and early 1990s.[2] The Commute Clot, as it was initially called, was first proposed as an event meant to join bike commuters with other cyclists who sought visibility on city streets.[3] These monthly gatherings quickly began to draw more participants despite a lack of formal organization or an overarching dogma. Initial rides drew around 50 or 60 people but within several years the numbers often swelled into the hundreds and thousands.

Since early rides were designed to celebrate biking, it was and still is common for people to ride with costumes, decorated bicycles, signs, noise-makers, and, in some cases, with sound systems and live bands. Halloween rides, for example, consistently feature some of the most elaborate festivities and parade themes. Critical Mass has also been used to pay tribute to cyclists killed by automobiles, and occasionally integrated into political protests and Reclaim the Streets events. The latter are guerilla street parties thrown to celebrate both car-free space and the act of celebration itself.[4] "Warfare" was never so much fun. Without a charter, a centralized network, or formal affiliation with any organization, the event spread to hundreds of cities by the end of the 1990s and has seen up to tens of thousands of "Massers" out on a single ride.[5] To wit, consider the case of Budapest, where an estimated 80,000 bicyclists rode through the city in April 2008.

Critical Mass is essentially a direct action, anarchic event in that rides are unsanctioned by city officials and riders are motivated by self-determination, self-rule, and a non-hierarchical structure. Bicyclist Michael Klett explains: "within Critical Mass itself there are no leaders; organizers, yes, we are all organizers – but we're not in charge ... that has been the key to its success."[6] His distinction between leader and organizer is a useful one because it points to the active role that participants are supposed to play in the event. Bike riders meet at designated spots on the last Friday of every month (in their respective cities and towns) to collectively decide on the route that will be taken; proposals are verbally solicited and sometimes circulated in the form of maps, before being put to a vote. Routes are occasionally decided in advance, but this practice is often discouraged in lieu of face-to-face, spontaneous decision-making.

Many of the techniques employed by Massers were developed in the early San Francisco rides, including the practice of "corking," which is when bikers position themselves at busy intersections to block, or "cork," traffic while the pack rides by. This tactic is intended to keep the Mass together while riding through stoplights, and though technically illegal, it is designed to maximize safety for cyclists (safety in numbers!) and minimize hassle for drivers (by keeping the Mass moving at a reasonable speed). Rather than causing vehicular bottlenecks, this "cork" actually opens spaces up. Still, this strategy – as well as the event as a whole – garners mixed responses, ranging from enthusiastic support, to indifference, to outright hostility. For example, police have physically assaulted riders and initiated mass arrests in a number of cities, whereas drivers have used everything from foul language to their own fists as a way to squelch rides. On several occasions, motorists aggravated at the temporary seizure of "their" roads have even run over participants with their cars (July 2007 in Chicago; July 2008 in Seattle). At the same time, rides have also been known to draw a variety of antagonistic cyclists, namely young white men eager to harass drivers, start fights, or take revenge on people's cars. Massers in San Francisco rightly dubbed this amorphous breed of participants the "testosterone brigade" in the 1990s.[7] Over a decade later, these and other bitter cyclists still pop up from time to time, but the vast majority of riders are there to enjoy themselves and to make a statement while doing so.

Interpretations

Part of Critical Mass's notoriety arguably stems from the difficulty faced by those who attempt to label and define it; scholars Susan Blickstein and Susan Hanson note that it has been called "a protest, a form of street theater, a method of commuting, a party, and a social space."[8] This slippery definition is both embraced and compounded by participants who also describe it as a "pro-bike, anti-car monthly action," a rebellion, a movement, a revolutionary act, and conversely, "just a bike ride."[9] The inability for people to accurately pinpoint what Critical Mass *is* does not necessarily reflect confusion (although it does do that) as much as disagreement over the ride's meaning and purpose. Oddly enough, this is not coincidental; Critical Mass was specifically designed to be inter-preted, shaped, and actively defined by its participants, regardless of whether they agree. Veteran Masser and bike advocate Jym Dyer writes:

> Participants are encouraged to implement their own ideas, and non-participants (including those who for various reasons are averse to the ride) are encouraged to join in with their ideas as well ... be prepared to discuss your missives and defend your arguments![10]

Xerocracy, or "rule through photocopying," is the dominant paradigm of Critical Mass and it rests on the premise that anyone can (and should) print, photocopy, and solicit media that advocate and/or explain the ride. This approach to grassroots communication creates an interesting space in which riders voice their opinions, debate their ideas, and collectively give meaning to the event through face-to-face communication and the active production and dissemination of writing, art, maps, and other self-produced media – some of which are passed out on rides and some that circulate online through a sprawling web of Mass pages. Artwork cele-brating Critical Mass and bicycle transportation is also common, par-ticularly images connecting bicycle transportation to environmentalism, autonomy, and critiques of the oil and auto industries. Xerocracy is thus not only a means to shape participant and public perceptions about bicy-cle transportation (through facts, statistics, images, and personal narra-tives), it is also a way for cyclists to actively "channel the energy and focus of the mass" as they see fit.[11]

While participants clearly articulate ideas about what Mass is and is not – what it does and does not do – the very nature of the event invites a level of interpretation that is completely unpredictable. The ride is con-tentious for precisely this reason: to its supporters, it symbolizes every-thing from pedal power to people power to the reclamation of public space, whereas its critics often see it as a symbol of disorganization and lawlessness ... even a hatred of drivers. In particular, there is an ongoing feud between cyclists as to whether the event is helpful or harmful to bike advocacy and the image of cycling, a debate exemplified in an archived 1999 email "flame war" between Critical Mass supporters, participants, and critics (mainly "vehicular cycling" advocates) on the West coast.[12] The debate – which has made as many rounds as a Japanese Keirin racer – tends to revolve around heated disputes over the questionable legality of Critical Mass, and from the ways in which the ride, its participants, and by extension all bicyclists are presented and *re*presented to the public.

Mass media – and the corporate press in particular – have thus significantly altered the stakes of Mass since its inception, namely by stoking the fire of a "Bike vs. Car" drama that journalists themselves have played a central role in cultivating since the 1980s, when urban bicyclists and especially bike messengers were routinely depicted as nuisances or safety hazards. This, despite tens of thousands of annual automobile fatalities and hundreds of thousands of auto-related accidents and injuries in the US alone. News audiences are now treated to a similar set of stories in which Critical Mass riders have taken the place of bike messengers as the two-wheeled clan most likely to be depicted as everything from casual troublemakers, to elitists, to zealots, chaos-loving anarchists, criminals, and even potential terrorists worthy of undercover police surveillance.[13] There is, of course, a small minority of belligerent (and, on rare occasions, violent) cyclists who are responsible for generating some of the bad press accrued over the years, but journalists have also churned out enough inflammatory news stories on the event to fill an Olympic velodrome. And this makes it all too easy to forget that the issue at hand is, after all, a short bike ride that only takes place once a month.

As a result of these and other factors, discussions about Critical Mass tend to slide into an overly simplistic set of pros and cons, love against hate arguments over whether it is "good" or "bad" for bicycling, despite the fact that Mass can exert a positive influence on bike advocacy even when it draws negative attention. For example, the perceived "radicalism" of Critical Mass can provide an incentive for transportation agencies and city officials to increase their dialogue with activists who they see as more "moderate." A sort of informal "good cop"/"bad cop" routine on wheels. Indeed, many bike advocacy groups have used the notoriety and contentiousness of Critical Mass to secure more influence and a louder public platform from which to express their views and policy recommendations.[14] Amy Stork, co-founder of Portland, Oregon's bike advocacy network Shift, speaks to this issue as both a cycling enthusiast and a specialist in strategic communication:

> I really appreciate Critical Mass because when you are going to change culture, it's good to have a radical wing, because that pushes folks towards the center. If people see Critical Mass and that appears radical to them, then putting a bike lane in seems reasonable. In places where they don't have Critical Mass, they think bike lanes are radical.[15]

Martin Wachs, a professor of engineering and planning at the University of California Berkeley, reiterates this point in his assessment of cycling infrastructure in San Francisco, noting that pressure applied by Critical Mass and other bike advocates in the late 1990s played a key role in the construction of a $147 million bike lane on the Oakland–San Francisco Bay Bridge: "it was included because a persistent, organized, and downright obnoxious group of advocates would not let go of the issue."[16] In short, while debating whether Critical Mass helps or hinders bike advocacy by sending the "wrong message" is not unreasonable or irrelevant, it is still only one way – not necessarily *the* way – to understand how and why this (or any other) collective action becomes meaningful.

Influences and Impacts

One of the reasons Critical Mass seems to irritate Americans like a fresh saddle sore is because the ride tends to raise critical questions about some of the dominant cultural norms and taken-for-granted privileges associated with mobility, the use of public space(s), and the sacred cow of Western society: the automobile. In this sense, Critical Mass is part of a lineage of bike activism that began in the late 1960s and early 1970s when groups like the Dutch Provo (Amsterdam), Alternative Stad (Stockholm), and New York City's Transportation Alternatives (among other US groups) began to actively imagine cities in which urban mobility would not have to be organized around the spaces, speeds, and trajectories of motorized traffic.

Then, as now, bicycling was not seen as a "cure all" as much as a utilitarian goal: a goal that speaks to the larger, interrelated problems brought on by air pollution, oil reliance, dwindling public spaces, and decades of unfettered political support for the auto industry and waves of urban development centered around the car. Building off the renewed popularity of leisure cycling and the urgency of both the environmental movement and the oil crisis in the early 1970s, this model of bike advocacy called for people to pragmatically intervene in the composition of the urban environment – through cycling, political organizing, and healthy doses of theatrical protest – to promote a more sustainable vision of city life. It was a basic expression of what Henri Lefebvre famously called the *right to the city*, which could best be described as the collective right for people to have a say in the ways that their cities (their homes)

are organized, and in the way they function. Importantly, having money or owning property is not a prerequisite for one's participation. It is a way of saying that citizens and urban dwellers have the intrinsic right to share in the exciting, challenging, and fundamentally political processes that make a city a city.

By the 1980s, the growing popularity of John Forester's philosophy of *vehicular cycling* – the notion that "bicyclists fare best when they act, and are treated in return, as drivers of vehicles" – marked a clear shift away from conceptualizing bicycle transportation as part of an environmental and political "right to the city," toward a paradigm that simply emphasized the right to bike.[17] Because while vehicular cycling is unquestionably a worthwhile skill for urban bikers, it is also a rather conservative ideology that draws passionate support from people who take pains to distinguish themselves from anything they perceive to be "anti-car." Progressive urban planners, environmentalists, so-called "political" bike activists, and even people who simply want off-road bike paths are often lumped together under the broad "anti-car" banner.

Fortunately, the resurgence of urban reform-minded bike activism in the 1990s began to gradually turn the tide away from advocacy bent on preserving the status quo of car culture. Critical Mass was and is instrumental in pointing many people in this direction, which is to say, toward a worldview that sees the bicycle as a tool for rethinking the logic of automobiles, as opposed to a tool one uses to simply imitate them. At the most basic level, Mass tends to spark people's interest in bicycling and it continues to nudge cyclists toward a more politicized engagement with transportation issues writ large.[18] That is to say, monthly rides bring bicycling advocates together, inspire other cyclists to get involved with local advocacy groups, and also provide an important network for activism that is as much tactical as it is social.[19] Cyclist and scholar Dave Horton sees the event as an important tool for enhancing the "activist identities of individuals" and building a wider political community:

> Individuals share an alternative culture, but – for as long as they remain anonymous to each other – are unable to develop joint projects from their shared ways of life, values, and goals. Critical Mass made – and continues from time to time to make – visible and tangible the connections between them, transforming anonymous inhabitation of an imagined community into meaningful and possibility-laden participation in a realtime face-to-face community.[20]

The advocates and activists who emerge from these networks have indeed played crucial roles in putting cycling on the public agenda and pushing bike advocacy in new directions. For example, Critical Mass has almost single-handedly created or rejuvenated widespread interest in using bicycles as vehicles for public expression. This is evident in the variety of creative bike demonstrations and protest rides that ensued since Critical Mass first gained popularity in the 1990s, from the somber memorial rides and "Ghost Bike" installations used to commemorate cyclists killed by automobiles, to the playful World Naked Bike Ride that activist and artist Conrad Schmidt founded as a protest against the *indecency* of oil. In particular, the often-playful nature of Critical Mass has shown bicyclists how they can use satire and humor to highlight the injustices, ironies, and bizarre "common sense" of car culture. Some prominent examples include the construction and public use of the Green Hummer – a pedal-powered vehicle that friends in Savannah, Georgia, built to the same ludicrous proportions of the Hummer SUV – as well as the creation of PARK(ing) Day: a now-annual event started by San Francisco's Rebar collective, in which activists roll out sod, benches, and potted trees to construct miniature public parks in metered, urban parking spaces.

By presenting bicycling as something different from a sport, a children's activity, or a means for simply getting one's butt into shape, Critical Mass has also helped to transform the image of bicycling and the common associations and stereotypes that resonate with the public. Charles Komanoff and other longtime bike advocates have taken note of this in recent years, arguing that Mass not only sparked new interest in urban cycling, it also helped to get cycling "out of its geek ghetto into someplace more appealing to the 99% of people who don't consider themselves 'cyclists.'"[21]

The fun, excitement, and even the rebelliousness of Critical Mass have contributed to a growing sentiment that biking can actually be cool (believe it or not). This is hardly an insignificant point when one considers that the most famous cyclist in the United States, aside from Lance Amstrong, is probably Pee-wee Herman or the 40-Year-Old Virgin. Because while environmentalism, physical fitness, thriftiness, and pleasure are all factors that influence people's bike-riding habits, it is safe to say that most people are not going to start bicycling simply because it sounds good on paper or is better for the environment (as unfortunate as this might be). Indeed, cultural norms play a profound role in our transportation habits and Critical Mass is one of the things that gives people a chance to potentially reassess what it actually means to be a "cyclist."

Such inroads may not change the negative social stigmas widely associated with adult bicycling (i.e., poverty, eccentricity), but they are especially vital in places where the moniker "cyclist" is exclusively used with reference to lycra hot pants, wacky old professors, or aging virgins.

Critical Mass is by no means a substitution for formal bike advocacy, nor does it offer a solution to transportation problems by any stretch of the imagination. Many participants are admittedly apolitical or gleefully disorganized, and the event does little to transform the social and economic aspects of car culture, or the actual "stuff" of urban planning, such as concrete, roads, and the like. But what it succeeds at doing is creating conditions in which people actively use bicycles to forge new ways of imagining, understanding, and ultimately utilizing both public and social spaces. Perhaps most importantly, it gives people who are marginalized on busy city streets a chance to "live the impossible" and immerse themselves in what cyclist Charles Higgins describes as a *festive rolling adventure*:

> Though it raises the blood pressure of some rush-hour commuters, Critical Mass offers a change, if only for a few moments, in the domination of the streets. In place of tons of steel and glass is a rolling community of people who can talk to each other and experience safety in numbers … Critical Mass provides an opportunity for average people to gather surrounded by other cyclists on the streets that otherwise threaten them.[22]

People who ride in Critical Mass frequently testify to the power of this experience because it obviously transcends the mere act of bicycling. Matthew Roth of New York City's *Time's Up!* states, "it is one of the few authentic experiences that I've had in a group setting," while Wisconsin cyclist Isral DeBruin reflects on the way it informed his sense of place:

> I began to truly appreciate seeing the city of Milwaukee at street level, moving more quickly than walking, but without any glass or the sound of an engine between the buildings and me. I started noticing things I'd never seen before and felt the city in an entirely new way. I could feel the streets. I could feel the pavement.[23]

Sharing a collective experience with a group of fellow cyclists and conveying one's right to the bikeable city can be a profound moment for a person, particularly one who is unaffiliated with, or simply uninterested in, formal cycling organizations, clubs, or traditional cycling events. It can serve as an introduction to a larger community of bike riders just as it can affirm, renew, or develop one's commitment to bicycling or one's identity as a bicyclist. In short, it can give people a reason to ride and a reason to take pride in doing so. Ayleen Crotty, a veteran bike advocate and co-host of the *Bike Show* on KBOO radio in Portland, Oregon, says that while Critical Mass has its limitations, it is also a "forum for cyclists to meet, feel supported and feel elated ... to know they're not the only ones out there."[24]

In creating a unique space where communities of cyclists can emerge through a common love of the bicycle, Critical Mass serves an important ritual function that gives a tangible, human expression to the slogan "Ride Daily, Celebrate Monthly." This is arguably the most cherished feature of the event and, incidentally, one of the characteristics its critics frequently overlook when they judge Mass by a set of standards better suited for measuring the worth of an old radio, that is, whether it transmits a clear message to a passive audience. Because ultimately, the value of Critical Mass is less contingent on what it *says* to the public than what it *does* for the people who show up to ride each month.

...We (Still) Are Traffic

If Critical Mass is judged solely by its capacity to live up to the rhetoric of its most adamant supporters, then one can hardly call it a success. But despite the bad press and the temptation to dismiss it as either a disturbance or mere street party, Critical Mass is much more than just a protest or fun ride. For short durations, cyclists disrupt the automobile's domination of the street and try to demonstrate something admittedly utopian: a vision of pedal power and human-scale community in action. Moreover, bike riders have often used this experience to actively question the functions and uses of public spaces, thereby thrusting the politics of car culture into the public spotlight in ways that are typically shielded from public debate or scrutiny. It may not prompt a revolution or usher in the post-automobile era, but at its best, Critical Mass is an expression of solidarity, passion, and critical thinking that is fundamental to the germination of any progressive moment; it pushes others to consider what is possible ... what *could* be.[25] At the very least, it is a demonstration of creative dissent and public experimentation with pleasure in an era of widespread apathy and cynicism about real change (not the kind promoted by politicians or advertisers). Even if these moments of dissent are fleeting, and at times poorly executed or misunderstood, they give people a unique chance to consider how they might use their voices, their bodies, and even their bicycles to exercise their collective "right to the city."

NOTES

1   Chris Carlsson, "Critical Massifesto," in *Critical Mass Essays, Flyers, Images from San Francisco, 1992–1998*. Available online at www.processedworld. com/tfrs_web/history/Index.html. (Originally published in June 1994.)
2   Rebecca Reilly, *Nerves of Steel* (Buffalo: Spoke & Word Press, 2000); Travis Hugh Culley, *The Immortal Class: Bike Messengers and the Cult of Human Power*, 1st ed. (New York: Villard, 2001).
3   Jym Dyer, "Flocculating in the Streets of Berkeley," *Terrain*, August 1993.
4   See John Jordan, "The Art of Necessity: The Subversive Imagination of Anti-Road Protest and Reclaim the Streets," in *DiY Culture: Party and Protest in Nineties Britain*, ed. George McKay (London: Verso, 1998), pp. 129–51.
5   The April 2008 ride in Budapest, Hungary, drew an estimated 80,000 bicyclists while rides in 2006 and 2007 both saw over 30,000 participants. See Zsolt Balla, "Critical Mass Wheels Away," *The Budapest Sun*, April 23, 2008.
6   Michael Klett, "A Uniquely Democratic Experiment," in *Critical Mass, Bicycling's Defiant Celebration*, ed. Chris Carlsson (Oakland: AK Press, 2002), p. 90.
7   See Steven Bodzin, "Politics Can Be Fun," in *Critical Mass*, ed. Carlsson, p. 103.
8   Susan Blickstein and Susan Hanson, "Critical Mass: Forging a Politics of Sustainable Mobility in the Information Age," *Transportation* 28, 4 (2001): 6.
9   Bernie Blaug, "Crit Mass," in *Critical Mass*, ed. Carlsson; Charles Higgins, "Critical to Recall Real 'Mass' Appeal," *San Francisco Guardian*, June 30, 2000.
10 Dyer, "Flocculating in the Streets of Berkeley."
11 Klett, "A Uniquely Democratic Experiment," 90.
12 "Critical Mass Flame War," in *Monkey Chicken*. Available online at www. monkeychicken.com/fwar.htm.
13 For examples, see: Alex Storozynski, "End the Anarchy: Critical Mass Deserves a Police Escort to Keep It Safe," *a.m. New York*, November 5, 2004; Elizabeth Press, Andrew Lynn, and Chris Ryan, *Still We Ride*, Tandem Production, 2005 (film).

14 Blickstein and Hanson, "Critical Mass," 360.
15 Amy Stork, interview with the author, August 6, 2004. Also see Dave Snyder, "Good for the Bicycling Cause," in *Critical Mass*, ed. Carlsson, p. 112.
16 Martin Wachs, "Creating Political Pressure for Cycling," *Transportation Quarterly* 52, 1 (1998): 6.
17 See John Forester, *Effective Cycling* (Cambridge, MA: MIT Press, 1993).
18 Adam Kessel, "Response to Boston CM Critics," *Chicago Critical Mass*, April 9, 2000. Available online at chicagocriticalmass.org/about/faq/adamkessel.
19 Dyer, "Flocculating in the Streets of Berkeley."
20 Dave Horton, "Lancaster Critical Mass: Does It Still Exist?" in *Critical Mass*, ed. Carlsson, pp. 63–4. See Guy Debord, "Report on the Construction of Situations and on the International Situationist Tendency's Conditions of Organization and Action," in *Situationist International Anthology*, ed. Ken Knabb (Berkeley, CA: Bureau of Public Secrets, 1981), p. 25. Originally published in Paris, June 1957.
21 Charles Komanoff, "The Need for More Cyclists," *Remarks to the Bicycle Education Leadership Conference/League of American Bicyclists in New York City, May 3rd 2005*. Available online at www.cars-suck.org/littera-scripta/LAB-talk.html.
22 Jeff Ferrell, *Tearing Down the Streets: Adventures in Urban Anarchy* (New York: Palgrave, 2001), p. 115; Higgins, "Critical to Recall Real 'Mass' Appeal."
23 Mindy Bond, "Matthew Roth, Bicycle Enthusiast, Time's Up," *Gothamist*, April 29, 2005; Isral DeBruin, "Critical Mass: A Personal Perspective," *University of Wisconsin-Milwaukee Post*, September 5, 2006.
24 Ayleen Crotty, personal correspondence, January 3, 2007.
25 David Pinder, "Commentary: Writing Cities against the Grain," *Urban Geography* 25, 8 (2004): 794.

STAGE 4

SPINNING WISDOM

CHAPTER 14

WARM UP

Are You Real? Tony Meets Bishop Berkeley

"Is that real?"

I could have laughed at the question from my 7-year-old son, but I considered it seriously. The buck was perfectly frozen, half in shadow beneath a young oak, up to his knees in grass and nettles. I hadn't been the first one to see him, focused as I was on keeping our tandem on the trail – we had already run into a patch of nettles. I should have known something was different when Tony stopped singing. After the wail of protest when I jammed his small, cleated shoes into the pedals and smashed his toes in the process, the singing had come as a relief, but not an unexpected one. We were old mates in the saddle by now, three-year veterans of off-road tandem rides. Tony's music and his stand-up technique helped to power us over impossible climbs. Rides of three or more hours did not deter us.

I flicked my glance at the buck, who might have been wondering if we were real, too ... a father and son Andy Warhol could have painted, draped in the plumage of modernity, too bright to consider without sunglasses, contemplating the wilderness. Aluminum and lycra, rubber and stainless steel, not to mention a grating self-awareness. Even the little boy's voice, daring to ask such a question.

"Are you real?" the buck might have responded.

"Is he supposed to be here?" Tony expanded the conversation.

"Of course he's real," I huffed. Most fathers want to stay ahead of their son's queries, but I prided myself on never being more than an answer behind.

I dropped the chain onto the smallest ring just as the front wheel dove into the stream. "Stand up!" I ordered. The water was shallow, but moved fast enough I couldn't see the bottom. Rocks leapt under our tires, but we were a perfect team, the tandem steady even as we side-slipped across. At the opposite shore the trail kicked upward, a brutal ascent that would test both of us until we reached the crest, or fell over with an "uh-oh." I pushed hard to gain some momentum.

"Is he supposed to be here?" Tony grew insistent, already dismissing my unspoken worry about the climb.

What the hell. I could be profound, too. "As much as we are," I responded.

"Oh," was his satisfied reply. He stood, and the bike surged from the stream, the front wheel biting into the incline.

I risked a glance behind us at the buck, but he was gone. I never saw him move.

"Water come down, water come down," Tony sang as he bounced on the pedals.

CHAPTER 15

MY LIFE AS A TWO-WHEELED PHILOSOPHER

My Last Race

The final race of my cycling career happened over 20 years ago, but I remember it quite vividly. It was a two-up track sprint on the now demolished 7-Eleven Olympic Velodrome in Los Angeles; both I and my opponent were trying to make it to the 1988 Olympics, where women's track cycling would be included for the first time. Women's road cycling had made its debut in 1984 and I had qualified for the Olympic Trials that year too, but this time I was much more experienced and better prepared. I had more or less dedicated my life to bike racing after graduating from college a couple of years earlier. I had raced actively throughout my college career, winning a national collegiate championship in this very event. Through cycling I had learned about training, nutrition, strategy, and mental preparation; but most importantly I had learned about myself. And it was a question about myself that was on the line in this race: had I become good enough to be "an Olympian"?

The race was only three laps of the 333-meter track, but match sprints almost always start out slowly because you can only hold your top speed for about 200 meters – if you charge ahead much earlier your opponent will ride through your slipstream and slingshot ahead to victory. You either need to force your opponent into the lead (indeed, some track racers actually stop and balance their bikes on the banking) or control the race from the front. I had a lot of explosive power, but not the best top end, so I went right to the front at the starting gun and then pedaled just ahead of and below my opponent, effectively pinning her to the upper rail. The higher up the track, the farther around it is, so when she accelerated to go over the top of me, I could easily stay ahead, and if she slowed to try to drop underneath me I could turn down the banking quickly and block her path. To keep an eye on her, I had to ride the entire track looking backward – which I had trained myself to do. I could tell it was unnerving for her to be watched in this way and at the beginning of the third lap she seemed to be getting antsy.

She began to accelerate around the top of the track, and I matched her speed to stay ahead. Then before the final turn I launched a surprise attack – I never planned exactly where to take off, figuring that if I surprised myself I'd be sure to surprise her. It worked: I could feel her freeze a bit as I jumped ahead and instantly she had a gap of several meters to close before the final turn. Going around the bend I soft-pedaled just a little, forcing her to ride the long way around the turn into the wind, instead of sitting in my draft. I could hear her breathing hard and saw her out of the corner of my eye, just above my rear wheel. Into the homestretch, I put the hammer down – confident in my slight lead and giving it everything I had. I'd ridden the race perfectly, I was on my way to the Olympic team! Then I heard what sounded like a train coming from behind and she blew past me just before the finish line.

According to conventional wisdom, I should have been shattered. So much time and effort dedicated to this one goal – so many miles, so much sweat, so many sacrifices – all, it would seem, for naught. But instead what I felt was a strange sense of satisfaction – it surprised me. I didn't feel as though my years of effort had been wasted; quite the opposite. I had ridden a good race – maybe the perfect race. I knew my strengths and weaknesses and played my cards as well as they could be played – my opponent was simply faster. And so my question was answered: I was not an Olympian. But in all those years of trying to become an Olympic athlete, I had been cultivating a kind of Olympic soul. Cycling was the medium through which I learned about myself and pursued lofty ideals. It was my path toward wisdom and excellence. It was a lived philosophy. And now that I am a professor of philosophy, immersed in books and lectures and conferences, I still ride my bike in pursuit of wisdom. The difference is that now I understand that cycling for me *is* philosophy; back then, I only knew that I could be satisfied even in defeat.

Rolling Up to the Starting Line

One of the first things you encounter when you decide to start racing is the question of whether you will be any good at it. To be sure, some athletes approach this question with more confidence than others, but no one rolls up to the starting line certain of victory. I had been a good athlete in all kinds of sports, so I was reasonably self-assured when I decided to start racing. But when the chips are down and that starting gun goes off, I, like everyone, had to confront the void. Of course, there are politics involved just getting to the starting line. Short criteriums start out fast, so everyone wants to be at the front and they rush to crowd the line as soon as the race is called. Some people ride around the pack and try to back their bikes in from the front – you have to have a lot of chutzpah to do this and it only works if the other riders respect you. Nobodies who try it are generally shunned. Sometimes the announcer will call World or Olympic Champions up to the line first – no one complains about this, no matter how hard they fought for a spot at the front. Those riders have what the rest of us are seeking – proof of their excellence. But once the group is assembled at the start, in those quiet moments before the gun goes off, even the champions must feel uncertain.

On the starting line we are all philosophers because philosophy is by nature rooted in uncertainty. The term "philosopher" means "lover of wisdom" in Greek, and it is said to have been coined by Pythagoras to describe those thinkers who acknowledged their ignorance, as opposed to those who acted as though they knew everything. To be a philosopher is to courageously immerse yourself in questions: questions about yourself, about others, about the world, about what, if anything, exists beyond the world. It means giving up the comfort of certainty and plunging into the immense and eternal struggle to learn – without any guarantee of success, and with the understanding that any knowledge you do achieve will only be followed by more questions. It is for that reason that philosophers and philosophical athletes have to take pleasure in the struggle and not just the victory (which, anyway, depends on the quality of the struggle). As a cyclist, my first and greatest challenge was simply trying to get the most out of myself.

I remember consulting one of the cycling elders in our Santa Barbara Bicycle Club. He was a former national champion and great source of wisdom, but if you wanted to learn from him you had to question him, just like Socrates. I asked about training for sprints – a crucial skill in my short races. He gave me some practical pointers: train for sprints early in the week, find a slightly downhill course, go all out the last 200 meters, and so on. All of this I could have learned from any number of sources. But then I asked a more philosophical question: "How do I know when I'm going all out?"

"When you really do a sprint right," he said, "you will feel it in your teeth."

Feel it in my teeth? I had no idea what he meant by that, but the phrase stuck with me as I twisted and turned the puzzle of my performance like some kind of Rubik's cube. I thought about people who lift up cars or perform other amazing feats of strength in emergency situations. We have so much more strength – in our minds and our bodies – than we ever use. How could I tap into this? Then one day, it happened. In Santa Barbara we had weekly training races in a local business park: men, women, juniors, seniors, we all raced together so it was a pretty hard test for me. At the end of one of these races, coming around the final turn, I launched my sprint and pushed hard for the finish line. I crossed somewhere in the top 10, but the real reward came as I was freewheeling in exhaustion after the finish: my teeth were buzzing! I'm sure there is some biological explanation for this, but the point for me was that I had pushed myself hard enough to make it happen. It was a breakthrough for me, and for the first time I wondered if I too might win a national championship someday.

The ever uncertain puzzle of performance dominated my racing career, but with knowledge and experience, my physical preparation became more predictable and less important. As you move up the ranks in any kind of sport, you find that talent and hard work no longer ensure success. At the top levels, all of the racers have talent and all of them work hard in training. Most are tactically astute and some have entire teams dedicated to their victory. Winning these kinds of races requires more than buzzing teeth – it takes everything you've got. And even then it is still uncertain. The first big race I won was a criterium on the national circuit in North Carolina. All the big teams and best racers were there. I was racing without teammates, but I profited from the other teams' tactics. On the next to last lap there was a big acceleration and the pack split in two. I was in the second group, but we caught the front runners just before the final turn. I saw one of the big team leaders eye the other and there was a moment of hesitation. I took off. It felt like diving off the high-board and being alone in mid-air. I got a gap and went all-out toward the finish. I could feel the pack approaching from behind, and as I neared the line some riders appeared in my peripheral vision, but I crossed the line first. I won!

Or maybe not. Was it in fact the final lap? What if I had sprinted a lap too soon? My fast-approaching competitors had now gone past me and I was waiting in hope and fear for someone to sit up and quit pedaling so I would know the race was over. Finally a rider pulled her hands out of the drops, looked back and said, "Good sprint – you caught us by surprise back there." I think that I nodded and said something, but I don't know what because, inside, my mind was screaming: "You won!!!" It turns out that even victory can be uncertain – at least for a little while. In any case the relief of victory is always short lived. After receiving my awards and seeing my name in print, the uncertainty would return. I had a series of goals written down with a timeline attached. By the time I reached one, I was already focused on the next. In fact, my biggest regret about my cycling career is that I didn't enjoy my victories more; didn't take more satisfaction in what I had achieved. I was always on to the next challenge – always wanting to do better and learn more. The true philosopher never completely reaches his goal. As the wisest man Socrates said right up until his death, "I know only that I do not know."

Racing Toward the Truth

I encountered another kind of uncertainty in my racing career that was anti-philosophical: the uncertainty caused by doping. Personally, I never took performance-enhancing drugs. But then, I was never offered them or pressured by coaches to take them. Most importantly, I never believed that it was necessary to take drugs in order to reach my goal of the Olympic Games. This may have been a mistaken belief, but it saved me from the trap that has snared so many others. I knew some of my competitors were taking drugs – we all knew. The drug of choice during my era was steroids, and the effects were pretty dramatic. I remember one woman who had been a slightly overweight also-ran appearing at the first race of the next season with half the body fat and twice the muscle mass of before. Her results improved spectacularly and she even made the national team. All we could do was hope that sooner or later she would be caught. She was; later rather than sooner. And after serving a three-month ban she married a steroid-dealing cyclist from another country and went on to race for their national team. Everyone always knew she was a doper, we even nicknamed her "Juicy Lucy." It really frosted me to see her name listed among Olympic medalists in a book celebrating the centennial of the Games.

I would argue, however, that even though some (maybe several) cyclists achieved by illegal means the goals I failed to reach, I ended up with something more valuable, namely, truth. Athletic contests are truth-seeking. They are constructed like scientific experiments, with equal opportunity and evaluation according to objective standards, because they are designed to find things out. There is a kind of truth about results obtained according to contest rules that overrides all the rhetoric and posturing that anyone cares to offer. I think that's why we love sport so much – it tries to satisfy our human desire for knowledge. But the secret use of performance enhancers interferes with the validity of the results and casts doubt over a process designed to produce certainty. People don't start sports wondering if they could win with the right drugs, they wonder if they could win on their own merits. Most riders who resort to doping do so because they believe it is necessary to stay competitive. Meanwhile clean athletes may be the real champions and never even know – but at least they know that their performances are truly their own.

The epistemological insidiousness of doping only hit home for me after my career was over. Someone gave me a copy of a magazine in which a former competitor of mine admitted that her cycling career had been fueled by all kinds of drugs: steroids, amphetamines, painkillers, you name it. She was confessing this as a warning to others; apparently she had damaged her body to the point that she was hardly able to walk. As I read, I thought back to an edition of the Nevada City Cycling Classic, a hard race on a hillside course in the California Sierras. I had crashed and broken my brake-lever. I went back to the finish line to see if I could get a spare bike, but the entire staff was mesmerized by the performance of this athlete – who was off on a solo breakaway, minutes ahead of the peloton. They had fitted her with what was then a new gizmo called a heart rate monitor, and the announcer was gushing that she was the fittest athlete they had ever tested. I remember standing there a bit dumbstruck myself; full of admiration for this great athlete.

Indeed, she made the Olympic team but was excluded at the last minute, not because she was sick, as the official story goes, but because (I heard later) she had failed a secret internal dope test. I felt numb reading the article – comforted that my own cycling inferiority was perhaps not as great as it had seemed that day in Nevada City, but also a bit like a victim of fraud. How "true" were my results if my competitors were doped? My competitor gave her own answer to that question in the article. She said that she believed she could have won everything even without the dope. The statement really took me aback. How could she believe

  HEATHER L. REID

that? Indeed, the one thing she'll *never* know is how good she could have been without the dope. What's more, she denied me and her other clean competitors the chance to find out how good we were in comparison with her. Perhaps if all of my competitors were clean, I might have reached more of my goals. But what's more important to me is the certain knowledge that what I achieved I did on my own. My performance – imperfect as it was – was still a kind of truth.

Climbing Up Mountains

As a philosopher, I am more satisfied with a hard argument than quick agreement. And as an athlete, I was more satisfied with an honest performance than a hollow victory. In the end, the awards and homage paid toward the victor are merely a veneer for what's really valuable in sport: the cultivation of excellence. When we dream as young athletes about championship rings or Olympic gold medals, what we want is not the trophy itself, but rather to *be the kind of person* worthy of such awards. We want to be persons of virtue: filled with excellences such as courage, discipline, respect, and justice; and able to turn those capacities into action. Wisdom, the goal of the philosopher, is essentially the ability to put knowledge in the service of the good. As one of my student's grandmother says, "you may know that a tomato is a fruit, but it takes wisdom to keep from putting it into a fruit salad." One of the beautiful things I discovered from cycling was that striving for victory helped me to cultivate these virtues – even when victory itself was not achieved.

Indeed, cycling can help to develop virtues even without competition; all you need is a challenge – perhaps a steep mountain to climb. After I retired from racing and began graduate school in philosophy I got a summer job leading bike tours in the mountains of Europe. As a racer, I was never a good climber. I was a fast descender by necessity: I needed to catch back up after being dropped on the ascent. Even so, I didn't really like the hills and I certainly didn't relish climbing huge mountain passes like the Stelvio, Marmolada, Gavia, or Giau. But I now find that these mountains give me something like the challenge that I lost when I quit racing. They demand my virtues and keep me from going completely soft. I now climb these mountains annually on tours with my husband's and my company, CycleItalia. It's not about how fast you reach the top of such passes; it's about what you need inside to just make it up.

First of all, the mountains demand courage, not just because of the dangerous descents, but also because you undertake the climb knowing both that you will suffer and that there will be no external reward. The Marmolada (Passo Fedaia) climb in Italy's Dolomites has a long valley stretch that looks almost flat but really ascends at about 14 percent. It takes everything I have just to keep the bike moving and yet it seems as though I'm making no progress at all. It feels like climbing a downward escalator. When you finally reach the last few kilometers of switchbacks, you think maybe the grade will ease ... but it doesn't. In fact the last ramp, which looks flat as you approach it, hides grades around 15 percent. I don't think I've ever climbed the Marmolada without stopping – at least once – and hunching over my handlebars in exhaustion. The climb still tortures me even though I know all of its deceptions and tricks. Yet every couple of years I try it again, just to see if I can make it to the top one more time. The question is not about distance, speed, and elevation – it's a question about my virtues and the need to keep testing them.

As a professional philosopher, I frequently deal with rejection. I send out papers, book proposals, fellowship applications, most of which are rejected. The courage to keep trying is the same courage that keeps me climbing these punishing passes. Of course every climb has its individual character and demands different things from the rider. Passo Stelvio in Italy is 29 kilometers long and has 48 switchbacks – you can't see the top until you're about 20K into the climb and even then it's an imposing zig-zag up a steep mountain face. To do this climb you have to be smart – there are several places where the grade is easy and you are tempted to push harder, but it can take nearly three hours to climb this mountain and if you spend too much energy on the lower slopes you'll have nothing left near the top. Stelvio is a climb that rewards discipline and wisdom – I've learned to refuse her early temptations and accept her subtle gestures of help. I go the long way around the switchbacks, where the roadway is flatter, and take the time to catch my breath. When the grade eases up I keep it in the low gear and spin: when the mountain gives you a break – take it, I say. Climbing is as much about smarts as it is about sinew.

Perhaps the most important virtue in dealing with the mountains is respect. You must respect not just their athletic demands, but also the danger imposed by changing weather. In the Alps you can start out with a perfectly blue sky, and end up shivering in sleet or even snow. Once as a tour guide I was driving a support vehicle up France's Col d'Iseran –

HEATHER L. REID

one of the highest passes in the Alps. At the bottom of the climb in Lanslebourg it was warm and sunny and a couple of our guests were lingering over lunch in a café. I got the call that it had begun to rain on the climb and that I needed to drive ahead and rescue some guests who hadn't even brought rain jackets. The couple at the café didn't want to get into the van, but their protests ended when we turned a corner and the blue sky turned black. On the lower slopes it was raining, but near the top it was starting to sleet. Cyclists were crowded together under a narrow ledge, shivering. They had to hold me upright as I loaded bikes onto the roof of the van in the freezing rain and howling winds. I turned the van heaters on full blast and drove carefully down the mountain to our hotel. In an hour the skies had cleared again, but the lesson was learned. Great challenges demand courage, discipline, and respect; and great challenges build courage, discipline, and respect.

Keeping the Rubber Side Down

Of course I don't spend all of my time cycling in the Alps; in fact, I spend relatively small amounts of time on my bike compared to my racing days. Many of my athletic virtues are now channeled into my academic career, but I'm not quite as ambitious a professor as I was a young bike racer. Cycling also taught me to have perspective – to remember what's important and seek balance in my life. I remember one year racing the Tour of Denver, there was a huge hailstorm in the middle of a road stage. The pack broke apart and I was left pedaling alone in the darkness when I came up to the place where my grandfather had parked his big Lincoln Town Car alongside the course. My brother was standing outside, squinting in the rain and hail, trying to hand me a thin nylon jacket. The wind was blowing us both around, so I stopped to take it and started to put it on. Then I thought, "What the hell am I doing out here?" and got inside the car until the storm passed. My grandmother turned around with pity on her face and said, "I'm glad you got in, honey, it's terrible out there." There with my family, dripping wet, I realized that the race wasn't really so important.

After a time the skies cleared and I got back on my bike and finished the race. I remember the official saying "finished" as I crossed the line. I didn't care in what place I finished, but I did care that I finished. To be a philosopher, as I said, is to pursue wisdom – and that means sticking with it when times are tough and systematically seeking your goal. But the reason philosophers pursue wisdom in the first place is the belief that it will improve their lives, and those of others. To treat any sport, cycling included, as something more important than health, or family, or friendship is to abuse the sport and to abuse yourself. The ancient Greeks used to say "nothing in excess" – the same Greeks who invented the Olympic Games. Probably they needed to warn themselves to keep their own ambitions in check. Done right, cycling promotes physical and mental health. It doesn't have to dominate a person's life in order to make that life better.

These days, much of my cycling gets squeezed into a busy day in the form of a commute to work. Often I ride a fixed-gear bike just to make it more of a workout. But the greatest benefit of the commute is mental: quiet time to think. Even when I was in college and training quite seriously, I did a lot of thinking and even composed papers in my head while pedaling through the hills around Charlottesville, Virginia. I heard once that cycling promotes integrated left and right brain thinking because it makes use of both sides of your body equally. That sounds a bit preposterous to me, but there is something about the rhythm of pedaling that gets the wheels turning inside my head. My short commutes and weekend rides provide empty mental space where I'm not focused on anything in particular – space big enough for philosophical thoughts about the nature of life or flexibility of justice. Cycling may not create philosophers, but it at least provides a space for philosophers to think and grow.

My Best Race

Looking back over nearly three decades of cycling, I think that my best race was neither a victory nor a defeat, but one that expressed the philosophical nature of cycling. It was the weekend before I graduated from college, the long-running Twilight Criterium in Athens, Georgia. 7-Eleven, the best women's team in the world at that time, was there with reigning Olympic champion Rebecca Twigg and World Sprint Champion Connie Paraskevin. I had squeezed my training between a heavy course schedule and was satisfied with the balance in my life, but I was a little afraid of racing against these champions. I felt that familiar uncertainty as I waited on the starting line – I was not among those called to the front for introductions, so I had to crowd up afterwards. A few laps into the race, I saw Twigg attack on a little hill and I went after her. It took all I had to bridge the gap and when I reached her wheel she looked back at me with what seemed like disappointment. I held on for about a lap until we got to that little hill again, then she glanced back, stamped a few times on the pedals, and dropped me like a rock. There was a kind of truth in it – the same satisfying truth I felt at the end of my last race – she was Olympic champion for a reason.

As the pack absorbed me again, I reflected a little. It was disappointing that I couldn't stay with Twigg, but great that I could go with her. Maybe I was going to be good enough to make the Olympic team some day, but the only way to find out was to keep trying. I went to the front and then took off on my own, thinking maybe I could bridge up to Twigg before the finish. I got to where I could just see her going around the turn at the other end of the long finishing straight, but I never did catch her. On the other hand, I stayed out in front of the pack and finished second in front of Connie Paraskevin who, unsurprisingly, won the field sprint. It was a time of hope and optimism standing on that podium with those two champions – I still have the pictures. I felt like I was standing at the foot of a mountain of possibility, when in reality I was probably at the peak – in terms of cycling.

What makes this my best race, however, is precisely that sense of wonder I felt about what I could achieve, not just as a cyclist but as a person. It was the courage to face uncertainty, the willingness to work hard for the truth, and the ability to retain balance and perspective that got me on that podium. And it is those same qualities that make a philosopher. One could say that my goal changed from the extrinsic reward of an Olympic gold medal to the intrinsic reward of wisdom, but really wisdom was always the goal and for me cycling will always be a form of philosophy.

CHAPTER 16

CYCLING AND PHILOSOPHICAL LESSONS LEARNED THE HARD WAY

Riding Out of the Cave

The first serious cycling trip I took was from where I live in Pennsylvania to a town named Carlisle, near the state capitol of Harrisburg. I was talked into this by my friend Tim, who had an aunt and uncle living down in Carlisle and was just starting to get into cycling. We decided to do the ride down in one day – 95 hilly miles and two mountain crossings. The longest bike ride I had taken before this trip was maybe 30 miles. Well, I thought I was in fairly decent physical shape; I was playing singles tennis two or three times a week, was riding my bike the six miles to the tennis courts, and walked to work every day. My cycling gear at that time consisted of a Schwinn World Sport 18-speed with a fat padded seat. I figured I needed to do a couple of longer rides before the big Carlisle trip, so I stretched out by riding to the neighboring town, a scenic, flat ride by the Susquehanna River that was 23 miles round-trip. I did that a couple of times. I felt ready to go. I can hear you veteran cyclists already laughing.

In Plato's allegory of the cave, chained prisoners see only flickering shadows on the walls, and mistake them for how things really are. It is philosophy that lets us climb – painfully and with resistance – out into the blinding sun of knowledge. Like Plato's prisoners, I had a lot to learn. Here are six philosophical lessons I've managed to learn pedaling out of the cave.

Tim showed up at my place, I strapped a book-bag-sized backpack to my back and we took off. The first 40 miles weren't too bad, and we rode them without pause, until we pulled into a sandwich joint for lunch. We threw down some calories and decided we deserved a good rest. After an hour, when I stood up, my legs had the flexibility of Frankenstein's monster. OK, not a good sign. We got back on the bikes, and after 20 miles I couldn't believe how wiped out I was. My butt hurt, my legs hurt, my back hurt, and I was just plain exhausted. We pulled off for another rest. Then we did another 10 miles, and needed a break. Then five miles. We were both bonking. Did I mention that one of the long uphills had been repaved that very day, and our tires were sinking into the hot asphalt?

Besides exhaustion, the other thing I hadn't really been prepared for was boredom. My whole family plays golf, which as a teenager I gave a good, fair try. It bored me silly. Plus the fact that after a crappy shot, I had a 150-yard walk while cursing myself before I had a chance to improve things. Tennis was my sport. The great thing about tennis is that it is fast-paced: hit a bad shot and you can redeem yourself within seconds. Two hours of tennis is a high-concentration, high-action workout. Numerous hours on a bike saddle slowly grinding through the rolling Pennsylvania countryside was boring. And painful.

Finally, finally, we pulled into Tim's aunt and uncle's house. My butt felt like I had spent two weeks as a new fish in gen pop in Sing-Sing. My neck had the remaining strength of a piece of limp asparagus. Tim's aunt had assumed we would be famished and laid out a huge spread for dinner, but I was so tired I could barely eat a thing. Even passing out smacked of too much effort. For weeks afterwards I would be fearful at even modest inclines in the road, even though I was driving a car. The psychological scars took a while to heal.

Discipline and Diet

In *Beyond Good and Evil*, section 188, the great German philosopher Friedrich Nietzsche wrote that, "What is essential 'in heaven and on earth' seems to be ... that there should be *obedience* over a long period of time and in a single direction: given that, something always develops, and has developed, for whose sake it is worthwhile to live on earth; for example, virtue, art, music, dance, reason, spirituality – something transfiguring, subtle, mad, and divine." In part Nietzsche means that nothing of value comes easy, and even the appreciation and understanding of what is valuable is rarely seen in advance. I understood and enjoyed the fast-paced, variable action of tennis. But the relatively slow-paced, systematic action of long-distance touring on a bicycle required not just a different kind of effort, but a changed mindset.

It wasn't enough to choose to go on the ride, or even attempt it. In *Thus Spoke Zarathustra*, Nietzsche writes of "the laughter of creative lightning which is followed obediently but grumblingly by the long thunder of the deed."[1] That is, there is a joy and excitement in a new idea, a new project, ambition, or adventure, but carrying it through to fruition is something else again, often arduous and slow. With cycling, I had to learn the devotion, almost the meditation, of the long thunder of the deed.

On one 80-mile ride in a rainstorm I remember feeling like a mechanism, tucked in, my legs rhythmic pistons, water sluicing over me like machine oil, hammering out the miles. There was a sort of perverse pride I felt, riding all day in the cold rain and getting coated in road grit. It was only through obedience to the implicit orders of cycling that I could learn its virtues, the silent, solitary, almost survivalist nature of riding far from home. To ride is to reduce life to simplicity, with no other demands but to keep pedaling. "Why should we live with such hurry and waste of life?" Thoreau writes in *Walden*.[2] Simplify, simplify.

The following summer Tim tried to talk me into another bike ride, this time from Providence, Rhode Island, out to Provincetown at the end of Cape Cod and back again. After all the climbing on the Carlisle trip, Tim swore this trip would be flat as a corpse's EEG. Well, the memory of pain from the previous summer had sufficiently faded and I told him I was in. I had learned from the previous year, though. I had to train. I determined my training ride would be a fairly short 11-mile loop, but it had a killer climb (for me!) in the middle – over 400 feet in a mile. It took me half a dozen attempts before I could get to the top without having to stop and catch my breath halfway up.

The training paid off. I still wasn't strong on distance, but I wasn't fazed by any kind of incline. One thing I was starting to notice was the huge calorie burn of days of distance riding. Halfway through the Cape Cod trip, we bunked overnight with friends Jim and Lynn, who were astonished at the amount of mussels, clams, lobster, and chardonnay we could put away. Jim started thinking about taking up cycling too, after seeing us knock back a pâtisserie's worth of breakfast pastries. But I really didn't figure out the incipient lesson here until the following summer.

STEVEN D. HALES

The next year Tim wanted to take a big ride. We decided to ride from Montréal, Canada, to Providence, Rhode Island, over 450 miles. We boxed our bikes, took a bus to Montréal. The first day's ride would be my very first true century: 105 miles to Derby Line, Vermont. Now, I was still riding the Schwinn with the spongy seat, I had flat pedals and no clips, and was carrying the backpack on my back. My advanced cycling gear was two water bottle holders, a little pack under the seat, and bike shorts. I think I was using old weightlifting gloves as cycling gloves. Obviously, my learning curve was steeper than Mont Ventoux.

We got up, had a hearty breakfast, and lit out. Once we got out of the city into the countryside, we discovered that cycling in Canada is a true pleasure, with wide shoulders, reasonably courteous drivers, and many bike lanes and paths. We made good time and rode into Granby for lunch; we'd had nothing but water since breakfast. We saw a charming crêperie, and thought that was the kind of quaint French Canadian nosh perfect for … a couple of hardcore cyclists in the middle of a century ride? Alright, we were stupid – what the heck kind of sports nutrition are crêpes? If only we had first pursued Nietzsche's idea that what we really need is a philosophy of nutrition to study the moral – and, more generally, the psychological – effects of different foods.[3] But we had our lunch and went on our way.

About this time my back was really starting to bother me. I had ridden about 80 miles that day laden under this green book bag and my back was aching. Tim, marginally smarter, at least had a rack, and his backpack was strapped to the top of it. I finally told Tim that we had to stop at a bike shop, because I had to get a rack. In fact, I had been entertaining fantasies of this item called "panniers" that I had vaguely heard of. It was like a Penthouse centerfold for a computer science major – glorious, unattainable salvation. We found a bike shop in Magog, with a vast wall of panniers, racks, and other exotica. At this point my back hurt so much I was willing to pay literally any price for a rack and panniers.

If "you have to train" is lesson number one, "you have to have adequate gear" is lesson number two. Not necessarily carbon fiber frames, Shimano Dura-Ace derailleurs, and a GPS unit, but something better than a grungy backpack for a multi-day tour.

We were in the home stretch for Derby Line. The problem now was that we had long ago burned off those crêpes and our brains had forgotten the sweet taste of glucose. So we would look at the maps and try to memorize "we go three miles, turn right at the light, and then make the first left." We'd ride three miles and couldn't remember what we were supposed to do, which meant laboriously stopping, getting off the bikes, pulling out the maps, and trying again to memorize two turns. We were like two Alzheimer's patients escaped from the nursing home and taking a road trip. That night, after having finally, somehow, made it to Vermont, there was not enough food in the world to feed us. We went to a pizza place, ate salads, split their biggest pizza with all the toppings, then had dessert. Even then, after we walked back to the Bed and Breakfast, Tim was still so hungry he ate all of the candy from the B&B's candy dish. He just couldn't stop himself.

The next day we found out about this magical food called Powerbars. Our lives would never be the same. You would think that a couple of Ivy-educated PhDs would be smarter than this, but apparently not. As a philosopher nobody expects me to have any contact with the empirical world, but Tim's a physicist and has less of an excuse. In any case, it turns out that the factory schedule of three meals a day is not what cyclists need. Regular, steady calorie intake is what keeps your legs churning those pedals and keeps the brain working well enough to retain directions.

The idea that our rational minds (useful for remembering directions) and our physical appetites (the need for regular feedings) are separated is an ancient one. In Plato's *Republic*, he argues that the soul is tripartite, divided into reason, appetite, and spirit. Reason is devoted to guidance and knowledge, whereas the appetitive part satisfies our animal instincts, primarily the desires for food, drink, and sex. The spirit is concerned with public recognition and honor. We may often have conflicting interests – to eat the chocolate cake and to stay on the diet, for example, or to hew to our moral principles or compromise them to get elected to office. Plato explains these conflicts in terms of the different parts of the soul at odds with each other, and argues that human excellence, the good life, is attained when the parts of the soul are in mutual harmony.

In the seventeenth and eighteenth centuries, philosophers tended to view our rational side and our emotional nature as in conflict with each other, and that our passions needed to be kept in check and controlled by reason. In 1649 the French philosopher René Descartes published his treatise, *The Passions of the Soul*. It in he argues, among other things, that there are six primitive passions: wonder, love, hatred, desire, joy, and sadness. "The chief use of wisdom," he writes, "lies in teaching us to be masters of our passions and to control them with such skill that the evils which they cause are quite bearable, and even become a source of joy."[4] The Scottish philosopher David Hume, taking a somewhat contrary view in 1739, averred that "reason is and ought to be the slave of the passions, and can never pretend to any other office than to serve and obey them."[5] So, is reason to master and dominate our emotions, or is reason simply a rationalizing tool at the subconscious beck and call of our arational passions?

What we learned on the ride from Montréal was that maybe neither Descartes nor Hume had it quite right. One needs to be adequately fed for one's reason to operate; reason is not exactly enslaved to the appetites, but it is not wholly master of them either. We are not pure creatures of intellect whose abstract logic is rudely corrupted by the parade of sensation and emotion. Nor does it seem right that we are merely instinctual animals whose reflective minds are merely a post hoc generation of those instincts. It may be that Plato was closer to the truth when he suggested that virtue is had in the harmonious operation of the components of the soul. I'm sure that Nietzsche, at least, would advocate a philosophy of cycling nutrition that included Will to Power Bars.

The third lesson of cycling is: keep fuel in the tank.

Toughing It Out

After the Montréal trip, our friend Jim decided that he wanted to give cycling a shot and go along on our next summer ride. I told him that was great, but I wanted to impart the little cycling wisdom I had acquired so far. No reason he had to learn everything the hard way like I did. So I told Jim that he needed to train, and train hard. We started going out on a 23-mile training loop with lots of climbing. I could hit 50 mph on one of the descents. Sometimes we did a double loop, or when we got to the bottom of the big hill we would stop, turn around, and climb back up it. We were getting strong. We decided to tackle Jonestown Mountain. Jonestown is one of the most challenging local rides, just over a 20-mile loop with a steep 850-foot climb in the middle.[6] Jim came over to my house to start the ride, but when he got there he realized he had forgotten his helmet. I lent him an old one of mine and we started out. There was a light drizzle, but we decided we were manly riders and didn't mind getting a little wet. We would just take the descent from the mountain slowly.

About four miles out we made a right turn onto an open-grate steel bridge spanning Fishing Creek. I was about 30 feet ahead of Jim in the middle of the bridge when I heard a sickening crash behind me. Jim had laid his bike down on the slick wet steel, and it looked like he had done a face-plant over the handlebars. His helmet was shattered, his glasses broken and the pieces missing, blood was pouring from his nose, his knee was gashed open, and it looked like he might have broken his wrist. Jim staggered to his feet and knew he was messed up. He kept asking me how he looked. I felt like I was in one of those war movies where some private has his guts blown out and keeps asking his sergeant if he was OK. "You're gonna make it, buddy," I said. I tried to sound reassuring. I took a handkerchief and tied it around the gaping wound in Jim's knee, mostly so I wouldn't be grossed out by looking at it.

Jim had broken his nose, took stitches in his knee, severely sprained his wrist, and needed new glasses. Three weeks later he saddled up to ride with Tim and me to the New York Finger Lakes, and the very first day Jim pedaled a heavy Trek hybrid 115 miles through very hilly terrain. That is still my longest one-day ride.

In *The Enchiridion*, Epictetus wrote that "With every accident, ask yourself what abilities you have for making a proper use of it … If you are in pain, you will find fortitude … And thus habituated, the appearances of things will not hurry you away along with them."[7] Epictetus was born a deformed Greek slave in Imperial Rome in the first century AD, and probably had some knowledge of pain and suffering. But here he expresses the Stoic ideal that the flourishing life is to strive for what is possible, with a sense of imperturbability. A Stoic sage is insulated from misfortune because he does not value the objects of the external world, and believes it is virtue alone that ensures the good life. For the Stoics, one undergoes emotions: they are things that happen to you, and are to be distinguished from actions that one performs. The proper attitude toward the emotions is to not be buffeted and controlled by them, but to be self-sufficient and even-keeled. The Stoics tried to live apathetically, meaning in its original sense unmoved by *pathê*, the passions. Thus we can live in accordance with nature. As the fellow Stoic and Roman emperor Marcus Aurelius wrote, don't say "'this is a misfortune,' but 'to bear this nobly is good fortune.'"[8]

The fourth lesson of cycling, as I learned from Jim and the Stoics: quit whining and tough it out. Also: always wear a helmet.

Surprises Down the Road

A couple of years later I had a further occasion to learn from cycling. Tim and I had planned a ride from Reading, Pennsylvania, to Ocean City, Maryland. This time our friend Pete was going to join us. Pete was an experienced rider who once attempted the Nightmare Ride (a double

🚲 STEVEN D. HALES

century around Lancaster County), and had logged thousands of miles on his bike. The first day we rode about 90 miles or so with a big headwind, and the sun was setting as we neared Dover, Delaware. We were taking a breather when we saw on the map that there was some sort of racetrack in Dover. We had no clue what they raced there. Horses? Was it a dog track? We joked that maybe it was bicycle racing. As we rounded a curve, the stadium came into view. And then we knew. NASCAR.

Yes, we had managed to arrive in Dover during NASCAR weekend. The stadium seats 135,000 people, and it was jam-packed. Before we left Pennsylvania, we figured that nobody was going to be in Dover on a random weekend after Labor Day; there would be plenty of places to stay and we would just grab a convenient motel. We rode to the first hotel we saw and the clerk literally started laughing at us. Dover – every single place in a 40-mile radius around Dover – had been booked for weeks. We were seriously thinking that we would be sleeping in the park. We got the Yellow Pages and started making calls. Finally we found some Motel 8-grade place down the road that had had a last-minute cancellation. All three of us could share a room for the special NASCAR rate of $350 for one night. But clearly, if we wanted a hot shower and a bed, we had no choice. After that, we referred to the town as Ben-Dover.

The next day we rode to Ocean City. Tim assured us that he had been to Ocean City before, that it was a huge resort town, and there would be thousands of hotel rooms. We would find something easily when we got there. After another day of grueling headwinds, we pulled into Ocean City only to discover that it was Sun Festival Weekend, and, yes, every hotel room was booked. To make a long story short, we did finally find a place to stay, a fairly dodgy motel flying the gay pride flag in front of its office.

The philosophical problem that we had failed to adequately appreciate is the problem of induction. When we reason inductively, we use our past experiences and past knowledge to reach conclusions about what we can expect in the future. For example, when you turn on the tap at your kitchen sink in the morning, you expect water to come out, not chocolate. That's because, in the past when you have turned on the tap, it was never chocolate and always water. We, too, reasoned inductively – in the past, on a non-holiday weekend after Labor Day, in a non-resort town, there was no difficulty finding a place to stay. Therefore we would have no difficulty on our trip.

As David Hume writes, "From causes which appear *similar*, we expect similar effects. This is the sum of all our experimental conclusions. Now it seems evident, that, if this conclusion were formed by reason, it would be as perfect at first, and upon one instance, as ever after so long a course of experience. But the case is far otherwise."[9] In other words, if the way that we formed expectations about the future on the basis of past experience were a matter of pure reason alone, then we would never be wrong about what the future holds. But we are often wrong. The British philosopher Bertrand Russell comments that a chicken that associates the farmer with the arrival of food is surely surprised when one day the farmer comes and the chicken, instead of receiving dinner, becomes dinner instead. Induction, as we found in Ben-Dover and Ocean City, is unpredictably fallible.

The fifth lesson: expect the unexpected.

From Tribulation to Wisdom

The last summer cycling trip I took was from Watkins Glen, a tourist town at the southern tip of Seneca Lake in upstate New York, out to Niagara Falls and back. It was a good four-day ride, including two centuries. Jim was riding with me, along with a new rider, Todd. Todd had done some local rides, although nothing over 50 miles. Yet he had trained and was ready to go. Todd asked me what sort of gear he should pack along, and I sent him the list of things I was bringing: a set of civilian clothes and shoes, rain jacket, swimsuit, two biking shorts, three biking jerseys, two water bottles, biking helmet, gloves, and shoes, sunglasses, link remover, CO_2 cartridges, two spare tubes, patch kit, tire levers, dozen Powerbars, multitool, black plastic tape, chain lube, cable lock and key, panniers, shaving kit, wallet, camera, and cell phone. According to Ronny at our local bike shop, The Dutch Wheelman, the most important tools to carry on a big bike ride are a cell phone and a credit card. With those two you can get everything else.

I don't think we got five miles before I had my first flat. Of course it was the rear tire, which meant taking the panniers off and getting greasy from the chain. All right, I put in a new tube and we were off. It was a beautiful sunny day with gorgeous views over the long glacial lake and I was in a good mood. A few more miles and I had another flat. Crap. This was bad luck. We all got off the bikes and I changed it again. Now I had used both of the tubes I brought with me (I hate patch kits, and regard them as a last resort). We went maybe another 10 miles and I had another flat. I couldn't believe this. Was I underinflating and getting snakebite flats? Was there something in the tire itself? I inspected the interior of the tire. It looked

🚲 STEVEN D. HALES

clean. I borrowed a tube from Jim, put it on and blew it full with the CO_2. I examined the dead tube – just one little hole, no snakebite.

But it kept happening, again and again, over 100 miles. I had seven flats, used up all the spares we had brought with us, all of my CO_2 cartridges, and was immensely frustrated at being unable to figure out the root problem. I was tired, hot, greasy, and cranky. We hit a bike shop and resupplied. Finally, the next morning, we were looking closely at my tire when Todd saw a minute pinhole in it. Then we figured it out: under pressure from an inflated tube, the pinhole expanded enough that when the tire flexed, the pinhole would pinch the tube and cause a puncture. I pulled out the black plastic tape and lined the interior of the tire, covering the pinhole. Problem solved – I had no more flats.

Todd stared at me, shaking his head. "When you put *black plastic tape* on the packing list I thought 'who does he think he is, fucking MacGyver?' But I guess that's about right." We all laughed. I realized that that's something I've come to appreciate about cycling; there's a sort of pioneer self-reliance that one needs to get through. I've gotten flats, broken spokes, thrown bearings, and once snapped my rear derailleur cable. If you're 20 or 30 miles from the nearest bike shop, then you're on your own and you have to rig a solution.

In *Concluding Unscientific Postscript* (1846), Søren Kierkegaard reflects upon the technological wonders of his age, the railways, steamboats, encyclopedias, and telegraphs that "benefit mankind."[10] They make our lives easier for us, so easy, in fact, that we might actually wish for difficulty to overcome. Kierkegaard thinks that his contribution to humanity might just be to provide that difficulty. One wonders how Kierkegaard would react to modern ease, with Google, flat-screen TVs, and climate-controlled homes. Kierkegaard thinks that it is rumination upon philosophy, thoughts on what it means to be an individual and not merely a member of a mob, contemplation on how to live, and the nature of truth – *that* is what is difficult. This study, this contemplation, will never be aided by any amount of web surfing. Cycling has the same sort of challenge, demanding a kind of measured attention to the task. The joy in difficulty that Kierkegaard has in mind is not climbing a hill at mile 85 when your glutes are long since shot, but the larger, expansive satisfaction of having completed the trip. Analogously, there is little pleasure in parsing Kierkegaard's own obtuse prose, although there is the happiness of wrestling with his thoughts once they have been revealed.

What good is your Blackberry or Blu-Ray when you've blown a spoke in the middle of nowhere and it is getting dark and pouring rain? Your credentials, your ego, and your money will not get you home again. It is in this situation that you learn something about yourself, about your ingenuity and self-sufficiency. The condition of the cyclist is the human condition, writ small – all of us must craft for ourselves the kinds of lives we wish to lead, we must decide how we are to live, what we will do, and how to pull it off. Like Kierkegaard, we can find exhilaration and self-knowledge in this challenge instead of ennui or despair.

The sixth lesson I have learned is that cycling is a way to Delphi, with the demand to know thyself inscribed over the portal to the oracle. Take heart in Emerson's words from *Self-Reliance*: "He cannot be happy and strong until he too lives with nature in the present, above time."[11] With the happiness of riding, that strength of character, you can find your way back.

NOTES

1 Friedrich Nietzsche, *Thus Spoke Zarathustra*, trans. Walter Kaufmann (New York: Viking Press, 1884), part III, "The Seven Seals," 3.
2 Henry David Thoreau, *Walden* (New York: Houghton Mifflin, 1854), p. 89.
3 Friedrich Nietzsche, *The Gay Science*, ed. and trans. Walter Kaufmann (New York: Vintage, 1882), section 7.
4 René Descartes, *The Passions of the Soul* (1649), in *The Philosophical Writings of Descartes*, vol. 1, trans. J. Cottingham. R. Stoothoff, and D. Murdoch (Cambridge: Cambridge University Press, 1985), section 212.
5 David Hume, *A Treatise of Human Nature* (1739), ed. L. A. Selby-Bigge, 2nd ed. (Oxford: Clarendon Press, 1978), book II, section III.
6 Readers will find the map I made of the Jonestown ride at www.gmap-pedometer.com/?r=2363457.
7 Epictetus, *Moral Discourses, Enchiridion, and Fragments* (New York: E. P. Dutton, 1910), §10.
8 Marcus Aurelius, *The Meditations* (New York: Modern Library, 2002), book IV, 49a.
9 David Hume, *An Enquiry Concerning Human Understanding* (1748), ed. L. A. Selby-Bigge (Oxford: Oxford University Press, 1975), sec. 4, pt. 2, ¶20.
10 Søren Kierkegaard, *Concluding Unscientific Postscript* (1846), trans. David F. Swenson and Walter Lowrie (Princeton, NJ: Princeton University Press, 1974).
11 Ralph Waldo Emerson, *Self-Reliance*, from *Essays: First Series* (New York: Charles E. Merrill, 1841), p. 98.

CHAPTER 17

FROM SHOES TO SADDLE

What happened to me? How did I become someone who spends as much money on one bicycle as
I used to spend on *ten pairs* of running shoes? And
what's the deal with my new wardrobe of bright
(and tight) lycra and spandex clothing? After back
surgery derailed my running career of over 20
years, I decided to buy – and actually ride – a bicycle. In the process of becoming a road cyclist,
I discovered and am discovering several things
about who I am. I now think of myself as more of
a cyclist than a runner, and deftly use words like
souplesse, panniers, and peloton, all of which were simply strange foreign
words to me only a year ago.

A Runner is Born

My desire to be a runner was first awakened, I think, at the end of my
fifth grade year. It was field day at my school, and one of the last events
was the 400-meter dash. For the seven of us who entered, this was a long
way to run, and so "dash" was not really an accurate description. But
I remember coming through the final straight and winning this race, and
how I swelled with pride after that victory. For the next few years, I ran

track during the summer and for the school team, but it was after my first year in high school that I decided to really *become* a runner.

I'd always played football in the fall. My last season was my first year of high school, however. I was on the freshman team, and one day for some reason I was lined up as a nose guard in practice, even though I played wide receiver and defensive back and was a razor thin kid. When my much more rotund teammate who was playing center fell on my arm and broke it, a chain of events was set in motion that led to my decision to give up football for cross-country.

For the next 25 years, I was a runner. I ran a marathon, a half-marathon, and many shorter races. When in graduate school I entertained the idea of running an ultramarathon, I began running as seriously as ever, and loved every minute of it. Not only did running keep me in good physical condition, it provided time and space in my life for reflection, stress reduction, and was generally good for my psychological health. Even though I was inconsistent compared to many runners over those years, running was not just a part of my life, it was a piece of my identity, a part of my self-concept. I knew that I'd probably have to give it up someday, though stories in *Runner's World* magazine of runners in their eighties gave me hope that the day was a long way off. That hope turned out to be unfounded, however. Life sometimes has a way of tripping you up.

It was around Christmas 2007. I'd had lower back trouble off and on for years, and so I assumed the pain I was having was just another flare-up. But when it started shooting down my sciatic nerve into my foot, I went for an MRI and the picture was not a pretty one. One of the discs in the lumbar region had ruptured like Mount St. Helens. I'd done enough research to know that surgery was likely, but what I really wanted to know was whether or not I'd have to give up running. My physician recommended that I give it up, and at the very least tone it down. I remember being in the elevator and the sadness and loss I felt at thinking that my running career was over. While much worse can happen to a person, this was a hard thing for me to face. Many runners are skeptical of such advice from their doctors, and sometimes rightly so. But when I've tried to run, my back and sciatic nerve start barking, and so at least for my particular case the doc was right. This was difficult for me to accept. I believe the difficulty stemmed from the fact that running wasn't just something I did, it was a part of who I was. I was a *runner*.

But what does it mean to be a runner? There are perhaps as many detailed answers to this question as there are runners, but for me it meant that running was one of the important commitments in my life. I felt better about myself when I was running regularly, especially if I was training for an upcoming race. Running was meaningful to me in a way that other sports I participated in were not. When I was taking time off, either intentionally or not, I would wish I was running, feel like I should be running, and think about a new challenge that could provide new motivation for me to run. I also got into the science of the sport, reading about the impact and benefits of running, both physical and psychological. And I read about runners, enjoying books about Steve Prefontaine, Roger Bannister, John Landy, and other prominent people in the history of the sport.

A Runner's Conversion to Cycling

Of course, being a runner wasn't the sole or even the most important aspect of my identity. My religious and moral commitments, the fact that I'm a husband, father, and philosopher are more central parts of who I am. But running was right behind this lead pack of my commitments. I suspect the same is true for most people, insofar as our ultimate commitments, family ties, and career – if we are fortunate to have one that we are passionate about – constitute the most significant aspects of our identities. As a philosopher (literally, a lover of wisdom), the fact that the wisest choice seemed to be giving up the sport I loved was more painful than the last six miles of a marathon or a finishing sprint in a 5K race. Rather than wallow in the loss, however, it didn't take too long for me to seek something to try to fill this new void in my life. I ultimately found that replacement on the saddle of a bicycle. But I'm getting ahead of myself.

My conversion to cycling was a forced conversion, brought upon me by that accursed ruptured disk. Forced conversions aren't usually a good thing, of course, but in this case it has turned out to be a great thing. The benefits of cycling are many, from the larger quads and more defined calves to the fellowship of shared suffering on two wheels. I also reaped a *philosophical* benefit from the bike. The entire episode led me to think more deeply about my identity, or self-concept. In thinking about identity and the self, I came across the work of contemporary philosopher Charles Taylor. He has explored the notion of identity in modern life, focusing on the sources of the self that we depend upon to constitute our identities.[1]

Taylor claims that a key part of one's identity is made up of what he calls "strong evaluations."[2] These include our judgments about right and wrong, better or worse, and higher and lower. They are value judgments about what is worthwhile and valuable in life, and we can be wrong about them. Our strong evaluations are our judgments about what is good, what is moral, and what does or does not have value, especially as it relates to what makes life meaningful and worthwhile. These sorts of evaluations are also crucial parts of our identity, of our selves, and so it is important that we know what we believe about such things and why we believe what we do. As Taylor puts it,

> To know who I am is a species of knowing where I stand. My identity is defined by the commitments and identifications which provide the frame or horizon within which I can try to determine from case to case what is good, or valuable, or what ought to be done, or what I endorse or oppose. In other words, it is the horizon within which I am capable of taking a stand.[3]

Unfortunately, we can get caught up in the small everyday obligations and activities and not take time to reflect upon our strong evaluations, and on the extent to which our lives align with them. This is one advantage that can come from doing a little bit of philosophy; it can help us reflect upon and improve the quality of our lives.

Taylor's discussion of strong evaluations explains a lot about why my commitments related to God, family, friends, and my career are more important to me than running was or cycling is. But it also helps explain why cycling is still very important to me. In my judgment, these strong evaluations, or ultimate commitments, have greater value than sports. For me, the fullness and meaning my life now possesses would be greatly diminished if I were no longer a husband or father, for example. As Taylor says, if I were to lose these commitments and identifications, I "would be at sea" and "wouldn't know anymore … what the significance of things was"[4] for me. And while I experienced a feeling of loss when I gave up running, it was relatively small compared to the loss of these more central parts of who I am. However, for me the loss was still significant, which is why I am so glad that cycling was able to take the place in my life that running had held for so many years. Even though being a cyclist has less significance for me than my family and philosophy, it still enters into my value judgments and choices in a variety of ways. Because of this, some of the insights offered by Taylor are relevant. Cycling is very important to me in part because of the joy it produces in my life. One reason that riding is a source of joy, I think, is that it is one of the sources of my self, of my identity.

Part of the joy of being a convert to cycling for me includes reading and learning about the sport and its history, watching bike races, and exploring the different cycling disciplines. As a cyclist, people like Major Taylor inspire me in a variety of ways, just as Emil Zatopek, Steve Prefontaine, and Jesse Owens did for me as a runner. I like reading about Lance, LeMond, and Bobke, because I share a passion with them (if only I shared some of their talent!). I also feel that I've just begun to appreciate and even view my life in small ways through the interesting and colorful traditions embedded within this great sport. With a little bit of personal experience in the bank, I can appreciate the challenge of a technical descent, an unimaginably painful and yet beautiful climb, the cooperation that occurs among teammates and members of the peloton, as well as the precision of a time trial. These connections enrich my life, as well as my experiences on the bike. They also inspire me to acquire some of the moral virtues that can be exemplified in this sport, including courage, perseverance, patience, and even an occasional dose of humility.

When I ran, it was not only a form of exercise and a way to deal with stress. It was also an expression of who I was and it was something I felt that I needed to do. Now, I have a similar need to ride my bike, and for the same reasons. I enjoy seeing the areas around where I live from the perspective of the saddle, even when the occasional dog thinks he needs to chase me down. At least on the bike, I can outpace the dogs, which wasn't generally true in running shoes! Plus, in all honesty, screaming down a descent is just plain fun! My newfound need to ride my bike has taught me something else about myself. Prior to May of 2009, the longest single ride I'd ever done was 26 miles. With a couple of friends, I signed up for a nearby charity ride. We opted for the 35-mile course, rather than the metric century or century ride. I enjoyed the casual start of this charity ride, especially since it was my first ride with more than four other people. With my water bottles full and some Hammergel in my jersey, I took off to set my own new distance record. And while the 35-mile course ended up being 40 miles, the sense of accomplishment and the sheer pleasure of the ride motivated my friends and me to set our sights on a metric century as our next goal. While for many reading this chapter, 40 miles might be a recovery day not worth the chamois cream, this was a significant first step for me as I move toward doing a century, and I loved the experience as well as the challenge.

This is where the lesson comes in. I've realized that I think of myself as an athlete. I came to see in a clear manner that this has been and is a part of who I am. And I'm grateful that this part of who I am is now primarily expressed on a bike. Many of us who have the time and freedom to do so pursue projects that are separate from our job and family obligations. For some, this may involve music, art, or dance. For me, it involves being an athlete. This is manifested in my life more specifically through cycling, as this is where I have chosen to express this aspect of my self.

This takes us to some important related points raised by Charles Taylor in his book *The Ethics of Authenticity*.[5] Taylor points out that there are some facts about me that may be unique to me, but do not constitute a part of my self-identity. For example, I may be the exact same height as a particular tree in Siberia, but this has no significance for me or for who I am. By contrast, as Taylor argues, there are some things that truly and objectively matter, such as the duties of citizenship, history, the needs of other human beings, or the call of God. Many seem to think that being *authentic* involves being completely original, unique, and rejecting the idea of objective value. However, we can be authentic selves without being solitary, original, or rejecting objectively valuable ideals. Authenticity and our choices about how to live and who to be make sense only within a framework of things that *matter*. We must use reason to find out what matters, and then seek our identities with these discoveries in mind. If we're successful, this can help us to avoid at least some of the narcissism and self-centeredness present in much of contemporary culture.

This is where an endurance sport like cycling can be a threat, as it can make us more self-centered and lead us to neglect our ties to those who need and deserve our time, attention, and love. There are times when I've rescheduled or sacrificed a ride because of some other obligation. While there is nothing wrong with devoting significant time and effort to cycling, and I do organize some of my days around my ride when this is possible, I want to be sure that it isn't harming my close personal relationships or undermining the fulfillment of my obligations to the significant others in my life, such as my wife, daughters, and friends. This is not to deny my identity, but rather to properly express it from within my various commitments. As Taylor points out, the significant people in our lives – parents, spouses, children, close friends – not only fulfill us, they also help to define us. This doesn't entail that we are locked into the values and commitments that are central to our significant others, but rather that we form our values and commitments – our identities – in dialogue with them. Sometimes this dialogue only occurs in our minds. But it still occurs. This is just a feature of human life, and being aware of it can help us as we reflect upon our self-identity and how we express it.

As I said, I came to realize that it is important to me that I am an athlete. I have a need to excel as an athlete, and I am grateful that my wife and daughters realize the significance riding now has for me. I want to improve my skills, my fitness, my form, and the distance I can ride. Something about this experience is fulfilling to me, in large part because I think it is an expression of a part of my *identity*. I imagine this is how a musician or artist might feel about her pursuits, even if they never arise above the level of a serious hobby. Cycling is an outlet where I can express creativity, face and overcome challenges and adversity, and seek physical and psychological health. However, given my other commitments and values I don't aspire to be a champion of any sort (well, in all honesty, I might fantasize about winning a local crit). Given these commitments in my life, I don't think at present that I would be justified in devoting hours each day to riding. However, I am seeking to improve my form over time as my other values and primary relationships – the other and more important parts of my identity – allow. Cycling is not the highest good or even among the highest goods in my life, but it is an important part of the next tier of my identity. As such, it is important. Part of its importance comes from the fact that cycling can teach some valuable lessons, both philosophical and non-philosophical.

A Few Lessons from a Relatively New Convert

One interesting thing about a conversion, whether religious, political, or, as in this case, athletic, is that you open yourself up to a new set of experiences, and you see the world in a different way. Sometimes these experiences are not entirely pleasant.

I hadn't been on a road bike since college when I test rode a bike at my local bike shop.[6] This bike wanted to move. I was so busy trying to figure out how to shift and not hit the chainstays with my heel that I didn't enjoy the ride all that much. One word aptly describes the entire experience – awkward. But as any rider knows, something strange begins to happen as you spend more time in the saddle. In some way, the body and the machine become more strongly linked to one another, the bike becomes an extension of the rider. A kinesthetic sense is awakened. Now that much of my riding is more automatic, this allows for more meditative riding, and I can enjoy other aspects of the riding experience that I couldn't when I first started to ride. I just love being outside on the bike. Kentucky, the state where I live, has beautiful, scenic, rolling green hills. Some of those hills ask a lot from my quads, but they also offer up natural beauty just waiting to be enjoyed from the saddle. I also enjoy the time to reflect that cycling provides, away from cell phones, email, and the Internet. With the closer union between rider and bike, I am now able to relish carving turns at higher speeds without worrying that I'm going to be catapulted off my bike into oblivion.

Another small change is that I find myself no longer appalled by the gear cyclists wear. I used to wonder why in the world anyone would wear a pink jersey. And while I still don't own a pink jersey, the bright colors and loud designs found on some gear can serve an important function, namely, making me stand out to the cars eating up pavement at 50 miles an hour right behind my rear wheel. I've found some functional and fun gear from both Eleven Gear and Twin Six that I like because it isn't a neon explosion of corporate ads. And while I'm on the subject of gear, though I never thought I'd ride at dusk or night, having my Planet Bike light makes me feel a bit more secure. Plus, 25 percent of their profits go to cycling advocacy, which is something I've come to care more about now that I consider myself a cyclist. These are small ways in which my cycling conversion has changed my perceptions, judgments, values, and budget(!). Often the cumulative effect of a number of small changes is a change in the identity of a self.

I've also learned that, contrary to my first impressions as a newbie, it is possible to suffer … no, suffer greatly, on a bike. While I don't feel as beat up at the end of a long ride as I did after a long run (because of the high-impact nature of running), I've found that if I expend enough effort the suffering comes. During my first months of riding, I was talking to Jesús – the co-editor of the book in your hands – about how I wasn't experiencing as much pain on the bike as I did as a runner. It just didn't seem as hard. He knew better, and now so do I! I think this element of cycling is a major part of what attracted me to the sport. It requires something of you, it demands that you push into and through pain. The challenge posed by suffering in endurance sports repels some, but attracts others, given who we are. As an athlete, I would rather suffer on a bike out on the asphalt than endure the different kind of suffering that sports like golf or tennis inflict.

More importantly than perceptions about the colors of jerseys or even learning how to suffer on a bike, cycling has reinforced for me the importance of being part of a community. This is another point brought out by Taylor in relation to our self-identities. Our contemporary culture, at least in the United States, has emphasized individualism over community when considering self-identity. Taylor argues that a full definition of a person's identity involves her stand on moral and spiritual concerns, and that it must also include some reference to a community that defines her. Someone might be a Catholic, an anarchist, an American, a Spaniard, or some combination of these. The important point is that our identities are also constituted by the communities to which we belong. The significance of community is wider than this and is something many philosophers, both past and present, insist upon. Plato's *Republic* is focused on the significance of community, Aristotle's *Nicomachean Ethics* contains an extensive discussion of friendship, and contemporary philosophers have continued to focus upon this important aspect of human life. Cyclists know the importance of this as well. Whether we're talking about a peloton of elite riders or a small group of friends who ride together when they can, it is true that cyclists need each other to fulfill their potential. Sprinters need lead out men, climbers need their teammates to help them gain ground in the mountains or at least get to the bottom in the right place in the pack, and anyone who ends up on the podium cannot accurately say he or she did it without help from others. No one can win the Tour de France on their own. And sometimes the recreational riders and enthusiasts need the help of friends just to finish a long weekend ride.

This is also true in life. We need our family, friends, and members of the community if we are to be fulfilled and flourish as human beings. And we need to remember this as we seek to contribute to the wellbeing of others. Everyone needs to take a pull at the front, and everyone needs some time in the slipstream as well. This is true for any community of people: families, companies, schools, religious groups, political organizations, community service groups, and even towns, states, and nations.

The End of the Tour

I believe that ultimately, the best life is one in which we love what is good. As Taylor writes of the good, "Love of it empowers us to be good. And hence loving it is part of what it is to be a good human being."[7] For me, cycling is something that brings fulfillment to my life. But in the end, perhaps the most valuable lesson for me is that even though cycling is not *necessary* for me to live a full and meaningful life, it can contribute to such a life in a variety of ways. And hopefully I'll never have to find a replacement for it, even if that means that as an old man I'll be exchanging my road bike for a fat-tired comfort bike that I'm only able to take on relatively safe bike paths instead of the narrow and winding country roads I now frequent. In my 75-year-old mind, if I'm able to ride even in this way, I'll still be satisfied that I'm a *cyclist*.

NOTES

1 Charles Taylor, *Sources of the Self: The Making of the Modern Identity* (Cambridge, MA: Harvard University Press, 1989).
2 Ibid., p. 4.
3 Ibid., p. 27.
4 Ibid.
5 Charles Taylor, *The Ethics of Authenticity* (Cambridge, MA: Harvard University Press, 1991).
6 Props to Mike's Hike and Bike in Richmond, Kentucky, which is for me the ideal LBS (www.mikeshikeandbike.com/).
7 Taylor, *Sources of the Self*, p. 93.

FAIR PLAY ON TWO WHEELS

CHAPTER 18

WARM UP

Pushing the Envelope

The dirt track split just ahead of me and pitched upward through fir and alder, but the mustang held her line, the leaves snapping against her shoulders. She needed no coaxing. I had come so close to her on the flat, spinning my middle chain-ring and skirting most of the loose rock, finding the smooth spots. She didn't like that. She turned back and sniffed at me, I thought first as a challenge, but mostly she just wanted to know where I was. She saw the climb ahead and knew I'd be pressed, especially as the grade stair-stepped and spun back to the north. She'd been here before, and her memory was better than mine.

As a veteran in the mountain bike-racing scene in the 1980s, I was used to getting beaten by younger and stronger riders, but also used to riding well enough to stay within screaming distance of the leaders. I could scream pretty loud. Theatre training and all that. I was, however, of an age where riding alone and wallowing in introspection while pushing my threshold was becoming less and less fun.

Enter Robbie and Breezy. Robbie is an American mutt of Scottish and French descent, blonde: my best friend and wife. Breezy is Arab by conformation, Mustang by disposition, and a horse with the heart of three. Robbie chose to introduce her to endurance racing about the same time I was regularly hammering my quadriceps – alone. Robbie and I had ridden together over the years, both on horses and bicycles. She suggested the hybrid of training, since Breezy always slowed down on the flats, and most cyclists slow down on the climbs. I suggested her horse's problem was a lack of motivation, while mine was gravity, but a sneer of disbelief suggested I may be suffering from both. I would not argue.

I knew if I could skip abreast of Breezy on the lower part of the climb, find the breath to talk to her and maybe mellow her pace a bit, I might be able to cut inside on the first turn and beat her to the next section of single track. There, I could dictate the pace, my only need being to out-distance the snot she blew in her impatience to get past me. The trail split and Breezy gave me the smoothest lane. I stood on my pedals as the way kicked up, refusing to drop from my middle chainring. I had 50 yards in which to take the lead. I cheated a glance at my competition. She was breathing harder than me, but only because she was pissed off at my proximity. I cooed at her, or maybe it was a gasp, but I disguised my labor well. Shoulder to shoulder. I envied her traction. I knew well Breezy's heart, that she would climb on her knees if she had to. She probably knew I wouldn't go that far.

The turn loomed. This was my only real advantage, that I knew the trail narrowed. My lungs seemed to shrink. I dropped into the small chainring. Breezy huffed beside me. I executed a flawless shift, lost no momentum and jacked through a smooth rut, bouncing onto firm trail, shouldering in front of Breezy as I leaned into the corner. I struck the single track first, rewarded myself with a gasp of breath, and sighted up the next 100-yard pitch. Steady, smooth. Once crested, I could smoke that four-hoofed hay-burner across the ridge. I began to celebrate. The tightness in my calves slackened. I settled onto my saddle, shifted up, and stroked the gear with ease.

The ground began to shake. A palpable tremor. I looked over my shoulder for Breezy. Limbs snapped beside me, in the woods. Small trees swayed. Breezy left the trail, fighting through salal and alder saplings. But that was on my right shoulder. The rumble was on my left.

Ride, I told myself. Just ride. Oxygen deprivation can deceive even the most alert mind.

Breezy blitzed past me 20 yards from the top. I swallowed dust and, I think, inhaled part of her tail. The strangest sensation, feeling the long hairs descend my throat and then slide back out. Breezy accelerated away from me and leapt up to the crest, where she turned broadside and stopped.

"What the hell?"

I thought it more than said it, as oxygen was not then available for such a wasteful display. She blocked me. Robbie held her palm down to slow me. Like I could be settled as easily as a horse? Higher life-form and all that. One of us was a higher life-form.

I dismounted, huffing and frankly pleased for the respite, but unwilling to admit it. Breezy was perfectly still, the bellows of her lungs settled, her heart a whisper. She turned once to me, as if to say, "Stay." She stepped away and nosed up to an elk calf that had separated from the herd – all that rumbling that shook the forest. I looked for the herd. They, too, had settled, nearly invisible in the dense stand of fir and alder.

The calf sniffed at Breezy, paying no attention to my scent or Robbie's presence. He licked up one side of Breezy's face. The horse lowered her head, gently nudging the calf toward the woods. The herd made little sound, but even I caught their scent now. The calf spun on his knobby legs, swung his head so hard he nearly toppled over, and stepped off the trail. He disappeared into the herd, and the herd disappeared into the woods.

Robbie pressed her knee into Breezy's side and the two of them started across the ridge. Humbled by a horse, in so many ways. I followed her lead.

CHAPTER 19

WHAT TO DO ONCE THEY'RE CAUGHT

Why Give a D*** about Doping?

Not many people seem to be aware of how deeply connected doping has been with professional cycling. Almost from its inception, professional cyclists began using anything and everything that could help them survive some of the most grueling sporting events ever invented. Although today most cyclists and followers of the sport currently reject doping and all that it represents, the previous world of cycling's subculture both knew about and tolerated doping by professional bike racers. This shift in views has resulted in the Union Cycliste Internationale (UCI) – the international governing body of cycling – implementing increasingly severe punishments, arguably the strictest of all sports, intended to dissuade athletes from using certain performance-enhancing substances.

I believe that cycling's sanctions for doping may have gone too far. Despite the cycling community's legitimate desire to strongly punish those who cheat by doping, certain largely unexamined attitudes towards doping are driving the trend towards unjustifiably harsh punishments. These harsh punishments are ethically questionable in terms of justice for the individual and also for the harms they may bring to the sport of cycling. Unless the cycling community changes its attitudes towards doping, it will struggle to fairly punish doped cyclists.

Presently, I hope to accomplish two things. First, take the "juice" out of doping by criticizing the well-intentioned but misguided attitudes that are driving these harsh punishments, and second, show how an "enhanced" view of doping will generate more effective punishments that both preserve fairness and deter doping.

From Acceptable Vigor to Absolute Vice

Doping is not a new phenomenon in cycling. It did not start with Richard Virenque and the "Festina Affair" in 1998. Nor did it start in the 1950s with admitted doper and first five-time Tour de France winner Jacques Anquetil.[1] In fact, almost from its inception in the late nineteenth century, professional cycling has had an ongoing relationship with doping. News reports indicate cyclists doped with brandy and strychnine as early as the 1880s, and the popular six-day track racers in the 1910s and 1920s openly used "chemical help" during their competitions.[2] Even famed Tour de France founder Henri Desgrange believed doping was acceptable "in a case of absolute necessity to give you for a period artificial vigor."[3] Before World War II, amphetamines, cocaine, heroin, and strychnine would have been but a few of the drugs in most professional riders' toolkits.[4] However, the 1960s witnessed a change in popular opinion towards doping.

The 1960s ushered in a turbulent era, both for society and cycling. With the rampant drug use of 1960s counter-culture and a general change in societal attitudes towards health, in the 1950s and 1960s the general public grew less accepting of drug usage in sport.[5] Up to that point, cyclists doped openly and broke no rules by doing so. Only in 1966 did the UCI actively begin testing riders.[6] Initially, riders protested, arguing that doping was a professional hazard no more dangerous than the normal health risks associated with racing bicycles.[7] However, the suspicious drug-related deaths of cyclists Knud Jensen in 1960 and Tom Simpson in 1967 along with shifting cultural views encouraged the UCI to create, at minimum, the appearance of a "clean" sport.[8]

While the professional peloton has at times rebuffed the UCI's efforts to remove doping from bicycle racing, today the cycling community appears to accept anti-doping rules as a fixture of the sport. The UCI and cycling sponsors along with the athletes, managers, and racing officials portray a culture that believes doping does not belong in the sport of cycling. It is this belief in the ideals of dope-free cycling that justifies the sport's doping prohibitions. Yet, these very beliefs have also given rise to today's overly severe sanctions.

The UCI currently enforces stricter anti-doping measures than can be found in any other professional sport.[9] In order to catch the athletes who dope, the UCI subjects professional riders to both in-competition and out-of-competition testing. Four times a year riders must provide the UCI with a schedule listing their location every day during the upcoming quarter and a specific 60-minute window when they will be available for an out-of-competition test.[10] If a rider tests positive for doping after a race, the sanctions for a first-time offender include disqualification from the competition, a *minimum* two-year suspension, and a fine equal to the rider's current yearly salary, leading in all probability to loss of sponsorship contracts to boot.[11]

Although these measures are severe in their own right, some in the cycling community are considering more extreme penalties. In 2009, the UCI raised the ban for a positive drug test from two to four years. Moreover, the Italian Association of Professional Cyclists Union (ACCPI) proposed that "the way to fight doping isn't simply to increase penalties, but rather life bans [sic]."[12] Lifetime bans are needed, according to the ACCPI, since "only extreme remedies can hope to restore credibility to our beloved sport."[13] Some professional teams have also adopted "extreme remedies" by writing fines for doping into an athlete's contract, fines that are up to five times the athlete's annual salary.[14] With such punishments, why not just bring back the Inquisition?

These harsh punishments, however, pose a number of ethical and practical problems. First, the quality of evidence used to convict riders of doping is far from being "beyond a reasonable doubt." Recently, scientists have openly questioned the science behind anti-doping tests.[15] Explaining how some tests may produce false positives, these scientists show that these tests are closer to voodoo magic than reliable science. Additionally, many riders admit to regularly beating doping tests, further calling into question the tests' accuracy and fairness.[16] Clearly, a system where sometimes the cheaters go free and the innocent riders serve two-year bans has some flaws. Given how these unreliable tests are affecting athletes, the cycling community should rethink imposing penalties that would end an athlete's career or dramatically affect his or her financial status.

That cycling is banning innocent athletes harms not only those athletes wrongly convicted but also the ones who are still racing. Cyclists – and their fans! – now witness major races with diluted talent pools.

Superstar riders like Tom Boonen, Alessandro Petacchi, and Michael Rasmussen have all been suspended for doping despite the absence of evidence that any of these riders had intentionally doped. Moreover, in 2008, the 2007 Tour de France champion Alberto Contador could not defend his title since the Tour de France organizing company, Amaury Sports Organization (ASO), decided to ban him and his team, Astana, from that year's race due to Astana's past doping problems. The rub is that Contador and many of Astana's coaches, managers, and other riders who transferred to the team in the off-season had no relationship to Astana's past doping offenses. Arguably, they did not deserve to be the victim of such penalties. With some of the best athletes wrongly sitting on the sidelines, the yellow jersey or the rainbow stripes lose a little luster for those who pull them on.

When thinking about these bans, we must also consider commonsense justice. Often the evidence used to charge athletes with a doping violation would not stand up in a court of law since it relies heavily on hearsay, indirect proof, and circumstantial evidence. Occasionally the evidence convicting a rider does not even prove that the rider ever raced while benefiting from doping. Even if an out-of-competition test shows a rider positive for illicit drugs, finding him guilty of doping outside of a race is akin to finding someone who drinks guilty of drunk driving even though he had never actually gotten behind the wheel of a car. Just because they had dope in their system does not *prove* they would have ever raced doped. The UCI's current "biological passport" system – it records a rider's tests and suspends the rider if his test results show minor fluctuations that indicate doping – exemplifies this point.[17] Biological passports cannot show what substance an athlete has taken or actually prove that the athlete ever took a banned substance. The biological passports, in short, produce no direct evidence of doping. They only indicate the likelihood doping occurred. Cycling should reconsider forcing athletes to pay such hefty prices for doping if the evidence doesn't prove the athlete cheated.

To Head-Butt or Not to Head-Butt?

In order to prevent anti-doping sanctions from harming cycling, one needs to understand how sanctions work in sport. Sanctions are applied to rule violations and typically come in two forms: penalties and punishments. In essence, penalties and punishments help athletes to determine whether they should or should not commit a certain foul, like head-butting an opponent in a field sprint. Penalties are sanctions that restore fairness to competition when athletes acceptably break certain rules. For example, if a basketball player fouls an opponent who is shooting, the officials penalize the player by awarding their opponent two free throws. We assume that these free throws restore fairness to the competition, if only in a rough and ready kind of way.

Usually a sport applies penalties to acceptable infractions considered part of the game – either accidental violations or benign varieties of strategic fouls. A type of strategic foul in cycling comes when a cyclist drafts off of (or sometimes grabs onto) a team car to get back to the race. For this behavior, they receive only minor fines or small time penalties. It is understood in cycling that this "professional foul" is often not caught, and when it is the penalty remains rather small in most cases. If the cycling community wished to eradicate this behavior, it would instead apply punishments.

Sporting communities add punishments to their penalties to prevent undesirable behaviors from occurring during the competition. Punishments often incorporate penalties so as to restore fairness but are more severe and, thus, go beyond the function of restoration. An example of a punishment is the red card in soccer. Red cards are given for unacceptable behavior such as fighting or malicious tackling. If a player receives a red card, the player must leave the field and his team plays with one less member. Unlike penalties, punishments seek to not only restore fairness but also prevent unwanted behavior. Ideally, the punishment's severity deters players from breaking that rule. Perhaps this explains Robbie McEwen's choice to only head-butt Stuart O'Grady in the third stage of the 2005 Tour de France rather than punch the rider in the face – an infraction that certainly would have had McEwen kicked out of the race. McEwen only received a relegation to the end of the peloton, losing no time and paying no fine. Perhaps the threat of the punishment for punching a rider prevented the hot-tempered Aussie from going directly to blows.

In the case of doping in cycling, it makes sense to sanction dopers with punishments in addition to penalties for two reasons. First, given the way that doping affects the competition, it appears very difficult, if not impossible, to undo the effects of a doped athlete's improved performance. During a race, a doped cyclist can attack the peloton causing opponents to expend extra energy to chase them down. Doped riders may chase down breakaways for their own team, thereby significantly affecting the competitive status of their allies. A doped rider's effect, in short, radiates far beyond her placement on the results page because of her effect on opponents and her service to her team. If the doped rider were not racing, in other words, the competition would unfold very differently.

Since officials can catch a doped rider only following a race, the finely honed penalties that we find in other sports are not useful in cycling. Officials cannot easily undo a doped athlete's effects on the outcome of a race. Under the current system, the best that can be done is to honor the rightful victor through disqualifications after the race. Thus in the sport of cycling, punishments – not penalties – seem to be the order of the day. If it is difficult to restore fairness once a certain behavior has taken place, then the best option is to deter the behavior. And this is exactly the aim of punishments. Yet this also adds to the likelihood that some resort to excessively aggressive punishments.

Second, the cultural views of the cycling community show the sport does not want doping. Because the cycling community appears united *against* cyclists using dope, the community is justified to aim to prevent doping rather than to tolerate it. If cycling does not tolerate doping, then it should use sanctions that prevent athletes from doping.

Helping Hands are Strangling the Sport!

While the majority of the cycling community supports the rules banning doping, many also perceive doping – almost with unwavering certainty – as morally reprehensible. Unlike their views on other rule infractions, some believe that those who break anti-doping rules are moral deviants whose behavior is much worse than those who violate other rules. The over-reaction to doping has undoubtedly contributed to the overly harsh punishments for doping that are harming the sport. Moreover, Danish doping expert Verner Møller warns that "the greatest danger to sport are the many people of good will who do not seem to understand that their helping hands have sport in a stranglehold that will eventually choke the life out of it."[18] Unless the cycling community revisits its emotionally laden attitudes towards doping, its draconian anti-doping sanctions may actually harm the sport of cycling more than help it.

What cycling needs is a different way to approach doping. Rather than using "extreme remedies" and absurd punishments, the cycling community should view doping instead as a simple rule violation – that is, as simply another form of cheating dealt with like all the other forms of cheating. Thus, a better way to handle doping in the sport of cycling is to imagine anti-doping rules are *just another* rule in the UCI rulebook.[19] In fact, the UCI specifically states that in cycling, "anti-doping rules are part of the competition rules, i.e. sports rules governing the conditions under which sport is played."[20] According to the UCI, anti-doping rules are a condition of participation just like all of the other rules that make a cycling race possible.[21]

Think about it. Although doping is undesirable, a form of cheating and illegal outside the boundaries of cycling, it is *actually not much different* from other types of behaviors we tolerate but punish in sports. Fighting in hockey is a case in point. If two people brawled outside a bar on a Friday night, they both would likely go to jail. Yet inside an ice rink with skates on, these same men could duke it out on national television and receive only a few minutes in the penalty box. In the Tour de France, riders blatantly take "natural breaks" on the side of the road, yet has a police officer ever ticketed a rider for lewd or indecent behavior?

The action's illegality and the related societal disapproval of fighting (or peeing in public!) does not factor into a sport's determination of the *fairness* of the sanction for the rule infraction. Instead, sports regulate certain immoral behaviors such as fighting, spitting on an opponent, and using abusive language often because if those behaviors occurred, the sport would be less fun. In other words, sports provide punishments towards the end of preventing behaviors that detract from fair and enjoyable contests. Thus, those seeking harsh punishments for doping should remember that the point of punishing doping is not to address issues of social morality or civil legality – other avenues are available for addressing those issues, such as legal courts or loss of sponsorship dollars. The point of punishing doping is to prevent behaviors that harm the sport. How ironic, then, that the punishments cycling designed to *prevent* harm to the sport are actually *causing* harm to the sport.

By viewing doping as a rule violation rather than a moral sin, the cycling community can focus on creating fair punishments that prevent doping but also fit within the sport. Holders of this view see that they should punish the actions of dopers with the same rationale that they would use to punish the actions of those who attempt to gain an advantage by intentionally breaking other rules of a sport. In order to prevent damaging the sport of cycling with overly harsh punishments, cycling should punish dopers who cheat, *but that is all that it should punish*. When cycling tries to do more, it runs the risks of creating bad punishments.

How Far Should We Go?

Since the sport of cycling seems to be establishing punishments that are too harsh, we need some way to determine how far is too far. However, it appears possible to establish better criteria helpful for establishing more appropriate sanctions. First, we must remember that punishments cannot violate an individual's rights since a sport is always subject to the larger rule of moral justice. We can all agree that the rules of ethics are more important than the rules of sport. Thus sport rules must comply with common ethical standards. An ethical punishment is one that respects the rights of all affected by the rule infraction in accordance with all applicable ethical standards.

Second, the severity of the punishment ought to be proportional to the severity of the infraction. Given the fact that doping can affect the outcome of a race in significant ways, it must be regarded as a serious infraction. Thus an athlete who cheats by doping deserves a rather serious punishment compared to other infractions. Yet the punishment should not be so serious that the athlete who violates a rule becomes a victim. On the contrary, the punishment for doping should fall within the range of sanctions levied for other serious infractions. Perhaps the punishment for taking a short cut, like the first Tour de France winner, Maurice Garin, did in 1904 when he boarded a train in the middle of a stage, is analogous. The Tour de France organizers later discovered the incident, stripping Garin of his 1904 title and suspending him only from the Tour for two years (since Garin could still race across Europe, his punishment for that infraction was less severe than today's doping sanctions).[22]

Additionally, cycling should consider the intent of the athlete. While intent is hard to determine, it still plays an important role in identifying an appropriate punishment. In today's cycling world, intent is irrelevant. Accidental doping through the use of medication for a cold is punished the same as intentional use of erythropoietin (EPO) to artificially boost hematocrit. Now, doesn't that seem a bit absurd? If the athlete's intent was not to cheat or gain an unfair advantage, his punishment should be lighter compared to the athlete who doped intentionally and took steps to avoid detection.

On the other hand, repeat offenders – who have shown multiple times their intent to dope – should face stiffer punishments than those who are caught the first time. If an athlete continues to violate the doping rules, she exhibits a sustained attitude of selfishness and a consistent disregard for the integrity of the sport. These are the athletes that should really feel the brunt of harsher punishments. This method is already employed by the World Anti-Doping Association (WADA) and the UCI, and should be continued. As noted, punishing second-, third-, and fourth-time offenders more severely makes sense since the intent is clearer in these cases and the harm produced by these individuals is greater.

Last, the severity of the punishment ought to relate to the accuracy of the call. In the case of doping, where the quality of evidence may be suspect, the punishments must reflect the possibility that it may be wrong. Given the imperfect nature of the tests used to document doping, the use of discretion, as previously argued, is appropriate. If we are not cautious, we risk overly punishing an innocent athlete. Softer punishments may mean a guilty rider returns to competition sooner, but it also will protect an innocent rider's career and not destroy his accomplishments. Additionally, the more conclusive the evidence against a rider, the harsher officials can be when they apply the penalties. For example, we should punish an athlete caught doping and in possession of doping supplies, like David Millar – who was found with vials of EPO and used syringes in his house in 2004 – more harshly than an athlete who can prove that he accidentally took the drug or is convicted using questionable evidence.

New Ways Forward

Clearly, we can all agree that as long as doping is against the rules, there must be sanctions – both penalties and punishments. Moreover, in cycling, the penalties must attempt to restore fairness while the punishments for doping must be strong enough to act as a deterrent. Yet current punishments, for all their unjustifiable harshness, seem actually ineffective in deterring doping. Rather than promoting longer bans and harsher fines, we need to find a new approach towards punishing doping in cycling – one that fairly punishes the infraction while reducing its occurrence.

A better approach is punishing both the individual who dopes and that individual's team. Given the fact that professional cycling is a team sport, it is logical that doping punishments apply to the team as well. Think of this like the red card in soccer, which makes the whole team play with one less player. Some may argue that punishing the teammates of a doper is unfair since the teammates did nothing wrong. However, the team certainly benefited from having the doped rider as a teammate. Think about it. If the entire team benefits from doping, then shouldn't the entire team also be punished?

One way cycling can put these team punishments into practice is by reducing the number of racers a team could start in a future race. Following an athlete's positive test for doping, the team would have to start races with fewer riders than their opponents. Fewer riders in a race would force the team to race with a handicap similar to a red card in soccer. Imagine having to start Paris–Roubaix with one less rider ... or even worse, a 21-day stage race. I would bet teams would spend a lot more energy trying to prevent that type of punishment.

Additionally, the UCI could impose punishments on teams and their individual riders by deducting Pro Tour points. The UCI awards Pro Tour points based on a rider's placement in certain races. These points are very valuable since they determine whether certain prestigious races invite the team to participate. Pro Tour points are also frequently used to determine an athlete's salary and bonuses. Deducting Pro Tour points from riders reduces their team's status in the sport and individual riders' financial gain. Unlike fines that apply only to the doper, having teammates lose Pro Tour points punishes all of the individuals who benefited from their teammate's doping. If one rider's actions hit all of their teammates in the pocketbooks, I bet teammates would spend much more time discouraging doping.

Clearly, then, team punishments discourage doping in the first place. The internal climate whereby cyclists discourage their teammates from doping acts as a better deterrent. The fear of having one rider negatively impact their career gives teammates a reason to police each other. Also, the sense that one's choice to dope would harm one's teammates may dissuade others from doping. In the case where the entire team agreed to dope, applying sanctions to the whole team would be especially effective since it was a team effort in the first place.

While team punishments present an appealing new punishment for doping, we should also continue to punish the individual caught doping. At the very minimum, the UCI should ban a doped rider from competition until the physiological benefits from doping have disappeared. For example, when riders boost their hematocrit using EPO, they should at least be banned until their hematocrit returns to normal levels. The same applies to other drugs like testosterone, steroids, or human growth hormones. Moreover, it makes sense that the UCI increases scrutiny on riders caught doping by subjecting them to more in-competition and out-of-competition testing.

Cycling's Constant Battle

The overall problem of doping defies easy answers. Once the cycling community banned performance-enhancing drugs, it pitted itself against the riders who explore every avenue for success. With their desire to win, the prospect of financial gain, and their relentless pursuit of the ultimate performance, some riders may continue to be lured towards breaking the doping rules. On the other hand, the sport of cycling has a vested interest in creating fair and desirable contests that appeal to its many fans, but its severe punishments are damaging the sport and unfairly punishing its athletes. By moving from unduly severe to more measured and better targeted punishments, we can take a step towards resolving the current problems caused by doping. Yet it is essential that the cycling community joins together in demanding not only fairer punishments, but also better treatment of the athletes who give so much. Although the rules should punish doping so as to prevent it from occurring, they have become too harsh. By calling for new ways, such as the ones defended here, the cycling community can continue to punish riders who dope but in an ethical manner that works to prevent doping. Professional cycling may never eradicate doping altogether, but it can certainly punish doping more effectively, and do so in a way that better preserves a sport loved by so many.

NOTES

1   For a discussion of Anquetil's drug use see Howard Paul, *Sex, Lies and Handlebar Tape: The Remarkable Life of Jacques Anquetil, the First Five-Time Winner of the Tour de France* (New York: Mainstream Publishing, 2008). Or see Christopher Thomson, *The Tour de France: A Cultural History*, 2nd ed. (Los Angeles: University of California Press, 2008).
2   Ivan Wadington and Andy Smith, *An Introduction to Drugs in Sport: Addicted to Winning?* (New York: Routledge, 2009), 129–30.
3   Henri Desgrange, *La Tête et les jambes* (Paris: Henri Richard, 1930), cited in Thomson, *The Tour de France*.
4   Wadington and Smith, *An Introduction to Drugs in Sport*, pp. 129–30.
5   For more on this issue, see Verner Møller, *The Doping Devil* (Copenhagen, Denmark: Gyldendal, 2008).
6   Pat McQuaid, *The UCI and the Fight against Doping: A Long History of Cat and Mouse* (Switzerland: Union Cycliste Internationale, 2008).

7   In fact, Luis Barrios, a US Postal Team medical consultant, claimed that "one stage of the Pyrenees will do far more damage to a cyclist's health than a therapeutic dose of certain performance-enhancing drugs" (*Cycling Weekly*, December 15, 2001).

8   For the discussion of shifting views towards doping in cycling, see Wadington and Smith, *An Introduction to Drugs in Sport*. In the case of the alleged doping deaths of Jensen and Simpson, Tom Simpson openly used amphetamines but his death was caused by a head injury he sustained after falling off his bike. This was likely due to dehydration exacerbated by his use of amphetamines. For the most insightful discussion of the death of Jensen, which shows that he most likely *did not* die of doping despite common assumptions, see Verner Møller, "Knud Enemark Jensen's Death During the 1960 Rome Olympics: A Search for Truth?," in *Drugs, Alcohol and Sport*, ed. Paul Dimeo (New York: Routledge, 2006), 99–118.

9   UCI, *Anti-Doping Rules of the UCI* (2009), 1. See also UCI, *Information on the Biological Passport*. Available online at www.uci.ch/Modules/ENews/ENewsDetails.asp?MenuId=MjI0NQ&id=NTQzOA&LangId=1.

10 Ibid., p. 18.

11 Ibid., pp. 43–52.

12 Associated Press, "Italian Cycling Group Suggests Lifetime Bans Needed to Combat Doping," *ESPN*, October 23, 2008.

13 Ibid.

14 Agence France Presse, "Three Top Katusha Riders Oppose Team Rules," *VeloNews*, June 7, 2009.

15 D. A. Berry, "The Science of Doping," *Nature* 454, 7205 (2008): 692–3.

16 Hedwig Kröner, "Kohl Tells All About Doping," *Cyclingnews.com*, June 9, 2009.

17 UCI, *Information on the Biological Passport*.

18 Møller, *The Doping Devil*, p. 192.

19 For this chapter, I am omitting discussion of the legal side to doping.

20 UCI, *Anti-Doping Rules of the UCI*, p. 1.

21 Ibid.

22 Les Woodland, *The Unknown Tour de France: The Many Faces of the World's Greatest Bicycle Race*, 3rd ed. (San Francisco, CA: Van der Plas Publications/Cycle, 2009).

CHAPTER 20

OUT OF CONTROL

The Pirate and Performance-Enhancing Drugs

Proud men must spurn charity. On July 13, 2000, during stage 12 of the Tour de France, leaving the rest of the field far behind, Lance Armstrong and Marco Pantani stormed up the unforgiving Mont Ventoux. A study in contrasts, the confident Armstrong, on the cusp of the second of his seven consecutive Tour de France victories, and the disgraced Pantani, desperately seeking redemption, sprinted against harsh winds toward the finish line. Suddenly, Armstrong relaxed and conceded the stage win to Pantani. From Armstrong's perspective, the gesture was a classy tribute to a rival who had undergone a year of torment. From Pantani's vantage point, Armstrong's actions were redolent with condescending altruism: Pantani had been denied an uncontaminated triumph. The Italian Pirate seethed.

Three days later, on stage 15 at Courchevel, Pantani attacked the mountain with deranged avidity. Once again, he was the swashbuckling, ferocious king of inclines. Pantani dropped his rivals like scalding rocks and flashed through the finish line alone. He had resurrected his greatness and regenerated his glory. Pantani's family, friends, and countrymen wept at the roadside.

This was to be Marco's final big score. After the 2000 Tour de France, Pantani raced only sporadically and without distinction. On February 14, 2004, he was found dead at a hotel in Rimini, Italy. Acute cocaine poisoning had caused a cerebral edema and heart failure. Marco Pantani was 34 years old.

Life and Times

Weighing only 130 pounds after stuffing his pockets with bricks, Pantani savored mountain racing. With a seemingly endless capability of punishing his scrawny body, he would at times drop to the rear of the pack to luxuriate in the extraordinary delight of passing everyone to win. Although he was always at a disadvantage in time-trial events, Marco's climbing style was unique, exhausting, and thrilling: staying on the drops the entire way, often pedaling out of the saddle, casting a maniacal – half-masochistic, half-sadistic – leer at his competitors, and sometimes insolently throwing down his bandana as an explicit challenge, Pantani exhilarated spectators and disconcerted rivals. He enjoyed peering into the eyes of his competitors as they suffered during the climb up the mountains.[1]

His early cycling career was marked by unpredictable, spectacular glimpses of greatness, recurrent injuries, and the prospect of promise unfulfilled. In 1994, Marco finished second at the Giro d'Italia and third at the Tour de France. In 1995 and 1997, he won two stages each year of the Tour de France, finishing third overall in 1997. Around this time, the legend of the Italian Pirate began. Relishing the attention, he amplified his image by shaving his head, sporting a goatee, piercing his ears for silver hoop earrings, and donning a knotted bandanna that brandished the skull-and-crossbones insignia of *Il Pirata*.

In 1998, it all came together for the Italian Pirate. Injury free and at the peak of his form, he blew the competition away at the Giro d'Italia and Tour de France. Marco was the first Italian since Fausto Coppi in 1952 and only the seventh rider in history to win the Giro and the Tour in the same year. The French team Festina was banned from the Tour de France that year when a member of its medical staff was detected at the France – Belgium border with a host of illicit doping products concealed in his automobile. Ironically, untouched by the scandal, Pantani was widely viewed as an untainted hero and the savior of cycling. "Then Marco had appeared, a ball of inspired chaos, full of subversive trickery – full of *style* and capable – who knew how? – of Promethean accelerations whenever the road turned skywards."[2]

However, like a shooting star, Marco Pantani's brightness quickly evaporated. In 1999, at the Giro d'Italia, Pantani was well on his way to earning the *maglia rosa* for the second consecutive year. Shockingly, he was expelled from the race and suspended after a drug test revealed his hematocrit level was too high and suggested that he had used r-EPO, a commercially produced recombinant form of the human hormone erythropoietin (EPO). Despite his protestations and vague allegations of a conspiracy against him, the Italian Pirate was forever stained.

Performance-Enhancing Drugs

Discussions about performing-enhancing drugs (PEDs) generally assume that (1) the use of PEDs, combined with physical training, facilitates better athletic performances, and (2) PEDs pose potentially serious health risks for committed users. The precise levels of athletic benefits and health risks are a matter of some dispute in many cases.

Like most banned substances, r-EPO has established clinical uses. For patients suffering from chronic anemia, r-EPO can raise dangerously low red blood cell counts to a healthy level. Patients for whom rising out of bed was a major challenge can resume almost normal lives after receiving proper dosages of r-EPO. When used by healthy cyclists, r-EPO boosts red blood cell count, thereby enhancing the athletes' aerobic capability so they can work much harder and longer without oxygen debt and lactic acid build-up in their muscles. The dangers of increasing the number of red blood cells in healthy athletes result from thickening the blood, which facilitates clotting and may result in heart attack, stroke, and pulmonary embolism. Additional dangers include sudden death during sleep, which has killed about 20 pro cyclists in the past two decades, and the development of antibodies directed against EPO, which causes anemia.

The first, common objection to the use of PEDs is that their unprescribed use violates the rules of sport. To use an illegal substance to gain a competitive advantage is unfair because it is a form of cheating. This objection, though, is circular: it uses the current status of PEDs – they violate the rules of the sport – as the basis to conclude that PEDs *should be* against the rules of that sport. An advocate of PEDs could respond that if PEDs were permitted by the rules of sport, then no competitive unfairness would result.

However, a cleaner objection can be advanced: unprescribed use of PEDs violates not only the rules of sports but also the law of the land. Some PEDs are legally dispensed only by prescription from a medical doctor. How can the rules of athletics permit that which the law of the land prohibits? The rules of professional cycling, for example, could not permit heroin use or accept the use of any illegal substance. In one way, this objection is decisive. Professional cycling does not even have the option of permitting the use of r-EPO because that substance is generally allowed only through medical prescription. However, relying on the illegality argument obscures some of the deeper reasons why use of PEDs may be objectionable.

The Paternalistic Argument

Some people argue that cycling should be concerned with the health of participants and that harmful substances such as r-EPO should therefore be banned. By focusing only on short-term performance and ignoring long-term health risks of using PEDs, sports diminish respect for athletes as people. We should not place a higher value on better athletic performances than we do on the health of our athletes.[3]

Critics of paternalism, though, have a ready response that I will call "the libertarian manifesto": athletes, not the rulers of cycling or society, should be the judge of the relevant risks and benefits. Inform athletes of those risks and benefits, but let individuals make their own call. Remember, John Stuart Mill's famous harm principle insists that the only sound reason to legislate is to protect others from harm. The individual is the best judge of his own interests. Society should not be permitted to substitute its judgment or tastes except where doing so protects the wellbeing of others. Individual autonomy and freedom of choice are paramount. We may rightfully act paternalistically only toward those who lack full rational capabilities because of age or mental incompetence. Besides, taking risks in sports is not automatically foolish. We permit risky sports such as mountain climbing, sky diving, and professional boxing.[4] We allow power meters and strenuous interval training in cycling that increase risk of injury. Taking risks in sports is as "today" as a triple-decker burger with blue cheese dressing, extra processed cheese, and a side order of fries!

As an extreme view, the libertarian manifesto is susceptible to criticism. As a matter of fact, societies do often justifiably act paternalistically.

The state refuses to permit anyone to agree to his or her own disablement or killing. The state will not recognize contracts to sell oneself into slavery, or to become a mistress, or a second spouse. Prostitution is illegal almost everywhere. Any citizen may use reasonable force to prevent others from harming themselves or committing suicide. We cannot purchase certain drugs without a physician's prescription. Other drugs, such as heroin, are not permitted at all.[5] The state decrees seatbelt laws for automobiles and motorcycle safety laws. Professional cyclists are required to wear protective helmets during races. Mill's harm principle is a terrific beginning for understanding the proper scope of regulating conduct, but it is not the final word.

Libertarians are, typically, unconvinced. Where do we draw the line? Should we ban whiskey, cigarettes, fried foods, and triple-decker burgers with blue cheese dressing? Once we begin crawling down the slippery slope of paternalistic regulation, do we not end up in a conceptual morass?

Not automatically. Numerous arguments end up with someone raising the specter of a slippery slope leading to disaster. Usually, distinctions can be made and tests can be formulated that prevent our stumbling into ruin. We can retain our freedom to pound down deep-fried junk food while accepting the law requiring seatbelt use in automobiles.

I would offer the following factors as elements to consider when determining how strong a reason paternalism provides for legislation in a particular case: the probability of harm if professional cyclists, say, consume r-EPO; the severity of that harm; the immediacy of that harm; the directness of the link between harm and taking r-EPO; the benefit cyclists will enjoy if they use the drug; the amount of freedom restricted if we prohibit r-EPO; and the enforceability of the legislation.

The results of applying this test in good faith would often be contestable. Some of the factors would sometimes cut in different directions. But that is a function of most regulation. We resolve the matter in the usual way: argument, negotiation, and compromise.

Libertarians may be correct: the great value we properly place on individual autonomy and freedom of choice suggests that the paternalistic argument cannot conclusively establish a ban against PEDs in sports. But advocates of such a ban can point out a difference between risks *inherent* to sport – those that are an intrinsic part of the competition – and risks that are *extraneous* to sport – those that are not part of the competition and are brought into play for external purposes. They could argue that the risks inherent to cycling help make the sport what it is. Some racers take much bigger risks descending mountains and put grave pressure on competitors who are less proficient or less daring. For example, Marco Pantani would sometimes descend recklessly by putting his chest on the saddle to get lower and increase momentum. Less experienced imitators of *Il Pirata*'s style courted unfortunate results. Still, this and other such risks – such as training injuries, accidents, muscle pulls, exhaustion, dehydration – are internal to the sport of cycling and partially constitute its allure. The use of PEDs such as r-EPO is an extraneous risk, not part of the inherent framework of the sport.

We should not fall prey to one rhetoric device common to these debates. Often, once an argument seems unable to establish *conclusively* that PEDs should be banned, the argument is tossed aside. The underlying assumption seems to be the following: *If an argument cannot clearly establish that a drug should be regulated, then that argument is irrelevant to the debate.* Applying this assumption to our case: If an argument cannot *prove* that cycling should ban competitors from using r-EPO, then that argument can be summarily dismissed.

Instead, I would argue that such an argument may provide a *reason* of varying strength, depending on the argument's power and context of application. So, the paternalistic argument probably cannot conclusively establish that r-EPO should be banned in cycling, but the argument is not irrelevant. It provides a non-conclusive reason for banning r-EPO.

The Argument from the Harm Principle

PEDs, in fact, could be banned in accord with the harm principle itself. The harm principle is grounded by the primary values of individual autonomy and freedom of choice. But numerous professional cyclists do not consume r-EPO after rendering informed consent. Instead, they are subtly coerced into using PEDs because they know opponents are doing so and they cannot afford to yield the competitive edge. These competitors would prefer not to take r-EPO, but reluctantly consume PEDs out of fear that they might otherwise lose their livelihood.[6] Accordingly, the choice of some lunatic athletes to risk their health in service of better performances harms others who are coerced into following suit.

Jan Ulrich in 1997 became the first German to win the Tour de France. He also finished second in that event five times and fourth on two other occasions. Along with a passel of other riders, including Ivan Basso, Francisco Mancebo, and Oscar Sevilla, Ulrich was suspended one day prior to the 2006 Tour de France as evidence mounted against him in a Spanish doping scandal, Operación Puerto. Spanish authorities sent the race organizers over 40 pages summarizing police investigations into a ring, headed by Dr. Eufemiano Fuentes, that allegedly supplied professional cyclists with a panoply of PEDs. The winner that year, Floyd Landis, was stripped of his title after a test demonstrated a stunningly high ratio of the hormone testosterone to the hormone epitestosterone (T/E ratio) after his stirring performance in stage 17. Unsurprisingly, drug expert Dr. John Hoberman has noted that "long-distance cycling has been the most consistently drug-soaked sport of the twentieth century ... the Tour [de France] is a virtual pharmacy on wheels."[7] To conclude that numerous professional cyclists are subtly coerced into resorting to PEDs is reasonable.

Libertarians would rejoin that every new training regime, advance in equipment, and athletic technique puts similar pressure on competitors. For example, at one time, serious weight training in most sports was nonexistent. Once a few players assumed heavy weight programs with clear positive results, competitors had to follow suit or fall behind. Innovations always carry risks to health, also.[8] Just because a decision is made more difficult – to pick up the new technique or to risk falling behind – does not mean the resulting decision is not free. Athletes of normal human capabilities and above the requisite age can still make informed decisions, even though knowing that others are using and benefiting from PEDs must be factored into their decisions.

A typical argument pattern, called *tu quoque* (roughly, "you, too"), is in play here: you already allow activities of a certain sort, so you are not in a position to deny privilege to my favored similar activity. For example, many permitted dangers accompany professional cycling such as strenuous training, so race organizers are not in a position to deny competitors the benefits of using r-EPO. Moralists have no problem accepting the risks and "subtly coerced" choices involved in training regimens, yet they throw up their hands in horror at the difficult decisions athletes are confronted with regarding PEDs. Are not moralists being hypocritical and logically inconsistent?

Maybe. Maybe not. Readers should not succumb to a simplistic application of *tu quoque*. They should ask whether, for example, heavy weight training involves the *same likelihood* of harm, *equal severity* of harm, and *similar extra health benefits* beyond enhanced performance as does serious use of PEDs such as r-EPO. If consuming PEDs has a greater likelihood of harm, more severe possibility of harm, and fewer extra health benefits than strenuous training regimens, then the *tu quoque* argument is less impressive than libertarians imagine. In general, libertarians tend to find a currently accepted practice that they can claim forces moralists to also accept PEDs. They claim that accepting the argument against PEDs would also force moralists to outlaw a host of practices uncontroversially considered permissible. I am cautioning that the claims of parallel risks must be examined more closely.

The Argument from Distorted Values

Some thinkers argue that use of PEDs alters the balance between process and outcome values in sport. Sports embody inherent goods and values, which are attained by performing in accord with standards of excellence integral to them. The *process values* of cycling are critical: maximizing one's athletic potentials, striving to do one's best, achieving health and fitness, deserving victory based on superior skill and expenditure of effort, and viewing one's opponent as a necessary partner in mutual self-discovery and self-creation. The use of PEDs pushes process values to the side in a wrong-headed obsession with *outcome values*: victory at all cost, celebrity, and wealth. Accordingly, PEDs alter the balance between process and outcome values in sport. Sport becomes nothing more than the rush for higher, faster, farther by any means necessary. In so doing, we denigrate the beauty and creativity of sport in deference to glory and riches purchased at the cost of our integrity.[9] Such a bargain should be beneath those who view sport as not fundamentally about wins and losses. The old Grantland Rice slogan may seem corny to cynics, but it still reflects a basic truth: it is not whether you won or lost, but how you played the game.

Libertarians, after wiping tears from their eyes at the invocation of Grantland Rice, would remain unconvinced. First, we already permit training techniques and regimens (for example, training at high altitudes, heavy weight training, power meters and intervals) that help users exercise their skills at higher levels without altering the character of sports.[10] No competitor ignores a new training technique or renounces better equipment or a superior diet because it focuses too much on outcome. Second, PEDs are not magic bullets. Effective use requires extra effort and training, which implicates process values, on the part of athletes. Third, professional and big-time collegiate athletics already stress winning. Coaches and administrators lose their jobs if their teams win too infrequently. Players are cut if their performance wanes. The imagined ideal of athletics mirrors the rhetoric, but not the actual practice, of sports as we know them. And we might well include the Olympics in that category. Medal winners from virtually every country are showered with privileges and acclaim that are withheld from other participants. Use of PEDs does not alter, but merely reflects, the balance between process and outcome values in sport. Of course, we must exclude purely recreational sports.

Moralists are correct in arguing that use of PEDs strains further the balance between process and outcome values in sport. They should insist that strenuous training techniques and regimens, unlike PEDs such as r-EPO, do not privilege enhanced performance over the health of athletes. Also, how we achieve victory still matters. To view the manner and means of victory as more important than simply attaining victory is reasonable. Still, a libertarian might retort that this argument is circular: it *assumes* PEDs are undesirable and thereby taint the glory of victory, as well as distorting the role of process values in sport. Then it uses the alleged distortion of process values to *demonstrate* the undesirability of PEDs. Libertarians also have a point that in many venues the relationship between process and outcome values is already other than the ideal extolled by moralists. The argument from distorted values, then, cannot prove that PEDs should be banned, but provides a reason that remains relevant to the decision.

The Argument from the Prisoner's Dilemma

Some would argue that PEDs should be banned so all competitors arrive at the best situation of choice. The prisoner's dilemma is a well-known philosophical puzzle with many applications. When applied to athletes considering whether to inject PEDs, it illustrates how society and sports officials often feel justified in banning PEDs.[11]

Suppose two competing cyclists, call them "The Spider" and "The Flea," must decide whether to use r-EPO. Here are the possible results of their choices:

- *The Milan–San Remo*: Spider uses r-EPO, Flea does not. *Result*: Spider gets a competitive advantage, defeats Flea, but bears health risks. Flea suffers a competitive detriment, but bears no health risk.

- *The Settimena Coppi e Bartali*: Flea uses r-EPO, Spider does not. *Result*: Flea gets a competitive advantage, defeats Spider, but bears health risks. Spider suffers a competitive detriment, but bears no health risk.
- *Giro d'Italia*: Both Flea and Spider use r-EPO. *Result*: Neither Flea nor Spider gains a competitive edge, both bear health risks.[12]
- *Giro del Casentino*: Neither Flea nor Spider uses r-EPO. *Result*: Neither Flea nor Spider gains a competitive edge, nor do they bear health risks.

Although I have restricted the universe of discourse to two competing athletes, the same analysis applies to larger contexts. The best situation for athletes, taken as a whole, is the fourth: competitors neither gain a competitive edge nor incur health risks. But professional cyclists who are antecedently unwilling to use PEDs and unaware of how others will choose will not want to risk competitive disadvantage. As a result, both Spider and Flea will end up using PEDs and end up in scenario 3, the worst of the set. Neither athlete gains a competitive advantage, both incur new health risks. In the larger context, most athletes will choose to inject PEDs and end up, collectively, in scenario 3. By enforcing a ban on PEDs, society and sports officials increase the likelihood that all competitors end up in the best position, scenario 4. Thus, to ensure that sports protect its athletes from unnecessary risks and maximize competitive equality, they should ban PEDs and enforce the prohibition rigorously.[13]

To libertarians, the prisoner's dilemma looks like a variation of the moralists' earlier claim that consumption of PEDs subtly coerces the choices of athletes who do not want to inject PEDs, but do so to remain competitive with users. The prisoner's dilemma, though, requires independent arguments to sustain its main assumption: that if everyone uses PEDs, everyone is worse off than if no one uses them. The independent arguments available are precisely the previous ones that we have examined and deemed problematic.[14] Absent an independent argument to ground its main assumption, the dilemma begs the question – it assumes what it purports to be proving.

The argument from the prisoner's dilemma centers on the common good: taking an objective, all-encompassing perspective, what is the best result for competitors, taken as a whole? This approach is especially attractive to sports commissioners and societal reformers who aspire to advance collective benefit. Libertarians are correct in replying that an independent argument is required to ground the moralists' main assumption – that if everyone uses PEDs, everyone is worse off than if no one uses them. Libertarians are also correct in thinking that the main candidates for that argument are those previously discussed. But libertarians conclude that because the arguments previously analyzed were "problematic" – they could not conclusively establish that PEDs should be banned – they are irrelevant. I would submit that several of those arguments bear differing weights that should affect our decision-making, even if none of them can decisively prove that injecting PEDs must be banned. In life we rarely make decisions from a condition of proof or certainty. Typically, we pursue the action that is supported by the best reasons, even if no single reason constitutes a proof. To stigmatize a reason as "problematic" is to undermine its capability to establish a proof. But such a reason may well retain enough currency to be useful in discovering what alternative is supported by the best evidence.

Why r-EPO Should Continue to be Banned

First, let's stipulate that no single argument raised by moralists can prove that r-EPO should be banned by professional cycling. Of course, for argument's sake, we are brushing aside the general legal prohibition against non-prescription use of the drug. Second, remember that though an argument or a reason cannot *prove* a particular conclusion, this does not imply that the argument or reason is *irrelevant* to whether that conclusion is warranted. Third, when selecting an alternative in a situation where we must choose one or the other alternative, we should act on the alternative supported by the best reasons, even if neither alternative can be conclusively established.

Fourth, many reasons remain relevant to whether r-EPO should be banned: r-EPO has a *direct* causal link that results in a *definite probability* of producing physical and mental harms of a *specific severity* to non-prescribed consumers; use of r-EPO values enhanced performance over the health of cyclists: its use subtly coerces other cyclists, who would prefer not to use r-EPO, to inject the drug to maintain competitive balance; it distorts the proper balance of outcome values and process values in professional cycling; banning r-EPO increases the probability that competitors, taken as a whole, will end up in the best comparative situation – no one gains a competitive edge, no one bears added health risks; and, finally, widespread use of r-EPO upsets the balances that constitute the evolving structure of professional cycling: challenges versus aids to performance, innovation versus tradition.

Fifth, in light of the reasons sketched in step four, libertarians should bear a burden of clear and convincing evidence to earn a judgment that use of r-EPO should be permitted.

Sixth, the reasons, offered by libertarians, militating most strongly that use of r-EPO should be permitted center on individual autonomy and freedom of choice; the increased possibilities for some athletes of attaining wealth, athletic success, and celebrity; and greater opportunities for overcoming performance inhibitions such as passiveness and muscle exhaustion.

Seventh, no other training technique, type of equipment, food supplement, or athletic regimen that is counter-indicated by reasons as numerous and strong as those listed in step four and supported by the reasons listed in step six is permitted by professional cycling.

Eighth, libertarians have not met the burden of providing clear and convincing evidence for their judgment that use of r-EPO should be permitted.

Accordingly, professional cycling should continue to ban the use of r-EPO.

The Pirate's False Treasure

From his disqualification at the 1999 Giro d'Italia to his death in 2004, Marco Pantani's life was a descending spiral of drug use, failed rehabilitation attempts, self-destructive activity, courtroom battles to clear his name, and bouts of clinical depression, punctuated by rare reminders of his former greatness and charisma. His unsubstantiated, half-paranoid convictions of plots against him accelerated his romance with cocaine. In 2003, when Marco's self-image and self-esteem were nearing bottom, he underwent cosmetic surgery to straighten his aquiline nose and pin back his protruding ears (Armstrong had earlier mocked him with an old slur: *Elefantino*). No medical procedures were available, though, to mend his fractured soul or to restore his discarded honor.

That the worst human attributes are merely our best traits exaggerated is by now a cliché. At his best, Pantani's suspicion of others, eagerness to take risks, zeal to drive himself ever harder, relentless exuberance, zest for celebrity, and compelling panache conspired to create the Italian

Pirate, one of the most exciting, enjoyable performers in cycling history. At his worst, Marco distorted those same attributes and transformed himself into a paranoid, self-destructive, live-only-in-the-present, drug-dependent, flee-from-reality, self-parody.

At the times James Dean and Elvis Presley died, some insensitive observers snidely remarked, "Good career move." Although the comments were cruel, an element of truth persisted. Perhaps they had already reached their peak in life and more years would have only tarnished their legend; indeed, their deaths would amplify their mystique and underwrite their enduring appeal. If only the same could be said about Marco Pantani's final, alienated destruction on Valentine's Day, a block from the seafront in Rimini.

NOTES

1   My account of Marco Pantani's life and career is gleaned from Matt Rendell, *The Death of Marco Pantani: A Biography* (London: Orion Books, 2006); John Wilcockson, *Marco Pantani: The Legend of a Tragic Champion* (Boulder, CO: Velo Press, 2005); Manuela Ronchi, *Man on the Run: The Life and Death of Marco Pantani* (London: Robson Books, 2005).

2   Rendell, *Death of Pantani*, p. 3.

3   M. Andrew Holowchak, "Aretism and Pharmacological Erogenic Aids in Sport," in *Philosophy of Sport* (Upper Saddle River, NJ: Prentice Hall, 2002), p. 312.

4   W. M. Brown, "Paternalism, Drugs, and the Nature of Sports," in *Ethics in Sport*, ed. William J. Morgan, Klaus V. Meier, and Angela J. Schneider (Champaign, IL: Human Kinetics, 2001), pp. 138–9.

5   Joel Feinberg, *Harm to Self* (New York: Oxford University Press, 1986), pp. 24–5.

6   Robert L. Simon, "Good Competition and Drug-Enhanced Performance," in *Ethics in Sport*, ed. Morgan et al., pp. 122–3.

7   John Hoberman, *Testosterone Dreams: Rejuvenation, Aphrodisia, Doping* (Berkeley: University of California Press, 2005), p. 248.

8   W. M. Brown, "As American as Gatorade and Apple Pie: Performance Drugs and Sports," in *Ethics in Sport*, ed. Morgan et al., p. 144.

9   Holowchak, "Aretism," pp. 315–19; Michael Lavin, "Sports and Drugs: Are the Current Bans Justified?" in *Ethics in Sport*, ed. Morgan et al., pp. 176–9.

10 Brown, "American as Gatorade," pp. 149–52.

11 Ibid., p. 162.

12 Well, not exactly. Human beings are not equal in their ability to benefit from taking PEDs nor in the adverse effects they will endure for doing so.

13 Of course, a ban on PEDs cannot *guarantee* that all competitors will end up in situation 4, the best overall position. Some competitors will violate the ban, resulting in situation 1 or 2. However, even here, a ban decreases the probability of ending up in situation 3, the worst overall situation.

14 Brown, "American as Gatorade," pp. 162–3.

CHAPTER 21

IS THE CANNIBAL A GOOD SPORT?

We are from Belgium. Unfortunately, most foreigners associate our country with chocolates and Bruges. So when we travel abroad and people ask us where we come from, we end up in tedious conversations about bonbons or, if you're really unlucky, lace. But sometimes, you are lucky enough to meet cycling fans. When they hear where we're from, they immediately know what Belgium's real pride is: Eddy Merckx.

In Belgium, Merckx is not only popular among cycling fans. In both broadcast versions of the television poll "The Greatest Belgian," one for the French-speaking part of the country and one for the Flemish part, Merckx reached the top five even though he had explicitly urged the public *not* to vote for him. In both polls, he was by far the most popular living nominee. His popularity can be further illustrated by the fact that Belgians do not think of July 21, 1969 as the day Neil Armstrong became the first man to walk on the moon. Our compatriots rather see it as the day after Merckx's first win of the Tour de France. In short, every Belgian hails Merckx as the greatest sportsman of the twentieth century.

Readers now understand how difficult it is for us to write critically about Merckx. However, as philosophers, being critical is one of our major duties. The topic we tackle presently is Merckx's sometimes questioned understanding of sportsmanship. Specifically, whether his ambition to win each and every race he participated in was really a sign of true sportsmanship, as he himself believed. Of course, Merckx never denied that altruism was a virtue before, during, and after a cycling race. But at the same time, he held that such praiseworthy altruism differed substantially from letting your opponents win. On his view, all professional cyclists should be dedicated athletes, and dedication to cycling was almost synonymous with doing your best to win and to excel. As most readers can probably imagine, many journalists and some of his rivals had a different take on this issue. They saw it as culpable cannibalism. But before spelling out and analyzing the pertinent arguments, we should take a closer look at the aspects of Merckx's behavior that gave rise to this "philosophical" controversy.

The Cannibal

Writing about Merckx is easier than riding a bike with training wheels: just enumerating his victories reads like an epic story. Of 1,585 races as a professional cyclist, Merckx won 445 – almost one out of three. He triumphed seven times in Milan–San Remo and five times in Liège–Bastogne–Liège, he won Paris–Roubaix and the World Championship three times, and amassed two victories in Flanders, Lombardy, and the Amstel Gold Race. But apart from being the most successful classic rider ever, he also set an hour record that stood for 12 years, and won 11 Six Day races. Still, Merckx will be mostly remembered for his five victories in the Tour de France and the Giro d'Italia.

His almost unworldly list of victories seems more than enough to account for his nickname "The Cannibal." However, the main reason for this moniker was not his ability to win so often, but rather *the way* he won and his insatiable urge to outperform his rivals.

A striking example of Merckx's "cannibalism" is his first win in the Tour de France in 1969. After having won the third stage, a team time trial, Merckx seized the yellow jersey for the first time. The fifth stage that led over the Ballon d'Alsace was Merckx's first win in an ordinary stage. After the passage through the Alps, Merckx was already six minutes ahead of the other contenders, Gimondi, Pingeon, Poulidor – no lousy riders – who began to realize that they wouldn't win the yellow jersey that year. However, his greatest and most "cannibalistic" performance was still to come. After the 16th stage, Merckx led the race by more than eight minutes over Pingeon and more than nine over Gimondi. On the 17th stage from Luchon to Mourenx, over two of the most frightening Pyrenean cols, everyone expected Merckx to just secure his lead. But rather than saving some energy, Merckx decided to attack on the giant climb of Tourmalet with not less than 140 kilometers to go to the finish. Instead of defending his already comfortable position in the GC, as most cyclists do and did, Merckx took the risk of attacking. As he himself said in a recent interview, "If I could strike, I did it. That's the way I am. But I must admit that I have repeatedly deplored my eagerness while I was on the way to Mourenx."[1] He would arrive in Mourenx with a lead of more than eight minutes. Merckx's performance in the stage to Mourenx is still widely considered to be one of his most memorable exploits.

Nobody denies that this combination of athletic abilities and inordinate ambition made him the greatest all-round cyclist. His win in Mourenx underscores this point. However, what can be disputed is whether the very same combination made him one of the greatest sportsmen in cycling. There is little doubt that sportsmen make determined efforts to win. But what really distinguishes the sportsman from less virtuous competitors is the fact that the true sportsman competes gallantly.[2] This raises concerns with regard to Merckx's moral supremacy: can a cannibalistic winner really be a true sportsman? In this regard, it is telling that during the stage to Mourenx, something happened that stained the character and sportsmanship of Merckx …

Culpable Cannibalism?

After the finish in Mourenx, all cyclists, including Pingeon and Poulidor, admitted that Merckx was simply unbeatable. The following day, Jacques Goddet, the director of the Tour, wrote his daily piece in the newspaper *L'Équipe*. Under the title "Merckxissimo," Goddet promised never to say again that the Tour de France isn't won until Paris. "Merckx has ridden this legend to pieces."

For obvious reasons, Merckx's Faema team was delighted too. One teammate felt nonetheless a little disappointed. Martin Van den Bossche, excellent climber and Merckx's lieutenant during the mountain stages, attacked together with Merckx on the Tourmalet. Whereas Van den Bossche had expected Merckx to allow him to pass first on the top of the mountain, Merckx attacked a few meters before the top. Van den Bossche only saw Merckx back in Mourenx. Afterwards, Merckx explained that

ANDREAS DE BLOCK AND YANNICK JOYE

he held a grudge against Van den Bossche because the super-domestique was going to swap Merckx's Faema team for the rival Molteni team at the end of that season. That night, Van den Bossche told Merckx: "Today, a humble cyclist expected a noble gesture from you." Merckx didn't say a word. Despite this incident, Merckx and Van den Bossche never ceased to be friends – the two cyclists still go biking together every once in a while. Although Van den Bossche looks back on that historical 17th stage without rancor, the incident on the Tourmalet does show a glimpse of the seamy side of Merckx's character and ambition. He was a cannibal, with a huge appetite, in more than one sense of the word.

Most people agree that this attack on the Tourmalet was not a sign of genuine sportsmanship. Years after he ended his career, even Merckx acknowledged the same thing, expressing his regret. However, in two seemingly comparable cases of greedy cannibalism, Merckx showed no regrets at all. On his view, these victories were not morally reprehensible at all.

The first "incident" took place a few months before his first victory in the Tour de France, during the stage race Paris–Nice. Today, Paris–Nice is considered by many cyclists as training for Milan–San Remo. But in 1969, it was still a primary target, not least for three of the best then-active cyclists, Raymond Poulidor, Jacques Anquetil, and, of course, Eddy Merckx. After the penultimate stage, Merckx was leading the general ranking, ahead of Anquetil. Yet, Merckx was still far from sure to win "the race to the sun": the last stage was a time trial to the top of the Col d'Eze, and Anquetil's nickname was "Mister Time Trial" (*Monsieur Chrono* in French). But that time trial turned out to be the scene of one of Anquetil's greatest defeats ever. Not only did Merckx win the time trial, he also passed Anquetil on the flanks of the Col d'Eze after starting one minute and 30 seconds behind. Afterwards, a journalist asked Merckx whether he shouldn't have spared Anquetil this humiliation. Merckx answered that this crossed his mind during the time trial. He had hesitated to pass Anquetil. But he decided to do it simply because not doing it would have been a more profound humiliation. On Merckx's view, the most appropriate way of showing respect was not some ill-conceived act of altruism, but rather to continue competing with Anquetil until the finish line.

Anquetil never blamed Merckx for what happened on the Col d'Eze. But there were cyclists who felt that Merckx's cannibalistic actions were sometimes morally irresponsible. This is probably nowhere more so than in the case of Roger De Vlaeminck. Even though De Vlaeminck admired his compatriot Merckx tremendously – he even named his son Eddy after his former rival – he had a long-standing feud with Merckx. The argument started because De Vlaeminck perceived himself to have been wronged by The Cannibal in the Giro d'Italia of 1973. In that year, the final stage of the Giro d'Italia ended dramatically for De Vlaeminck. The Belgian cyclist was keen on winning the points competition leader's jersey, which he had already won the previous year. The only rival left in the points classification was Merckx. But since Merckx was already sure of the overall win, De Vlaeminck assumed that Merckx would let him take home the *maglia ciclamo*. However, Merckx wasn't satisfied with the overall win, and beat De Vlaeminck in the sprint of that last stage, thereby taking away the *maglia* from De Vlaeminck for good. De Vlaeminck was furious about what he considered to be a lack of sportsmanship on Merckx's part. Merckx himself countered De Vlaeminck's verbal attacks by claiming that what he had done was the only logical and moral thing to do for a sportsman. In his view, winning was one of professional cycling's intrinsic goals, and hence, trying to win was some sort of a moral obligation.

By now, the philosophical significance of these victories must be clear. They all hinge on what "winning with dignity" is. Although everyone agrees that there is a difference between winning in the right way and winning at all costs, it is often surprisingly difficult to determine whether and why an athlete finds himself on the wrong side of the divide. Of course, we all have intuitions about true sportsmanship. But these intuitions often differ substantially from other people's intuitions. For example, after the 1973 Giro, some Belgian cycling journalists took Merckx's side, while others felt that De Vlaeminck was right to complain about Merckx's behavior. And even when there is a consensus that the winner hasn't won the right way – as in the Merckx versus Van den Bossche case – it remains a challenge to spell out the moral principles that have been violated in the course of the action. After all, Merckx clearly was the better climber of the two, and Van den Bossche was hired as his domestique. So on what basis could Van den Bossche have claimed the right to the points of the first rider to climb the Tourmalet?

Winning the Right Way

It is widely agreed that winning is one of the primary goals of game playing. In a cycling race, the winner is the rider who crosses the finish line first or, in a stage race, the rider who completes all the stages with the lowest cumulative time, provided he or she has conformed to the rules of

ANDREAS DE BLOCK AND YANNICK JOYE

cycling races that dictate what can and cannot be done during a cycling race.[3] Riders who voluntarily break the rules are considered to be cheats. Cheats want to win at all costs, but if their cheating is detected, they are disqualified or receive other penalties. So, if you cross the finish line first, but you've swerved into your opponent during the sprint, the second cyclist crossing the finish line will be the official winner. And if you fail the UCI drug test or if you're caught sabotaging the equipment of other competitors, you will face even more severe penalties.

There is little doubt that cheats do not win with dignity, if they can be said to win at all. But the three examples above have little to do with cheating. In all these cases, Merckx conformed to the rules and regulations set by the UCI. Merckx didn't beat Anquetil by taking a shortcut to the finish line. And he didn't beat De Vlaeminck by punching him in the stomach. Hence, one might wonder whether there is really a moral problem left. When you're trying to win the game and you do so without violating the UCI rules, you are simply playing the game as it should be played. There is nothing wrong with that. Or is there?

This raises the question concerning any possible wrong with winning a game *as such*. Can we think of examples where the winner of a cycling race, who obeyed all the rules, can still be considered an unfair athlete? Yes we can. Suppose, for instance, that you organize a short road race in which only you and your two toddlers participate. Being a well-trained amateur cyclist, you are pretty sure that you will win hands down. After all, your kids are 2 and 3 years old, and you are riding your favorite Merckx Carbon CHM, while the toddlers have chosen their Thomas the Tank Engine Bike for this race. And indeed, you'll leave them biting the dust. You'll easily beat them by a long stretch. But if you really do so, most spectators will disapprove of your behavior.

What can you do to deal with this popular outcry? It would probably be a reasonable defense to argue that you wanted to teach your children something that is important for their future life, for instance that winning is not all that matters in sports. It's not that you took the game too seriously, but rather that you wanted your children to learn not to take sports too seriously. But suppose you just replied to the booing spectators that you conformed to the rules of road racing, and that, hence, you won the race the right way. In that case, chances are that none of them will change their mind about the moral irresponsibility of your behavior. On most people's view, there are at least a few things in life more important than winning a game, and one of those things is being a good and caring parent.

Hence, a judgment on an athlete's sportsmanship depends not only on his conformity to the formal rules of the game, but also on the social context and the intentions of the athlete.[4] The all-too-ambitious parent has violated a rule, and an ethically more important rule than the rules of the UCI or the racing rules the parent himself has made up. The parent's behavior is repugnant to our moral sense because he saw winning the race as something of higher importance than making his toddlers happy. He didn't win the right way, because he wanted to win at the cost of his children's happiness. A good sport must find a balance between sport-intrinsic goals (winning, excelling) and sport-extrinsic goals. The overly ambitious parent clearly is off-balance on this point.

How does this apply to the Merckx–Anquetil case? Merckx clearly took into consideration sport-extrinsic moral rules of thumb before he rushed past Anquetil. If Merckx's statement after that time trial was truthful – and we have no reason to doubt its truthfulness – one must conclude that he decided that the best way to show his respect to Anquetil was to ride as fast as possible. Rushing past Anquetil was his duty not only as a professional cyclist, but also as a human being and a friend of his professional rival. Hence, on Merckx's view, there really wasn't a moral dilemma. He didn't have to choose between rushing past Anquetil, on the one hand, and treating him with due respect. It seems that Merckx could have his sportive cake and eat it morally.

In Control Even after a Blowout

Some people might still object that Merckx did something morally irresponsible when he rushed past Anquetil, because he won by an *immorally* wide margin. Their argument would go as follows: "Merckx must have been sure of the victory in both the time trial and the GC of Paris–Nice long before he flew by Anquetil. When he nonetheless decided to maximize the margin of his victory, he did something that is *intrinsically* unsporting. He could and should have minimized the pain of defeat that Anquetil experienced."

This argument is based on what Dixon has called the Anti-Blowout thesis – namely, that there is something inherently unsporting about pushing your advantage once your win is clearly secured.[5] But together with Dixon, we believe this argument is wrong. In a professional cycling race, winning by a margin as wide as possible is part of the game, and

ANDREAS DE BLOCK AND YANNICK JOYE

there is nothing intrinsically unsporting about it. You can actually win by a large margin while still showing respect for your opponent. Dixon points out that the Anti-Blowout thesis itself leans on an almost reprehensible attitude toward sport, namely, that winning is the only thing that matters. Although winning is certainly one of the goals of professional cycling races, professional cyclists also aim to display their athletic excellence or set a new personal record during a time trial.[6] Hence, there is nothing wrong with Merckx widening the margin long after he had secured victory.

Now, suppose you are one of those who don't buy Dixon's argument. For some reason, you cannot get rid of the feeling that pursuing blowouts is somehow blameworthy. Even then, you will have trouble rationalizing your condemnation of Merckx in this case. After all, Merckx clearly did not pursue a blowout. When he realized that his win would be a blowout victory, he did a quick moral calculus, eventually deciding that he would hurt Anquetil more by slowing down than by passing him by. But if you still think that Merckx should have slowed down because rushing past Anquetil was an affront to the latter's status as a cyclist, please consider what happened in 2000 at the end of the 12th stage of the Tour de France. That stage was a 149-kilometer long stage through Provence, ending with the climb topping the infamous Mont Ventoux. A small field including Jan Ulrich, Marco Pantani, and GC leader Lance Armstrong began the climb. With about 4 kilometers to go, and after having attacked several times, Pantani again dropped the hammer and was able to finally get away from the leading group. Ulrich et al. were unable to close the gap, which was the sign for Armstrong to power away from the chasing group up to Pantani in one long effort. It was clear that Armstrong was the strongest of the duo: Pantani lost touch with his wheel a couple of times, but he showed *grinta* and was able to hang on. At the finish line, however, Armstrong subtly dropped the pace, thereby allowing Pantani to easily overtake and to secure the victory. Despite Armstrong's (apparent) generous gesture, the win felt bitter-sweet for Pantani; he clearly considered it as a humiliation.

The Armstrong–Pantani dispute shows that most cyclists would agree with Merckx: if the stronger rider lets the weaker competitor win, the weaker competitor often feels humiliated. But how does this square with the moral indignation of De Vlaeminck after Merckx had taken the *maglia ciclamo* from him? Wasn't Merckx the better rider? And if so, should De Vlaeminck have felt humiliated? Most probably, the answer to this question is that De Vlaeminck's moral outrage had little to do with his feeling humiliated.

But what, then, was the real reason De Vlaeminck accused Merckx of being a bad sport? Two possibilities need to be explored. The first is that De Vlaeminck felt that Merckx had betrayed their friendship by winning the points competition. Merckx was already sure of the *maglia rosa*, so why would he try to take the points classification as well? If this really was the kernel of their dispute, there would be some striking similarities with the Merckx–Anquetil case. In both cases, it's about finding a balance between the value of winning and the value of respect or friendship. However, De Vlaeminck never claimed that he was indignant *because* they had been such good friends before. After the incident, the friendship cooled down – at least for a few months – not primarily because Merckx had been a bad friend, but rather because Merckx had been a bad sport. This hints at a second, and philosophically more interesting, possibility: opposite interpretations of informal fair play.

Many rules of cycling are written down in official documents. If you conform to these rules, you are formally a fair player. But as we have argued above, conforming to the formal rules of the game is at most a necessary, and certainly not a sufficient condition for being a true sports-man. Sportsmanship also requires the right attitudes toward the game, even though these attitudes are not guided by explicit rules. However, because the exact nature of these attitudes is not laid down in some offi-cial document, conflicting interpretations can easily arise over what they amount to. Probably this was what happened in the last stage of the 1973 edition of the Giro d'Italia (and its aftermath). In his interpretation of the sporting attitude, Merckx put the emphasis on complete dedication to the intrinsic goals of cycling: winning, entertaining the fans, and exhi-bition of excellence.

Dedication to these ends is more than just a desire to win or to excel. It is a commitment not to succumb to temptations, desires, or intentions that lead away from these ends, even if it is the intention to let your friend win the points classification in an important stage race.[7] After the sprint, Merckx gave an interview in which he explained why he decided to go for the *maglia ciclamo*. In line with our interpretation, he did not talk in that interview about his desire to win. He just said that he considered it to be *immoral* not to seize the opportunity to win the points classification.[8] De Vlaeminck, on his part, clearly thought that Merckx's behavior was a sign of unsporting covetousness. He appealed to the long-established tradi-tion that GC leaders do not directly compete for other, less important, classifications. According to De Vlaeminck, the right attitude toward the sport of cycling was one that respected this tradition.

ANDREAS DE BLOCK AND YANNICK JOYE

These opposite interpretations of informal fair play do not imply that there is anything paradoxical about the informal fair play of cycling. They only point out that informal fair play is a bag of diverse values. Sometimes these diverse values collide, leading to long-standing arguments. But these arguments are difficult to resolve, because it depends on an individual weighing of the different values to decide in which direction the moral balance should be tilted. The case under scrutiny is no exception to this rule.

Still, we think that De Vlaeminck's appeal to tradition is not very convincing, simply because many traditions are morally reprehensible. To prove this point, one could refer to the mafia traditions. But, unfortunately enough, examples can be found in cycling as well. Think for instance of the feud between Armstrong and Filippo Simeoni. In stage 18 of the 2004 Tour de France, Simeoni attempted to close the gap with a breakaway of six riders who posed no threat to the GC contenders (Simeoni was also too far away in the GC). Nevertheless, yellow jersey Armstrong chased Simeoni, with the result that they both ended up with the six leaders. If Simeoni did not drop from the breakaway, the other teams would have been forced to organize a chase, which would eliminate the chances of winning for the six original riders. Simeoni dropped from the leading group. The backdrop of this dispute was that Simeoni had previously testified against the controversial sports doctor Michele Ferrari on the allegation of prescribing him erythropoietin (EPO) and human growth hormones. Armstrong and several other high-profile riders were known to be Ferrari clients, and Simeoni's doping allegations against the doctor raised suspicions about Armstrong's past performances and others in the peloton. Armstrong's "trailing" of Simeoni was his way of making clear that neither he nor the peloton would tolerate Simeoni destroying their alleged "clean" image and that of their sport. Ironically, a couple of days later, during the tour's last stage Simeoni attacked from the (easy-going) bunch over and over again, thereby forcing Armstrong's team to set up a chase. Simeoni's move was clearly intended to annoy Armstrong and to get back at him, as there is an unwritten rule in the peloton that on the last *étape* of the Tour racing only starts on the local circuit on the Champs-Elysées in Paris.

We think most cycling fans agree that Armstrong's behavior was not really testimony of his sportsmanship, even though Armstrong was by far the better cyclist of the two and even though he only tried to police the traditions of cycling. To us, it is quite clear why his behavior was unsporting. First, Armstrong didn't seek victory himself, but sought defeat and humiliation for Simeoni. Second, and probably even more important, the traditions Armstrong was defending are not particularly praiseworthy.

Last Pedal Strokes ...

Winning in an endurance sport like cycling constitutes a special case when it is the subject of moral analyses. When you compare the reactions to Merckx's cannibalistic behavior with the reactions to Federer's supremacy in tennis, the difference is telling. When Federer wins a grand slam tournament with much superiority and display, few would express any moral concerns about this – in fact, most would praise Federer for his genius. On the other hand, the cases we have discussed in this chapter show that something completely different is at hand with cycling. Merckx's cannibalistic way of winning not only evoked awe. It also led to moral indignation. We think there are several reasons for this difference. First, there is the fact that a peloton is, apart from a collection of individuals, also a social organization. During the act of sporting mutual friendships, alliances and feuds can arise – either spontaneously or, as in the case of domestiques, by forced means. Of course on a tennis court the players can be friends too, but that social relation is not elaborated upon during the game itself.

The specific way in which a cycling race unfolds can be morally evaluated against this "social" backdrop. For example, if Hinault hadn't specified a social role for himself as domestique in the 1986 edition of the Tour de France, then probably nobody would have reproached him attacking and wearing down Lemond. A second point is that the bodily activity of cycling in itself is much more prone to lead to moral judgments. When in a tennis match somebody loses, this could mean that the adversary just isn't fast enough to go after the balls or that he or she returns the balls badly. In cycling, however, winning, and especially the cannibalistic way of winning, often entails physical suffering on the loser's part. And because that suffering is clearly visible to the viewer, this can evoke quite strong moral sentiments and influence the moral perception of the act of winning – even if suffering is part and parcel of the game. A third point is that in a race, and then especially in a stage race, there are different classifications and (unexpressed) roles for each of the contenders aiming to compete for the classifications (e.g., leader, points, king of mountains). For example, if the king of mountains attempts to

ANDREAS DE BLOCK AND YANNICK JOYE

mix into a bunch sprint, chances are that his fellow sprinters will consider this as inappropriate behavior – everybody should stick to his role.

What these examples all make clear is that in cycling there is often moral ambiguity attached to winning a race. This could make it a hell of a task to get a firm grasp on the topic philosophically, but perhaps this *is* the reason why cycling is so interesting and why we get so excited about it.

NOTES

1 *De Standaard*, April 29, 2009.
2 James W. Keating, "Sportsmanship as a Moral Category," *Ethics* 75 (1964): 25–35.
3 Bernard Suits, "The Elements of Sport," in *Philosophic Inquiry of Sport*, ed. K. V. Meier and W. J. Morgan (Champaign, IL: Human Kinetics, 1988), pp. 9–19.
4 Heather Sheridan, "Conceptualizing 'Fair Play': A Review of the Literature," *European Physical Education Review* 9 (2003): 63–184.
5 Nicholas Dixon, "On Sportsmanship and 'Running Up' the Score," *Journal of the Philosophy of Sport* 19 (1992): 1–13.
6 Ibid., p. 3.
7 Paul Weiss, *Sport: A Philosophic Inquiry* (Carbondale: Southern Illinois University Press, 1969).
8 J. Tamboer and J. Steebergen, *Sportfilosofie* (Leende: Damon, 2000).

PEDALING CIRCLES

CHAPTER 22

WARM UP

Riding into Awe

Emily's wheels skid through a deep puddle of dust. The cloud buries me, and all I have left of the trail is my young daughter's laughter. Heat and sweat muddy my face. The bright air hides somewhere above me. No complaint.

After an eight-mile climb up an old horse trail and 12 miles of traversing the crest of Green Ridge, we have finally begun to descend. Birds and insects snap and buzz in protest as the heat rolls up the ridge on waves. On one side of the volcanic up-thrust we look down on pine forest; the other side shimmers into meadows and the Oregon desert. Shade offers little respite, except from squinting. Our water is warm and Emily bitches about that.

"What do you want me to do?" I whine in response.

The trail grows wider, picking up the remains of an old logging road. We pass the turn-off to the fire lookout and drop 300 feet on a smooth dirt track. Already the pines begin to crowd the road. A large meadow opens up to the east, and we climb the last pitch of the day. From the top, Fireroad 1490 plummets 2,000 feet to the Metolius River. The road is rippled and weather-beaten, exposed and gritty, a tire-eating run-out of red cinder. Four switchbacks punctuate the descent, and missing any one of them would mean a long flight to the valley floor.

Deer are common here, though more alert than me, and considerably more shy. A badger hissed at me once as I sped past his burrow. I've been buzzed by hawks, trailed by vultures. I watched a black bear and her cub rip the bark from a dead pine tree, but that was long ago and the distance was great.

Emily slides around the second hairpin. I follow her tracks, several bike lengths behind. Her back wheel bounces over the washboard at 20 miles per hour. Light on her saddle, her legs and arms supple, she reacts to the sliding scree and airborne moments like a gazelle. This stretch of road is straight, and I risk a glance away from my task to the river below and the jagged line of mountains to the north and west.

I've been spotting ghosts lately – that's what I've begun to call them, the shadows and movements just beyond my periphery. Things that resist identification because they're too fast or I'm too slow. And now I see another. A swatch of brown animal skirts the hillside above us, and I don't bother to react, until the smooth, muscled body drops down the embankment in front of Emily. Her response is immediate. She locks her wheels at first, then smoothly reigns in her bike like the veteran she is at 13 years of age. My ghost lopes onto the road, suddenly quite alive, not 15 feet from my daughter. A huge animal, all muscle and silky skin, made even larger by his proximity. His big paws settle into the cinder, little clouds of red dust climb his legs. I'm already with Emily, stopped at her side before I know I've touched my brakes. She straddles her frame as I loop my arm around her waist. Tears run off her chin – I know teenage girls can cry, but how do they cry so fast? Immediately I heft my bicycle in my left hand, and I'm ready to use it, a tiny shield between us and this impossibly beautiful and uncaged animal. The cougar halts in his glide, turns his face once in our direction, and apparently sees nothing worthy of his gaze. We do not share his lack of interest. He pads across the road and leaps into the trees.

"Fat and happy," I try to soothe myself. "Well-fed, don't you think?" I ask Emily.

Emily's tears don't stop her from watching the animal disappear. Her shoulders shake, her breath chatters, and she wipes at her eyes. She plants her face in my chest. We stand huddled on the empty road. I hide my own gasp, and feel blessed to have this moment with her.

CHAPTER 23

TAKING THE *GITA* FOR AN AWESOME SPIN

"That was *awesome!*" What cyclist hasn't uttered those words after thrillingly riding tight single track, ascending a tough mountain pass, or maneuvering in a tight pack in a complicated crit course? Awesomeness seems a natural and deep fit for cycling. In fact, a great deal of its appeal lies in this. But the simplicity of the utterance, particularly when followed by "dude," belies the complexity of understanding just what this awesomeness is about, and how it connects with cycling.

Now, you probably take this initial sentiment of cycling's awesomeness to be something of a truism, at least as a cyclist. But, and here is where your calf gets a big "chain-tattoo," this sentiment is also highly ambiguous. While many cyclists may all agree that cycling is awesome in one way or another, it's not entirely clear what the nature of this awesomeness is, or that it is something that cyclists really agree on. Do all expressions of the "awesomeness" mean more or less the same thing to all cyclists? Are they cut from the same philosophical fabric, or are they something different from one another? Just what *could* it mean for a cyclist to say that cycling is "awesome"?

We'll hop on this saddle in a moment. But before that, or perhaps in order to do that, I must first raise another group of more basic questions. The gist of these is: What is the *point* of asking about the meaning of the awesomeness of cycling in the first place? What exactly is accomplished by having a better understanding of the *ambiguities* of the term "awesome" regarding cycling? What can such questions *reveal* for us, and what do we hope such questions can *do* for us, as cyclists, as philosophers, or even as human beings? Why should we *care* about the meaning of the awesomeness of cycling? And, for that matter, *what* exactly is it that we are caring about when we care about the meaning of such questions?

Your head may be spinning like cranks with a fallen chain after such a barrage, so let's slow down and see why it is crucial to respond to these basic questions. First, basically, whatever we happen to discover in investigating the "awesomeness" of cycling will be shaped by the frame we ride, by how we structure the investigation. This opens up the possibilities of the concept by adequately orienting our wheels and thinking to those possibilities at the outset. Second is the simple fact that if these more basic questions can't be addressed in a satisfactory way, then the other questions are, at best, trivial.

So, after this intense start to our ride, what is the response to the basic questions? We (should) care about the meaning of the term awesome because its significance runs far beneath how we think it is used, even when those uses are of the most unassuming or superficial kind (again, often the case when they are followed by the word "dude"). The term awesome acts as a *conceptual marker* on a number of levels for a much deeper idea – the idea of *freedom*. Towards the end of this "outing," I will briefly refine what precisely I mean by the idea of freedom, and how it ties the various ways of talking about cycling's awesomeness together. The *Bhagavad Gita* will lead things there. For now, it is enough to say that the ambiguity of the term awesomeness has less to do with its lack of clarity than with the profundity of the concept of freedom it refers to, and the multitude of ways and levels that that concept it marks – freedom – finds physical, philosophical, and spiritual expression. We are in for quite a ride.

Now, to shift things into the proper gear, this does not mean that freedom and awesomeness are wholly synonymous with each other. As we shall see, the idea of freedom covers a far greater conceptual ground than awesomeness does, and awesomeness, in turn, does speak to certain things that are not directly related to freedom. However, it does mean that the idea of freedom grounds the essence of what we mean by the "awesomeness" of cycling.

To start our tour of cycling's awesomeness, it might be helpful here to briefly consider an analogy: we can think of the relationship between the idea of freedom and the awesomeness of cycling as the way the horizon orients and ultimately defines the direction, the pace, and even the heart with which we conduct our ride. For even when we're not perpetually focused on it, and although we will never reach it, it is always there in front of us, always giving rise to the emerging path before us, and always grounding the possibilities of the ground on which we grind up, glide down, and pedal ahead. Just as it is with the horizon and the ride, so it is with freedom and the awesomeness of cycling. By investigating these issues, we begin to see what is really at work when we talk about the awesomeness of cycling.

Etching Awesomeness on the Top Tube in Three Pedal Strokes

Let's quickly review the course we are going to be pedaling. Looking at the meaning of awesomeness insofar as it relates to our reasons for cycling is worth the effort because it articulates the deeper meaning we associate with the activity of cycling: not just *that* it is an important activity, but the *nature* of what that importance is to us and the *access* we have to that importance. Time to pedal in earnest and see the three basic levels that stating "Cycling is awesome" can mean. While each of these levels ultimately drinks from the same hydration pack, they express themselves in different ways and contexts.

The first stroke

Cycling is awesome because it centers us through its rightness. This is the most immediate and by far the most common use of the term awesome. It is the use that addresses the experience of the act of cycling as *pleasing*, *delightful*, or *enjoyable*, as in, "I had a really awesome ride today." This is clear enough if one considers the fact that any of these words (and a host of others that are closely related) might be exchanged for awesome, depending upon the particular context in which the sentiment was uttered. What holds all these ideas together in a tight pack, we can see, is the sense of satisfaction, specifically a satisfaction that comes through rightly performing and completing a kind of action, a bicycle ride.

But how exactly is this idea of a "satisfying" ride being used? This satisfaction does not come through *merely* performing and completing the ride, but *rightly* performing and completing it. Not all rides are awesome. Some can be disappointing, others downright nasty, still others just "blah." And what distinguishes these latter rides from awesome rides is not just that there is an element of pleasure in them; there's no reason that a mundane ride or even a horrible one couldn't have a pleasing dimension or two to it. Rather, it is that the different parts of the awesome ride, whatever they may be, have an integrity to how they constitute the endeavor of that ride itself. That is, everything about the way the ride was performed – pushing the pace, taking pulls, drafting, and whatever else went into making that ride the ride it was – the very way it came to be as an act and as an achievement fits together to give it a rightness; a "yes-that's-exactly-the-way-it-ought-to-be-ness," so to speak. No missed shifts or wobbly handling here!

So the experiences of pleasantness, enjoyableness, or delightfulness while we ride are secondary to the awesomeness of the ride because they are only indicative of that awesomeness in that they emerge from the rightness of it. It was the integrity of this rightness that ultimately comes to satisfy the cyclist as pleasing, delightful, or enjoyable. This is why it seems the terms can be exchanged with one another, at first glance.

Why does rightly performing and completing a ride satisfy cyclists? What is significant about the ride's rightness to this way of being satisfied? The answer, I think, has to do with a kind of centering or balance that occurs through the riding. And we all know that a sense of balance and identifying with one's rig is the trick that keeps the wheels going round. Remember that the rightness of the ride comes from an integration of parts toward a new, more whole, integrity – a whole new whole, as it were. Now, the achievement of this "whole new whole" (and it is an achievement) is *revelatory*. It uncovers and displays within our conscious experience a sense of identity – of ourselves as riders – that is complete and clear. It is unfettered by distractions or obscurities. Its rightness and its integrity lend a purity to this newly revealed identity, as riders, simply being what we are. And so, we are centered by this rightness of the ride because we feel that there is nothing but the center to us in this way of being.

Now, this doesn't mean that this heightened sense of centeredness and rightness is at the front of every cyclist's mind whenever they say that their ride was or is awesome. It means that *at some* level this centeredness informs their statement, even if it is fleeting or far away. Indeed, it is precisely because this particular way of using the term awesome can be so fickle in our consciousness that the deeper levels, those that ultimately find their source in freedom directly, exist as they do. The depth of our experience rides on this fickleness.

The second stroke

Cycling is awesome because it attunes us to our possibility and becoming in the world. The way I have just been speaking of the awesomeness of cycling does not stand alone. It needs a kickstand: an aspirational dimension that looks to a deeper way in which one might speak of cycling as awesome. Here the expression that cycling is awesome points to how it is *uplifting*, *intense*, *extraordinary*, or *ecstatic*, as in, "The way Contador took off when the road went up and how he dominated in the time trials blew my mind. He was totally awesome."

As with the first use, the connection between awesomeness and the emotions it connotes is not all there is to the picture. It is not enough that the riding was simply accompanied by feelings of intensity or ecstasy, because these feelings can also accompany rides that are decidedly unawesome. These emotions become associated with the awesomeness of the ride because of something internal to cycling itself. But what is this internal dimension that generates this second set of feelings and how is it different from the first? We are going anaerobic now, take a deep breath.

This second level emerges from the revelatory dimension of the cyclist's centering during an awesome ride. What separates these emotions from the previously mentioned emotions is *where* they stand in relation to the revelatory character of the ride. In the first use of the term the cyclist has the emotions he does because there is a revelation of his centeredness *to himself*. The emotions he refers to through the term awesome are aspects of this state of being. But while what is revealed is an *authentic* sense of self, it is, at the same time, *merely* a sense of self – a sense of centered purity as an *individual* and only as an individual. There is no greater sense of the world, no greater communion that occurs. There is only a sense of one's mind as one's own. We ride solo, and we know this only goes so far. There is nothing inherently problematic about this. It has its place and time. But right though it may be, there is also a certain lack of awareness that accompanies it. This lack comes specifically from the purity of self the cyclist feels in the first sense of awesomeness.

To engage an easier cog and take a breather. As the cyclist becomes more aware and centered in himself as an individual there is a tendency, if he looks *only* at his centeredness, to not realize the conditions that make it possible for him to embody the achievement that his riding is. This is ultimately a kind of trap. It will make you miss a shift when you least want it. The revelation and centeredness that go with the first way of speaking about awesomeness are, after all, fleeting, which can potentially be a problem. To become solely focused on this self-centeredness from a performance in some moment past is to plant the seeds of what could, if left unminded, transform into a kind of narcissism and obsession. A cyclist who is forever chasing after *that* ride on Mt. Evans he once had, unable to enjoy other rides because he is longing for that long-ago exploit, is a sad example of this. To avoid this, the cyclist must begin to have a sense of what is beyond him, and even beyond the ride itself.

So, regarding this *beyond*, what is it, and how is one supposed to have a sense of it? To put it compact crank size, the beyond is the larger world, and our sense of it comes through a kind of communion facilitated by the act of cycling. This happens by recognizing that the awesomeness of the ride is not just about the cyclist's personal satisfaction. Instead, his satisfaction must come from being acutely aware that his cycling is as awesome (revelatory) as it is precisely because it is a part of something larger than any individual ride or cyclist could be. Cycling greats like Lance Armstrong and Eddy Merckx are the best showcase for this. The awesomeness of these cyclists does not just come from the fact that they are capable of extremely impressive feats of speed, focus, and endurance. Rather, it comes from the way the exploits of such cyclists fire up our imagination. They help each of us point our minds and ambitions toward greater things, and bring us to the significance of our cycling endeavors against the backdrop of a larger world. Their achievements become a study in possibility, in what might be.

The result of this is that this second way of speaking about the awesomeness of cycling is qualitatively different from the first. It is like the difference in quality between riding a carbon frame versus an aluminum one over, say, chip-seal. While the first one absorbs the roughness, the second loosens your fillings. It is not simply about being, but about being-in-the-world. The emotions that arise from this second way of thinking about cycling's awesomeness are consequences of a deeper process going on just as those that arise from the first way are. But notice that the emotions from this second set are all emotions that suggest an outward trajectory, rather than static self-satisfaction. Instead of doing a track stand on the lower part of the banking, they jump for the upper reaches to launch themselves. Consider the words themselves – *in-tension* suggests a stretching across; *extra-ordinary*, beyond the mundane; *up-lifting*, a moving above; *ec-static*, a standing outside of the ground where we are set. Each of them speaks to becoming more, to the emotional states that precede radical transformation.

The third stroke

Cycling is awesome because it is a transformative spiritual achievement. There is yet a third and far rarer way of speaking about the awesomeness of cycling. This way of using the phrase treats awesome as *inspiring, wonderful*, or quite literally, *filling with awe*, as in, "When I think back on my life I don't always know where to place those rides I took just before I left for college. There I was, alone and ripping down Hwy 26 like a bat out of hell just before dawn. Even now as I picture the way the colors splashed across the sky, the wind on my face, it still makes me feel like there may be something to it when people talk about knowing that God exists. Man, those times were some of the most awesome of my life."

People do speak of cycling being awesome in this way, but it's rarer to hear because of the depth of the sentiment. Individual words and even elaborate descriptions almost seem to do an injustice to the gravity of what has taken place within us. The emotions that are used in connotation with this sense of awesomeness need to be taken with the fullest weight they can be given to even approach the sentiment they seek to carry, and still they seem inadequate. Unlike the first two uses, they don't reflect the significance of the sentiment's internal dynamics because there is too much to reflect. Instead they merely suggest it evocatively.

The senses of "rightness" and the "possibility" that marked the first and second ways of thinking about the awesomeness of cycling are both here too, but they are hardly exhaustive. Rather, this way of thinking about cycling's awesomeness subsumes the uses mentioned earlier. Just like when the peloton absorbs a breakaway rider and he becomes seamlessly integrated into the pack, these are drops in the bucket for a sentiment that seems to loom over others, circumscribing them through its significance and gravity for us, not just as cyclists but as human beings.

What we have in this use of awesomeness is a profound *transformative spiritual achievement*: a sense of the wholeness of ourselves in the world by virtue of a particular way of being in it. The paradoxical result of this is that this way of thinking about cycling's awesomeness places it both at the center of the cyclist's world and outside of it. It is both hub and rim at the same time. Here cycling becomes a way for us to begin considering totality as totality, and in this respect it is everywhere. And yet, at the same time and just because of the cosmic scope of this sentiment, it is nowhere in the cyclist's world; not because it is absent from that world, but because this sentiment cannot be defined or articulated by the practices that one uses to arrive at it, whatever it may be. Wittgenstein said the ladder must be kicked away once it is climbed; we must dismount the bike once we reach the summit to take this in.

Free Riding with the *Bhagavad Gita*

So far we have ridden over difficult but gratifying terrain regarding the different ways in which cyclists might speak about cycling as awesome. Much earlier in the ride, I suggested that inherent within all of this rightness, centeredness, and attunement there is a rather deep and pervasive notion of freedom that is found in the *Bhagavad Gita*. But before we take on this freedom in a two-man sprint and see what it is about and how it fits with the ground we have covered, we need to learn some tricks, and get some pertinent background.

The *Bhagavad Gita*, one of the great spiritual classics of the Brahmanical philosophic tradition of South Asia, has as one of its chief concerns the cultivation and articulation of the concept of *moksha*, or spiritual liberation. It's important to realize that "liberation" does not mean "freeing from oppression" here; it refers to a full realization of the true self *as* true self. That is, freedom is bringing to the fullness of consciousness all of what one is. This may seem as easy as pointing your wheels to where you want to go, but there is a huge philosophical tree standing in your way: the true self – what fundamentally makes you you (*Atman*) – is not identified with the mere individual self (*Jiva*), but with all that gives rise to the conditions of any one person or thing being who and what they are. Given that all things are causally interdependent with all other things, we are left with a startling conclusion: the true self is not limited to my body, my mind, or my spirit! The true self is the totality of all things. The saying "being one with one's bike" takes on a whole new meaning. It is only because we are deluded into thinking that we are *this* person, separated from the Being of the world around us, that we are denied the full realization of our freedom.

Realizing this can be harder than riding a 53 × 11 up a steep slope. And indeed, the *Bhagavad Gita* aims at addressing the difficulty in understanding and accepting this connection between the absolute but subtle, elusive presence of our freedom and our true identity. The strategy the *Gita* uses for this is a process of instruction that seeks to bring us through three phases in the journey to realize spiritual freedom. It is indeed a training program not unlike a cyclists' regimen to improve their climbing, sprinting, or cornering ability. They require discipline (Yoga also means that), and a plan.

It begins by addressing *Karma Yoga*, roughly translatable as "cultivation through works." The aim of *Karma Yoga* is to bring about an equanimity of mind, a state of centeredness where the mind neither grasps toward nor retreats from the objects which perpetually pass before it through senses and thoughts. We need to stay focused on the task at hand. If we get distracted we will run into the wheel in front of us or lower the intensity of our effort during intervals. It works so long as it can still the mind and keep it from reacting to those objects which perpetually delude it, thereby making the realization of spiritual freedom all the more elusive. Chasing every breakaway soon tires us out, and sees us spit off the back of the pack. What it cannot do, though, is hold the mind in that position of equanimity for long or offer it any insight beyond the mental stillness itself. We can't do a max VO2 intensity interval for a whole ride – our focus will waver and the level of effort will drop.

In order to begin doing that the Gita introduces a practice aimed at the second phase of the journey – *Bhakti Yoga*, or "cultivation through devotion." Here, the equanimity of mind is set down through giving oneself over wholly and completely to that which is greater than oneself. As cyclists we devote ourselves to our sport and its greater significance in our lives and beyond with resolve. Awesomeness begins to become part of the lattice of our experience, and this training regime is instrumental in this process. By doing this we begin to step beyond the egoism and self-delusion that come from our attachments to those objects which continually seem to rise up and stand so separate from our being. We become part of the race or the ride as a whole, or teammates, or members of the larger cycling community.

Even this is not enough to yield the insights required to realize *moksha* in its fullest sense. In order for that to occur, the *Gita* takes us through its third phase – *Jnana Yoga*, or "cultivation through wisdom." It is here, when the mind has been matured to a point where it is capable of regarding its objects and even itself as a mere reflection of the Absolute, that true spiritual freedom begins to find authentic expression. Here we find that deep transformation that occurs in those few and precious moments where our cycling experience becomes something to remember (without getting stuck on it).

Coming Full Circle

To sum this all up in one tight and tidy jump: the three basic ways that cyclists speak about cycling as awesome follows this pattern. I have treated cycling's centering rightness as a kind of parallel to *Karma Yoga*, its attunement to possibility and becoming as a kind of *Bhakti Yoga*, and its role as a transformative spiritual achievement as a kind of *Jnana Yoga*.

One last question remains: Why did I do this?

The sprint-distance answer is that I did it to answer the most basic question of all – why do cyclists ride bicycles? The answer is simply that they cycle because cycling functions as a kind of yoga for them. Cycling is a way to pursue the path of freedom in a fashion that is appropriate to whatever their intellectual, physical, and spiritual circumstances will allow. It is a way of coming to realize fully what one is in spite of the delusions and distractions we face in our existence. Cycling is a path to freedom and this is why it's so awesome.

CHAPTER 24

STRETCHED ELASTICS, THE TOUR DE FRANCE, AND A MEANINGFUL LIFE

 We turned the last corner, picking up our pace with the end only meters ahead. After slowly tapping out a rhythm up the 21.6-kilometer *hors catégorie* (HC) climb, we temporarily danced on our pedals side by side, knowing mere pedal strokes on our bikes carried us towards accomplishing something special together. Bob and Jeff, two members of our group, joined us at the finish and we shared congratulatory hugs and handshakes under the iconic weather tower overlooking breathtaking panoramic vistas. In the crowd gathered at the top Jeff spotted his son Dave – long since finished with our group's collection of mountain goats. "How was it, Dave?" we asked the young whippet. "Haaard," replied our new Aussie friend.

Other members of our group trickled in to the finish. Chris, after "training" in France for the previous seven weeks, exuded a sense of elation with his achievement. Later Lindsay pedaled across the threshold, followed by a jubilant and relieved Adam. Others did not make it. Adam's dad, Jeff, felled by the heat, disappointingly conceded and flagged down the tour company van carrying non-riders to the peak to see the view. Mechanical problems forced Sam to relinquish his goal of reaching the summit. Grahme stopped at the chalet six kilometers from the top to enjoy a bite to eat. After refueling, he got back on the saddle and headed *down* the mountain, rather than up, satisfied with his accomplishment – and his meal. Grahme's wife, Deb, also contentedly turned back with the climb partially completed.

At the top euphoric cyclists recounted challenges overcome along the journey – enduring stifling 37 degree Celsius heat for much of the ride, weaving through halted camper van traffic and wobbling pedestrians, trying to ignore drunken campers telling us to turn around, and, of course, dealing with the long climb's relentless, constant rising gradient averaging 7.6 percent. We also shared stories about strangers on the side of the road clapping, propelling us on with shouts of "*Allez! Allez!*"; how the names and messages written in chalk and paint beneath our wheels, although meant for other more famous riders, still inspired us to keep pushing forward; children lining the route slapping our hands as if the sweat-soaked purchased jerseys pressing against our bodies actually meant we represented professional teams like Astana, Saxo Bank, or Columbia HTC.

At the summit, we gathered in an altitude, loosely organized line over-looking the edge of the mountain. While patiently waiting our turn to take a photograph, we peered down on what looked like ants on bikes crawling across a lunar landscape towards us at the peak. Finally, as the newly self-anointed king and queen of the mountain, we found ourselves at the front of the line. Quickly we passed our camera to a willing stranger and posed with our bikes for a picture together, followed by more photos with Chris, Bob, Jeff, and Dave. The next day more famous cyclists would pass by this same spot – riders like Alberto Contador, Fränk and Andy Schleck, and, of course, Lance Armstrong. But *these* riders undoubtedly skipped posing for pictures snapped under the sign symbolizing the accomplishment we now all shared; the sign that meant we had reached the top of the "Bald Mountain," the *Géant de Provence*, riding our bicycle; the sign that read:

Sommet
du Mont Ventoux
1910 m

Under the sign we stood – everyday people named Jill, Tim, Chris, Bob, Jeff, and Dave who had just climbed the mountain Lance Armstrong once described as the only mountain that scared him and the ascent other seasoned professionals dread. And by the way, we were all on vacation.

The Bike as a Vehicle for Meaningful Suffering

In July 2009, we set off on our dream trip – ten days following the final stages of the Tour de France and cycling along portions of the race route. For months we alternated between excitement and anxiety, anticipating the challenging rides that lay ahead on our vacation. Injuries and commitments in the weeks leading up to the departure date left us unsure regarding our fitness levels' sufficiency to endure the tour's riding itinerary. Despite this, we eagerly awaited travel to France to *suffer* on the same roads we used to watch, from comfortable couches, professional riders suffer.

Family and friends warmly supported our ambition and enthusiasm, yet certainly must have found the whole premise a little strange – "training" and undergoing many hours of rehabilitation to prepare for a vacation revolving around the voluntary pursuit of pain. After all, people often go to great lengths to minimize or eliminate suffering from their everyday lives, let alone while on vacation. We are culturally conditioned to focus on costs and benefits – to use cold, analytical logic to determine good from bad, valued from inconsequential, comfortable from distressful (although virtually impossible as emotionally charged humans). So when humans think of vacations, of taking time off from their functionally driven daily responsibilities, most seek out relaxation and tranquility. Even when it comes to visions of riding a bicycle, most people imagine leisurely rides in relaxing settings. There is a welcomed sense of aimlessness to these moments, a break from life focused on results and necessity.

A few, however, willingly suffer while riding a bicycle in the name of utility. Members of the professional cycling peloton suffer through training and during competition to earn wages, win prizes, and keep paying sponsors happy. Some non-professional riders similarly tolerate physical discomfort in the name of quantifiable outcomes – measuring heart rates, counting kilometers ridden, determining "wattage" output. These riders extend themselves to evaluate their current physical status or push their corporeal limits: they use the latest techno gadgets to gather scientific data, focusing almost exclusively on the "ends" or outcomes of a day in the saddle. Such riders view suffering as "useful" – and "useful" becomes synonymous with "meaningful."

Pragmatic philosophers such as John Dewey, however, attempted to break away from the analytic peloton. Dewey, following the work done by his philosophic lead out men Charles Peirce and William James, found the emphasis of "meaning" on reductive, measurable ends as cold and mechanical. As he wrote in *Experience and Nature*, "the characteristic human need is for possession and appreciation of the meaning of things, and this need is ignored and unsatisfied in the traditional notion of the useful."[1] But he also championed something more than aimlessness and randomness when considering what humans needed to live the good life. Dewey instead emphasized "aesthetic experiences" as the source of human meaning.

For Dewey (and other members of his Team Pragmatism), human experience is a continuous, ongoing affair – we are always "experiencing" as we interact with the complex world surrounding us. Most of our "experiencing" happens without much lasting impact. But once in a while a moment stands out, lifting off the pages of our personal stories. These are the moments he refers to as "aesthetic experiences." We "feel" these moments rather than "know" them. In other words, aesthetic experiences immediately grab us; they make us see the world around us more vividly or in a different light altogether. Dewey uses the example of looking over a valley in the night as a lightning strike brilliantly illuminates the landscape below. Suddenly, fleetingly, the topography of the valley floor is revealed in a new light – never to look the same to the viewer again. The meaningfulness is immediate, resonating to the core of our embodied being. Only after the moment passes does reflection begin in an attempt to understand why a moment like this stood out from the rest.

Possibilities for heightened experiential moments are available to us in our everyday lives. Sometimes they occur during quiet, tranquil moments, such as when a gardener tends to her plot on a still summer morning, a reader consumes a moving novel curled up on the couch, or a cyclist casually rides along a riverfront path under a bright blue sky. Aesthetic experiences can also happen in less happy moments; the loss of a loved one, crashing while on a ride, or the failure to accomplish a long-desired goal can also serve as meaningful contexts. But all of these *extra-ordinary* moments resonate, becoming a "that moment" – *that* summer morning, *that* book, *that* ride, *that* loss, *that* crash, *that* failure. So in a life filled with risk and perils, with opportunity and comforts, of "doings" and "undergoings," experiencing life aesthetically demands that we live beyond the emptiness and dullness of an "anaesthetic" or meaningless existence. A meaningful life, from Dewey's Team Pragmatism perspective, is a life filled with meaningful moments – sometimes in quiet, sometimes in despair, and sometimes while living at the edge of our saddles.[2]

Voluntarily enduring physical and mental suffering riding a bicycle serves as a great opportunity to experience life in such a meaningful way. When we ride our bikes near the limits of our capabilities, we temporarily exist at the point where possible and impossible collide. To fully engage these moments in their fullness (rather than focus on quantifiable elements such as heart rate maximums) is to be at once aware of the precariousness of life and open to its opportunities to push at the boundaries of what we can (and cannot) do with our physical being. Consequently, we create projects to make such vivid, transformative, and ultimately meaningful moments possible – such as running marathons, white-water rafting, and cycling up Category 1 and HC climbs while on vacation at the Tour de France.

Suffering as the Hub of the Tour de France

Started in 1903, the Tour de France quickly emerged as cycling's revered race and among the most popular annual sporting events in the world.[3] Many also consider the three-week race as one of, if not the most, challenging athletic events. Organizers design *la Grande Boucle* both to elicit suffering and to test the riders' ability to endure its physiological and psychological effects while rolling through the long windswept roads of the French countryside, the twisting mountain passes of the Alps and Pyrenees, and the cobblestones of Paris. As the professional cyclists pedal along, they tap into a kind of suffering symbolic of the Tour's *raison d'être*. The cyclist's willing embrace of suffering and the celebration of his or her ability to endure the intense pace, unpredictably volatile weather conditions, and unrelenting categorized climbs that permeate the route thus stand at the core of the Tour de France.

Consequently, each autumn nervous anticipation and excitement surround the revealing of next July's official route. Its release prompts passionate discussion as enthusiasts envision how much riders will suffer in pursuit of Tour glory. Often the focus lies in the itinerary's final week, as route planners deliberately place the most difficult stages at the time riders must deal with the physical and mental effects generated by extreme cumulative fatigue. The 2009 Tour's final week, which Lance Armstrong described as sinister, was an extreme example. Cyclists ascended over 4,000 meters, riding over four Category 1 and one Category 2 Alpine climbs in the heat, rain, wind, *and* cold – on stage 17 alone. Relentless climbs in the Alps during stages 15 and 16 preceded this day, with the individual time trial and Mont Ventoux stage to follow (and an "easy" 178 km stage 19 to allow the riders to recover before ascending Mont Ventoux on stage 20). At least they get paid to do this.

The currency of the Tour is paid by the willingness of the riders to suffer. No rider escapes the pain; a few will endure more to reap the rewards of team and individual success. Breakaway riders leave the comfort of the peloton to suffer with the hope and slim chance they might win the stage; sprinters drag their bodies over the mountains for rare opportunities to sprint from the pack in the final meters of the stage; all riders must face the time trial without assistance from teammates, propelling their machines over the course as fast as they can; team leaders must stay in contention each day, making sure they can attack at the race's hardest points to justify the suffering undergone by their loyal domestiques.

It is here during these intense moments of suffering, where cyclists push their bodies to the edge of experience, that possibilities and constraints intersect. When the riders enter into the realm of pain, the possibility of a *that moment* heightens. These cyclists cannot know for sure what lies ahead, only that they must endure, to push at the limits of their physical and mental being. This pushing to the limits helps to explain the appeal of the breakaway rider, the time trialist, the sprinter, and the GC rider. We are drawn to their willingness to suffer, awestruck by their capacity to endure for the sake of a moment of glory for self and team. That is why a professional like Garmin-Slipstream's Christian Vandevelde can say before a 2008 Tour de France stage that the upcoming ride will be "terrible" with a twinkle in his eye. Vandevelde and the rest of the professional peloton willingly choose this life, this existence so dependent upon voluntary suffering – they wouldn't have it any other way. They will bear the radical weather changes; they will accept the exuberant fans dressed as Vikings or devils running alongside them, waving flags in their face, interfering with their forward progress; they will ride so high up the mountains the air thins and snow in July remains an ominous possibility; their bikes will break down; their legs and lungs will burn as if filling with acid; they will crack; they will crash; they will lose.

They will, however, also become one with their machine, feeling the bike and road beneath the wheels as if a living, breathing part of them; they will take in the passion of the crowd; they will savor the pain circulating through their bodies; they will achieve; they will push at the boundaries of their embodied possibilities. From Dewey's perspective, such a vivid, purposeful existence lived at the edges of experience makes a meaningful life more likely. And although professional cyclists must undergo long, monotonous days in the saddle, the presence of suffering can make their connection to the world anything but mundane or meaningless.

Share the Road! (And the Pain)

But the meaningfulness of suffering at the Tour de France extends beyond the riders coping with each grueling day for 21 stages and over 3,500 kilometers of terrain. There is suffering of varying kinds by non-racers everywhere you look at the Tour de France. From the masses of team crews and *soigneurs* who work endless hours involved in every aspect of bike and rider performance preparations and race management, to the staff operating the massive caravan that precedes the race, there is meaning generated by these willing "sufferers."

One obvious way non-racers tap into the meaningful suffering experienced by the professional peloton is by riding portions of the race course. Professionals certainly stretch the elastic further than the ordinary cyclist. They put up with excruciating training sessions to extend their ability to suffer in public competition as demanded by their vocation. But non-professional riders similarly embrace the challenge and suffering, although with some trepidation, to ride the same roads and cols as the *Géants de la Route*. And just like the pros, non-racers want to experience the tension of stretching of the elastic without it snapping – thus providing an access point to the experiential meaningfulness of riding in the Tour de France.

While suffering serves as a driving force of the professional cyclists' existence, the non-racers seek out something quite similar on the course. This becomes obvious by considering *where* non-professional riders choose to experience the race course: at the route's toughest points. Few would ride through the flat roads of Provence only to stop at the base of Mont Ventoux. Instead, riders start at the bottom of the Ventoux, the Alpe d'Huez, the Col du Tourmalet. Riders want to tap into the suffering experienced by the giants of cycling, to feel the same road under their machines, to endure something so challenging it places people at the edge of, and potentially over, their physical and mental limits. These rides provide ample terrain for *that moments* on a bicycle. So after experiencing the struggle to turn the pedal over and over again, of overcoming the psychologically daunting view of the far-off peak of a mountain, we buy the proverbial "I DID IT" jerseys and snap pictures under signs at the summit to symbolize the meaningfulness of our suffering.

Non-racers can also experience *that moments* while simply watching professionals on the rivet as they race in *la Grande Boucle*. One of the enduring aspects of the race is the proximity of the spectators to the race course, close enough to touch riders as they pass by. This happens because, unlike most major sporting events, the Tour de France takes place on roads used by common, "ordinary" people. A road cutting through the vineyards used by farmers, a highway traveled by commuters on their way to work, a pass over a mountain traversed by weekend vacationers, a roundabout navigated by locals en route to completing their daily chores momentarily becomes hallowed ground, the site of one of the world's great sporting events. So whereas elite football or hockey or track and field events occur in highly secured, rarely used facilities, grand bicycle tours such as the Tour de France, Giro d'Italia, Vuelta a España, and the Tour of California roll through on regular roads designed for everyday use.

Even for non-riders, suffering stands at the core of their attraction to the Tour de France. Spectators alongside the road often seek out places where the agony will be most palpable. Travel advice for Tour bystanders emphasizes locations where riders face extraordinary tests, where the challenge of the road separates those willing and able to suffer more effectively than their rivals. Although the speed of the peloton on flat roads certainly impresses, we want to see riders struggling up a mountain, to see up close in their strained faces, unzipped jerseys, and sweat-soaked bodies the level of physical and mental anguish they willingly endure. It's no surprise that fans by the hundreds of thousands camp out for days on the side of a mountain waiting, in rain, wind, or shine, to get a momentary glimpse of the unyielding challenge the riders accept.

Phil and Paul, and the Extension of Meaningful Suffering

But spectators need not travel to France and wait on a mountainside to appreciate the suffering embodied by the Tour de France. Television viewers can sit back and watch racers face the Tour's challenges from the comfort of their own homes. Thanks to fearless camera operators, instantaneous and continuous images of the race beam around the world. And for many English-speaking cycling fans, television commentators Phil

TIM ELCOMBE AND JILL TRACEY

Liggett and Paul Sherwen give depth to these pictures with eloquently presented insight and analysis. They connect viewers a continent away with the pain and distress the riders seek. Each race day they bring the anguish of the riders to light, using well-known "Liggettisms" and "Sherwenisms" such as "the elastic has snapped!," "he's wearing the mask of pain!," "the rider has cracked!," and "they're in a spot of bother!" (Some of these should be familiar to readers by now.)

With their vivid, colorful commentary, Phil and Paul essentially serve as the television spectators' super-domestiques of suffering, connecting them deeply to the trials endured by Tour riders thousands of miles away. As a result, their skill to lucidly capture the Tour de France's emphasis on suffering makes them as popular as the professional riders in many cycling communities. In fact, because of Phil and Paul's knack for conveying the idea that pain can deliver *that moments*, we used their voices in the hours leading up to the birth of our son. As labor progressed, DVDs with Phil and Paul describing stages featuring climbs and time trials during the 2007 Tour de France played in the hospital room, connecting the meaningfulness of suffering on a bicycle with the meaningfulness of suffering "we" were undergoing.

Even as spectators we find meaning in the suffering endured by riders in the Tour de France. Part of the explanation why we can experience *that moments* while watching others ride is because on some level the professionals represent us. They symbolize human possibility: what we as a species are capable of at our limits. But these riders encounter possibility at points we can only dream of as "ordinary" cyclists. Few people in the world can ride *that far, that fast, that intensely*. At the same time, they also represent our constraints, the frailty of humanness. Even the best riders in the world crack and suffer, sometimes to the point they can no longer go on. This frailty reminds us that they suffer like us, that there are limits to what they can do.

This appreciation for the human frailty of even the world's greatest cyclists helps explain the public's distaste for doping offenders. When we watch epic stage performances such as Floyd Landis's monumental 125-kilometer breakaway victory during stage 17 of the 2006 Tour de France, we marvel at their capacity to ride to the edge of cracking. Yet our awe and amazement for such performances quickly dissipate after news of positive drug tests becomes public. At first glance, Landis seemed to viewers willing to suffer far more than the rest of the peloton. And although he undoubtedly turned himself inside out, the advantage gained through the use of banned substances blurs evidence that Landis *clearly* suffered at a level beyond his competitors. So in a way, dopers do not suffer to the degree we first believed, and thus their achievements are lessened by them cheating, on some level, our human frailty.

On the other hand, the return of Lance Armstrong for the 2009 Tour and his treatment by the French press give insight into the centrality of agony and the appeal of human limitations. Although he is a cancer survivor and a legend in the sport of cycling, Armstrong's seven consecutive Tour victories failed to convince many of his greatness – his accomplishments long treated as suspicious despite never failing a drug test. Only following his return after more than three years in retirement did French fans start to gain respect for Armstrong. The French appreciated that he no longer dominated as in years past, his inability to climb with Contador and the Schlecks, and his willingness to return to the sport without guarantee of victory. In other words, Armstrong's frailty made him seem, for the first time, human and thus worthy of admiration and a source of meaning. We are amazed by how deeply riders such as Armstrong can dig in the realm of pain, yet we also want to see them at the edge of their limits, to witness their vulnerability. These are the moments when we best connect to the cyclists – and the Tour de France is made of such moments.

Of Suffering and Bicycles

There are many ways humans can realize meaning, and the act of riding a bicycle is one that resonates with many people. Recreational cyclists casually riding along a peaceful bicycle trail, "roadies" cutting through the countryside on a long Saturday morning ride, and professionals pushing the pace through switchbacks on a mountain pass in the Alps can all experience aesthetic moments. But riding to our limits, to feel the elastic stretched near its breaking point, seems to provide an especially powerful context in which *that moments* might happen. And interestingly, so can watching cyclists who, aching pedal stroke after aching pedal stroke, create opportunities to experience life more meaningfully.

The type, level, and depth of meaning may vary but experiencing struggle or suffering through cycling (as riders or viewers) opens space for a meaningfulness all cycling enthusiasts can share. As a result, a community develops through the suffering to be had on a bicycle – a community revolving around stiff headwinds, 8 percent grades, even crashes. Riders who may never meet, or who become great friends through cycling, can all tap into similar opportunities for meaning. Although worlds away, they share experiences as they extend a little further than in previous rides, push faster, and grind up a steep slope. For community members who experience these vivid moments of suffering, accomplishment, and sometimes anguish, personally, or by extension through watching others, the encounter can prove transformative to their being. The opportunity to live any or all of these is powerful and drives many to engage in them.

For us personally, the 2009 Tour de France seemed to capture the race's potential for meaningful experiences. For the first two weeks of the Tour, we sat at home and watched professionals tough it out through time trials, relentless cross and head winds, and Pyrenean climbs, while Phil and Paul brought the depth of the riders' struggles to life for us. And then we were there, cycling along the roads of France with other members of our group at such a pace and length that we finished rides with a sense of both fatigue and exhilaration. We rode up the Col de Romme, the Col de la Colombière, and Mont Ventoux with waiting spectators cheering us on. We stood along the race route in the hot and cold watching battles for stage wins and overall standing as riders turned themselves inside out on climbs and in time trials. We felt the same road beneath our wheels, the weather changes from the bottom to the top of a mountain, the energy and passion of the spectators, the gradient of the climbs. We experienced three weeks filled with an *extra-ordinary* number of *that moments* revolving around human suffering and the Tour de France.

Dewey and his fellow pragmatists believe this way of living, of seeking out and being open to increasingly more experiences that burst from the peloton, propel us to the good life. And while he believed these aesthetic experiences can come in all shapes and sizes, moments when humans engage in projects that push them to the limits of their possibilities, that create the conditions for personal growth, seem more likely to provide us with the context for *that moments*.

Each July we get a glimpse of humanity through the connection between cycling and suffering that holds the potential to change and amplify the way we live and the way we engage the world around us. And even though the 2009 race and our trip to France fade into the past and we return to a more "normal" existence, the meaningfulness of the Tour de France continues to resonate. Every aspect of the experience, from the challenges faced in our preparations, to the strenuousness of the rides, to the witnessing firsthand of the level of suffering endured by the professional riders, left a mark on us. We lived, if only momentarily, closer to the edges of our being, opened to a more meaningful existence.

NOTES

1 John Dewey, *Experience and Nature* (London: Allen & Unwin, 1929), p. 362.
2 For a more thorough discussion on Dewey's notion of aesthetic experience, see Thomas Alexander, "The Art of Life," in *Reading Dewey: Interpretations for a Postmodern Generation*, ed. Larry A. Hickman (Bloomington: Indiana University Press, 1998), pp. 1–22.
3 For an extended analysis of the Tour and its place in French and sport history see Christopher S. Thompson's excellent cultural history book, *The Tour de France* (Berkeley: University of California Press, 2006).

JESÚS ILUNDÁIN-AGURRUZA[1]
AND MIKE MCNAMEE

CHAPTER 25

LIFE CYCLES AND THE STAGES OF A CYCLING LIFE

A trip of a thousand miles begins with a pedal stroke.[2]

Child's Play

An unremarkable place, a back alley, frames the event for Tom Zoumaras, a master US champion. The wavering handlebars spelled self-doubt and doom. About to surrender to the safe defeat of the ground (again!), the front wheel found its purpose. Tom didn't know how, but bike and body joined in a common direction. Tricycle, training-wheels, just the bike: a pedagogical path toward self-reliance and achievement where toy became a vehicle for freedom and confidence beckoning him to explore new territory.

In stage races prologues are short, intense efforts, preambles that set the tone for what's to come. Childhood too is but one such dash. Before we know, it's over. Yet, our future passions are often moved by the muscular memories of those first pedal strokes that hold the secret reasons to our zest for both bike and life. Are we overplaying things? How can a bicycle, a triangle on two circles, as Pythagoras might conceive it, help us to live flourishing lives? An answer to this question must take on a narrative structure; an examination of the cycles of life and of life on cycles.

Adolescent Infatuation

It was love at first sight. The sculpted body, curvaceous where desired, lean where needed, made it all too easy. "Voluptuous" would have been the word, had he known it at the time. He wasn't quite ten and had fallen head over handlebars for her: a silver three-speed racing wonder. The baddest pro wouldn't have ridden a click on its hard plastic saddle, but love is blind (and accepting where necessary!). The GAC, that piece of engineering élan, cost fifty bucks – which meant a long, platonic courtship until his birthday. He named her Lola – after a racy comic book character he surely was too young for. He was Merckx and Zoetemelk rolled into one, till he had to follow his brother and friends off-road, they had all-terrain bikes, on that seat. With Lola he learned about (tough) love and how two could become one – in defiance of his math teacher's crude arithmetic economy.

Late adolescence: a stage full of turmoil where idealism meets that lust for all kinds of action (cycling and biological puberty needn't coincide). Typical of opening stages, this is flat and fast, ending in a crazy bunch sprint. Crushes and crashes are common, for we tend to overshoot our abilities on and off the bike. All hormones and acne, the adolescent is drawn to believing in (honorably) lost causes. So, falling in love, and eagerly tackling epic, perhaps foolish, rides are all rites of passage. Move over Don Quixote, Hales's tales are the adolescent cyclists' philosophical nutrition bars.[3] Unsurprisingly, many renowned champions – Eddy Merckx, Miguel Induráin, Lance Armstrong – throngs of racers, and generations of recreational cyclists, trace their amorous two-wheeled escapades to this time. A growing self-awareness brings intimations of what doing something for love (of the game) is about. It marks the origin of a cultivation and appreciation for the practice of cycling.

Tighten your helmet strap for a breakneck descent down the tricky switchbacks of non-instrumental values and intrinsic interest. Many thinkers have thought that the good life was to be found immersing oneself in activities that had some kind of fundamental or grounding value. Aristotle thought that there were layers of life, according to nature. Our needs and potentialities are more various and sophisticated than plants and other animals: whether nutritive, locomotive, or intellectual. Being at the front of the pack of plant and animal life, he thought that contemplative

JESÚS ILUNDÁIN-AGURRUZA AND MIKE McNAMEE

life was the most fulfilling for rational creatures such as ourselves. Others have embraced more fully the idea that we are essentially *embodied* rational creatures for whom action is as characteristic as reflection. Attempting to articulate the value that cycling can offer us on the way to living good lives – at all levels – is not easy but one necessary training element is getting clear on the nature and variety of value and valuing.

When we treat others – pets, people, possessions, even activities – as ends worthy in and of themselves, just for what they are, we value them intrinsically. They are not mere instruments. We take a spin "just because." This is how Genaro Zugasti, once a fantastic elite sprinter, rides today – hard and fast because it's fun – impressing local pros like 2009 Giro d'Italia winner Dennis Menchov and Caisse d'Epargne's Xavier Zandio. But when our interest in them is only as a way of getting to something or somewhere else, they have instrumental value. They become the means, the instrument, for what we really want to get. Tom Simpson and Rik Van Steenbergen "famously" raced exclusively for money: biking was for them the best means for money-paying fame. When the chosen ends striven for are extrinsic to cycling, racers justify the most efficient means whether they are good, bad, or indifferent. If all you really value your bike for is an external end, like getting to the shops quicker than walking or running, well, why not take the car? Wouldn't it be more efficient since it is faster and takes much less effort? But those who love life on two wheels don't ride this one-way road of efficiency-only thinking. And we all know that if all that matters is the results or the win, well shortcuts seem to be easily justified. Doping fits this pattern like a custom-made frame – something Gleaves and Belliotti handily dealt with earlier.

Before getting too romantic about things, the instrumental benefits of cycling should not be ignored. Here comes an outlandish but laudable example powered by Bartali's legs: during World War II, he helped smuggle Jews out of trouble by hiding documents and fake passports in his bicycle's tubes and delivering them while he trained and enjoyed the rides.[4] Tucked right behind comes Susan B. Anthony, who said that the bicycle had done more for the emancipation of women than anything else in the world.[5] Hyperbolic or not, women became liberated from the sartorial restrictions of corsets and gained autonomy while concurrently *enjoying* cycling amid protestations by certain Victorian "gentlemen" that it would *transport* them to prostitution.

Riding closer to home, cycling can be a wonderful means towards fitness, political, and ecological goals. The quartet of Haraldsson, Harris, Fox, and Furness, working like a tight four-man time-trial team, makes this clear earlier in our Tour. For Kona-tested triathlete Dan Rees it is a great way to channel irrepressible competitive urges. And let's not forget the camaraderie of cycling: from group ride to peloton, the bonds born on the road stick better than tubular glue – the reason that nabs the sprint for lifelong cyclist Julio Sanz. At the mercy of the vicissitudes of life, many of us began cycling because of the health benefits of cycling. Unlike running, cycling won't hammer your spine with repetitive rebounds; unlike swimming you won't have to endure the crushing burden of boredom, counting the tiles on the pool floor. But the instrumental value of cycling, like any other activity, rests on the value that is inherent in the activity. It's when you realize this that the love affair begins properly.

When things get serious there's nothing like a pair of carbon wheels. Let's bring them out. The non-instrumental, playful attitude reflected above is the front wheel of our mechanical steed, but the one that powers things, the rear one, is built on certain skills unique to cycling which we are willing to cultivate for themselves, even risk some nasty road rash: how to move in a pack, take the inside line into a tricky turn, feather the breaks, or become a Sultan of Spin. These are non-instrumental because they are pursued for themselves. The satisfaction we get comes just from doing it right (which can vary with the type of riding, as we see with Hopsicker, Larsen, and Dyer). Satisfaction: that's the word. Not just pleasure.

If adolescence is the time we experiment with who we are, who we have been, and who we would like to become, then things take on a different turn. The fun of taking a spin now becomes a stage of exploration: how long can I go; how fast can I take this bend; what is my top speed; and so on. We play with our bodies' capacities. Exploring our biological and psychological limits, we push the plasticity of our character and identity too. If your lungs feel like they are about to explode, when your legs are so awash in lactic they begin to cramp, begging you to ease off, well, you have to be a masochist to think of this as pleasurable. And yet, you know – as a cyclist – this is the process of becoming and belonging. "I can really call myself a cyclist now," says the adolescent. This emerging identification and dedication lead us to pursue excellence – whether in objective terms or in relation to our own best – like the most dogged pursuit track rider. Speaking of track riders, Steve Brown says, "It is a search for excellence … You cannot say you're a track sprinter if you are not committed to being the best." We have met Tom Zoumaras. He exemplifies this unerring dedication to excel, as he takes even the most ordinary turn to practice his cornering skills *while* experiencing every moment as valuable – even the suffering. The closer we draft behind these values, the more genuine our interest in the activity, and the more meaningful it is *independently* of other factors.

To quickly ingest all of this in the fashion of a paradoxical energy gel: the road itself, the getting there, is the end point that we should be aiming at, and we achieve the other goods when we do this. And all the time we also craft our own character as cyclists.

Flourishing Adulthood

Tchak! Tchak! Tchak! The axe rhythmically falls on the beech logs. Then it stops. The offensively bright, tight outfits have disrupted Aintzia's Sunday morning, a hamlet atop a ridge 10 miles as the vulture flies (that's what flies there) from Roncesvalles – where Charlemagne's rearguard got creamed by disgruntled Basques as payback for his ravaging of Pamplona. Woodchopper and wife, who pops her head out of a small window, eye Mike and Jesús with disapproval. Mike bets a Silca pump that he knows what they're thinking: all that energy wasted climbing the snaky road, it'd be better used on something useful, like chopping wood, instead of pedaling around. Jesús says, "'Axe-man' here ain't no mutant; he doesn't like the chopping." Mike adds, "He just wishes he could come out to play with us." As they discuss this, Jesús suggests a detour to add one more climb – one for the chopper. Mike adds another for kicks.

Early adulthood is an age for boundless ambition and overflowing enthusiasm. Ideally, courage and skills are matched. This mountainous stage – three Category One climbs and one *hors catégorie* – puts that to the test. After a difficult Tour de France stage, Miguel Induráin bemoaned the fact that at the end of the day, compared to a farmer's toil (his father was one), he had nothing to show for all his efforts and suffering: he hadn't produced anything.[6] Maybe we should opt to chop wood: at least something productive comes out of it. For the utilitarian ethos that exults tangible results, this is the case. Today's society frowns upon grown-ups who play with bikes. But there is a road we can take that legitimizes our riding and brings the Spanish legend peace of mind without succumbing to the pedestrian purpose of production.

José Ortega y Gasset, the Spanish philosophical powerhouse, argued that the utilitarian stance, while useful (by definition), is in fact not creative in a richer sense of that term. Work simply adopts previous playful explorations and efforts that are really derived from a vital disposition that is exuberant, joyful, and spontaneous. Instead of calculating outcomes, we playfully and willingly risk, without expecting anything in return, all that energy, perhaps even life itself. (Considering its injuries and fatalities, cycling *is* a risky pursuit.) The purest example of this creative ethos is sport, played for its own sake. At its best, it's not only the result that counts on its own, but the quality of the effort that goes into the achievement. This is a familiar route. Maybe Quixotic, but inspiring nonetheless. In fact, Ortega praises Don Quixote's will for the adventurous. Like a good Stoic warrior, the indefatigable knight says, "Enchanters may deprive me of good fortune, but of spirit and courage, never!"[7] Nowadays, he would set out on two wheels. Let's call this the *sporting spirit*.

Solo breakaways, built on relentless attacking until they stick or sink, best embody this exuberant spirit. These long jaunts are awesome and transformative, as we've seen following Tichenor. Jacky Durand and Fabio Roscioli excelled at these devil-may-care assaults on the peloton and themselves. But the award for greatest "won't-give-up bastard" goes to Claudio Chiappucci's 1992 Tour exploit at Sestriere (his status as favorite made this harder to pull off). He was a true *baroudeur* (brawler) who galloped over 200K to his win on an Alpine stage that looked like our woodman's bow-saw.

To throw a leg over competitive racing, the prevailing conception views competition in terms of victory alone – an instrumental stance. But there is a richer, non-instrumental notion of competition that, while preserving the struggle, has a more expansive view of what's worth celebrating. Andy Hampsten, the only American to win a Giro, in 1988, used to say that in cycling there's always a winner, but that there are never losers because 129 out of 130 cannot be considered losers.[8] To build on this, the *Lanterne Rouge*, the Tour's last GC rider, actually denotes a place of honor, because finishing the Tour *is* itself a near superhuman feat. The Belgian film *Ghislain Lambert's Bicycle* comically magnifies this idea, as it makes Lambert's last place in the Tour the point of the race for his team.[9] OK, OK. So there's losing and then there's tanking it!

Many efforts, even or particularly when they come to naught, are beautiful exploits created out of pain and sweat. As such, they honor that which makes us thriving beings: our vitality. Sometimes the "loser" is

JESÚS ILUNDÁIN-AGURRUZA AND MIKE McNAMEE

fêted more than the winner. Most French fans adored Raymond Poulidor and abhorred Jacques Anquetil. Poulidor was affectionately called "Poupou" (an ill-informed phonetic infelicity to their Anglophone arch-rivals). Poupou never won the Tour de France, finishing second three times and third five! His long 18-year career happened to span the reigns of five-time Tour winners Anquetil and Merckx (De Block and Joye made it clear why it was so unpropitious to coincide with Merckx). Talk about bad luck. Yet he said that to have lots of bad luck of this kind was his good fortune.[10] Some tough break to be a great rider in the company of the greatest. Fittingly, given the stance we endorse, Poulidor is one of the most contented riders to this day. He has said that he already rode a bike for the fun of it before the Tour, so the rest didn't matter ... but if to this you added money, well, "C'est formidable!"[11]

Midlife Crisis Pit Stop

We all know the type of rider. He could lose more than a few pounds; his car sits outside the garage because the dozen bikes leave no room. And yet, he is drooling for that new Italian wonder, light as a feather that comes with a mortgage plan. It is painted Ferrari red of course.

Many of us have or will go through a midlife crisis. On the road, the crisis usually sneaks up during a long climb or riding into a nasty gale, where we question – half ashamed – the sanity of our endeavors. Then, the red sporty cars popular with the midlife crisis crowd look appealing ... but we cyclists are of a different mettle, aren't we? So we grimace and plod ahead. There is only one way to ride a bike, as there is only one way to live life: always moving forward, as Cesar Torres remarks. And suffering is the chain that propels this. Competitors and pundits used to whiningly complain that Induráin made it look easy.

Well, he stated, "I have gone very far in the route of pain."[12] This applies to his racing *and* all those long, hard years preparing for his victories and defeats. We reap where we sow. In short, but not a shortcut, we need to embrace the pain. Biking, while fun, is built on discipline and training. What achievement isn't? This equals suffering (even recreational riders need fitness to fruitfully face mountains or headwinds). But, rejoice! Somehow, this seems quasi-masochistic and confounds outsiders, the pain transforms into joy. Elcombe and Tracey made this painfully clear. To sublimate suffering into enjoyment we need to take the road towards kinesthetic celebration, where movement and beauty combine to create an inspiring narrative. As with most pit stops and midlife crises (at least those that serve their purpose), it is over in a blink. The race and life do not wait for slow pokes.

Unreflective Maturity

> Alfonsina Strada. Her last name can translate as "road." She signed up for the 1925 Giro. If there ever was a machismo stronghold, Italy is it. Predictably, there were protests by many peloton members. Did they feel threatened? Surely not! They just made sure she encountered "extra" problems, mechanical or otherwise, on top of the daunting ones any three-week race presents ...

Like a good wine that has aged well, our maturity is best served so as to allow the nuances afforded by reflection to enhance the bouquet. Of course the trouble is that this comes at the end of a mountain-top finish. It's not so much a pity as an irony that fatigue mercilessly empties us, leaving us little or no energy even to appreciate the more sophisticated of refreshments.

Sometimes, the thinking is done for us, as if to show us what possibilities await if we will only stick at it. That is the beauty of tradition. Induráin's father once replied to remarks about his son's laconic nature that Miguel preferred to speak with his pedals. Indeed, talk is cheap and actions pedal louder than words. And yet. And yet ... sometimes we need the words. To the untrained eye, the one not honed by years of commitment to the internal demands of cycling, the flashy pulls, the apparently iconic breaks from the peloton, these movements and performances might look like the real deal. On a contested group ride someone jumps off the front. Did she do it to drop you, or to bridge the gap, thinking you'd be in her wake? Movements must be interpreted according to underlying intentions. We also need to look within.

Here is where the breaks grab the rim, threatening an embarrassing, painful dismount. Introspection and the life of action are not always good tandem partners. Indeed, they are naturally averse: the more active on the saddle, the less energy for contemplation and vice versa. It may be perverse, but for all the vitality cycling exudes, it stops here. To take the

JESÚS ILUNDÁIN-AGURRUZA AND MIKE McNAMEE

extreme line here, pros usually are about as reflective as the inside of an inner tube – perhaps this is inevitable given the time they offer up to the gods of cycling and the particular Calvary they endure. The closer to them in our cycling habits, the more our own reflective wheels will develop a nasty hop.

This has nothing to do with their intellectual gifts, but with the quality of their "cultural involvement." Most of them do like Induráin: stick to magazines and dailies. And we learned with Bassham and Krall that the same held for Armstrong. They would rather go up Mortirolo Pass in the big ring than read a book. Younger generations, less ambitious yet, opt for the PlayStation. As Tinley intimated, our athletic (quasi-)heroes are human, all too human. Whereas interviews seem like a great source for self-examination, a cursory inspection of decades of earnest outpourings typically reveal only pedaling platitudes.

But we hear protests: "There are exceptions!" There is Pedro Horrillo, a Spanish rider with a philosophy degree who writes a column, *From the Saddle*, for a popular daily; Thomas Davy, Tom Danielson, a few others, were or are pros who attended college; and there is bespectacled, two-Tour winner Laurent Fignon, a.k.a. "Le Professeur," who lived in Paris – awful for training, you know how they drive there, one hand holding a cigarette, the other waving around – because of the intellectual life it offered. Well done. But they are exceptions; that makes *our* point. By the way, Laurent Fignon said: "This job brought me a lot, except on the intellectual level, where I felt I regressed, and that was my biggest sacrifice."[13]

Only occasionally will one of the pedaling greats reveal their own Delphic Oracle. Lance Armstrong, in a moment of rare insight, once observed, "Suffering, I was beginning to think, was essential to a good life, and as inextricable from such a life as bliss. It's a great enhancer. It might last a minute, or a month, but eventually it subsides, and when it does, something else takes its place, and maybe that thing is a greater space. For happiness. Each time I encountered suffering, I believe that I grew, and further defined my capacities – not just my physical ones, but my interior ones as well, for contentment, friendship, or any other human experience."[14] Now the question remains open as to the extent to which we can know the joys of cycling excess that Armstrong has experienced without going through the particular (time) trials and tribulations that he has. Suffering, as he put it, can be ennobling. That is not a license for self-harm, merely a recognition that all things come at a cost. Cycling is no exception. Most of us, especially in these latter years, are able to count the costs more wisely; to reflect critically on which goods really were worth pursuing to the level with or without regret.

Maturity Cycles to Sofia (No, Not the Bulgarian Capital)

> Alfonsina made it to Milan, the finish. Over the allotted time, but to the acclaim of the crowds. Helmets off to her. Things haven't changed much in the 21st century, as the wife of one us can attest whenever she races in male fields. Some men unerringly complain, and would put a pump through her spokes if they only could catch her.

Felicitously, we can redress this skull-numbing tendency just in the way we'd like: by riding our bikes. The Socratic Team of Reid, Hales, and Austin leads the race here. Don't move away from us as if we are about to lose control of the front end in this turn. This works like counter-steering, push the handlebar left to dive right. To shift into a gear we're used to, it depends on the process, on how we ride: we can think reflectively *while* we cycle. On this stretch of road we're going to see how cycling can be a unique philosophical tool, a "sopho-cyclical" method (*sophia* – wisdom; *methodos* – way of locomotion, how fitting!). Incidentally, as Womack and Suyemoto intimate, women seem to have a leg up over men here.[15]

There are different ways of being in the world, and thinking molds around them like a skinsuit. We don't think in the same way lying on a couch, sitting alert, walking, or running (Aristotle thought best walking about, and his students … followed). The bike brings a rhythm of its own to our thinking: it usually takes place over longer periods of time and covers more terrain than strolling or jogging, and it is faster and usually less risky than mountaineering. In today's world of "busy-ness" this allows for fluid and even complex thinking to take place. We *know* the feeling of how a ride can untie emotional or logical knots and bring structure to our thinking. There's more: the bike itself is a tool that can become an extension of our body. This has implications for how we experience the limits of our selves and lives.

For Roland Barthes, the geological and atmospheric elements are central to the racer's experience, and the mountains tower over all the rest. As Matthew Hecht, former elite racer, says, going over the now familiar terrain, "Climbing the big passes in Colorado was exhilarating and yet

🚲 JESÚS ILUNDÁIN-AGURRUZA AND MIKE McNAMEE

peaceful. There was usually a small group together on the upper stretches. We were competitors, yet I remember a sense of camaraderie as much as a sense of competition. For me, there was a spiritual aspect to racing in the mountains." More importantly, for Barthes, it is not the muscle that takes victory, but "a certain idea of man and the world, of man in the world."[16] *Blade Runner*'s Roy Batty may have seen starships on fire off Orion's shoulder, but any cyclist worth his electrolytes can top his sappy account. These occasions open paths to experience the world that would be otherwise beyond reach. One of us was bombing a mountain pass when a large falcon soared right over his front wheel, matching speeds, barely at an arm's length, he could see the feathers ruffling. He almost flew off a switchback with the falcon as he communed with animal, terrain, wind, and "bodybike" unity – his circumstances, to say it with Ortega. It was sublime. Not all encounters are merry-making, as Vala tells in *Growl*, but they remain life-changing moments. This is sporting spirit too. It enriches our lives, adding facets to our *lived* perspective. And the beauty is that it holds true no matter the type of cyclist we are, racer, recreational, commuter. To spin it another way, even if the mystical has eluded you, as Lennard Zinn (who at 6 ft. 6 in. is almost larger than life) says, "Be at one with the universe. If you can't do that, at least be at one with your bike."[17]

Bicycling is not a better way to think – Campy, Shimano, or SRAM, they all shift well – but it is an additional mode that can be as fruitful as quiet contemplation if only we can find the right gear and terrain.

Old Age Re-Cycling

A dream: at 70, Mike rides a custom Henry-lugged steel frame by famed builder Javier González, Xabigo, who built bikes for the likes of Induráin and Delgado. Jesús's bones are holding up after being diagnosed with osteopenia, a precursor of osteoporosis, three decades ago. The hard riding and sweating bleached the calcium off. Genaro's still going hard and fast – some things don't change. Three-fourths up Goñi pass a lass – local pro, very talented – quickly closes on, and passes them as if they're sloths on sedatives. Mike latches on to the end of her saddle as Genaro hangs on to his and Jesús to Genaro's. She laughs, brightening the overcast day, and says, "Kids, you need to lose some weight, how about trying to pedal?" Released, she floats away. They all vicariously enjoy her vigor. Mike yells, "When you meet Irene [Jesús's wife] at the top, [pant] tell her, 'shame on her for [gasp] beating up on us old geezers!'"

Old age. Some would say it's time to slow down, watch the show from the side of the road, and reminisce. Fat chance. Philosophers are philosophical Peter Pans: children who never grow old in a sense. Cycling too shares that outlook. Old age is *another* childhood. Bodies are less flexible, more wrinkled, but having been around has its advantages, old folks can afford all the light carbon that the young guns lust after. Plato, towards the end of his life, lauded dance, sports, and the playful in life. He was a kid, only wiser. He'd ridden there and back. Italo Zilioli, Merckx's best racing friend, thanked God for giving him the strength to prolong, on the bicycle, his childhood dreams.[18] No doubt about it, life is a trip. A tiring trope, to be sure. But less so on a bicycle. And a lot more satisfying, even when it hurts. What goes around comes around; the bicycle has a Karmic allure. We're ready to roll. Again. Even if we are only dreaming it now.

NOTES

1 Jesús dedicates this to his wife, Irene Beyerlein: my much more talented riding partner on the bike and in life, I love to draft from you. Every ride you take the wimpiness out of me, pushing me to better myself on and off the saddle – no excuses – leading by example each painful yet joyful pedal stroke. (However, it'd help if you carried the tools ...)

2 Loosely paraphrasing Laozi's "A journey of a thousand miles begins with one step" (*The Essential Tao*, trans. Thomas Cleary [New York: HarperCollins, 1991], p. 49).

   At www.atisbos.com/cyclingandphilosophy readers will find an annotated bibliography that cross-references sources with the text. Cited comments not referenced presently come from the responses to a philosophic "cycling interview" undertaken by dauntless cycling comrades. Questionnaire (in English and Spanish) and full answers are posted here also. Feel free to take a philosophical spin, and submit your answers to jilunda@linfield.edu or ilunprof@yahoo.com. Responses will be uploaded as the vagaries of life permit. Further bibliographies by contributors, links to other cycling resources, and more are also posted there.

3 As readers get going they'll find some re-cycling as they run across names and comments referring to previous chapters – bringing themes together. Comments echoing our fellow cyclists' views are another cycle yet.

JESÚS ILUNDÁIN-AGURRUZA AND MIKE McNAMEE

4   See stanford.wellsphere.com/biking-article/gino-bartali-a-cyclist-who-saved-a-nation/190259 10/12/08; Philippe Brunel, *An Intimate Portrait of the Tour de France: Masters and Slaves of the Road* (Denver, CO: Buonpane, 1996), p. 37.

5   ladiescycling.net/news/content/history-of-womens-cycling/ (accessed October 12, 2008).

6   Induráin commented on this during an interview for Spanish TV, and once retired he echoed it again in conversation with one of the authors (Jesús Ilundáin-Agurruza).

7   Miguel de Cervantes, *Don Quixote*, translated by Edith Grossman (New York: HarperCollins, 2003), p. 565.

8   Samuel Abt, *Champion: Bicycle Racing in the Age of Induráin* (San Francisco: Bicycle Books, 1993), p. 142.

9   *Ghislain Lambert's Bicycle*, dir. Philippe Arel, with Benoît Poelvoorde, Jose García, Daniel Ceccaldi (Studio Canal, 2001).

10 Brunel, *An Intimate Portrait of the Tour de France*, p. 91.

11 *Vélo* 323 (August 1996): 56.

12 Javier García Sanchez, *Induráin: una passion templada* (Barcelona: Plaza & Janés, 1998), p. 67 (authors' translation).

13 Brunel, *An Intimate Portrait of the Tour de France*, p. 147.

14 www.estatevaults.com/bol/archives/2005/09/29/lance_armstrong_on_suffering.html 9/14/2009.

15 As their examples suggest, women's interpretations of their cycling experiences often are richer, more reflective, and dare we say, wiser than men's. The testosterone-endowed side of the readership would do well in following their line here.

16 Roland Barthes, *Del deporte y los hombres* [Men and Sports] (Barcelona: Paidós, 2008), p. 57 (authors' translation).

17 kba.tripod.com/quotes.htm (accessed September 14, 2009).

18 Brunel, *An Intimate Portrait of the Tour de France*, p. 102.

NOTES ON CONTRIBUTORS

The *Cycling – Philosophy for Everyone Peloton*

MICHAEL W. AUSTIN is an associate professor of philosophy at Eastern Kentucky University, where he works primarily in ethics. He has papers published or forthcoming in such journals as *Journal of Applied Philosophy*, *Journal for the Philosophy of Sport*, and *Journal of Value Inquiry*. He has also published three books: *Conceptions of Parenthood: Ethics and the Family* (2007), *Running and Philosophy: A Marathon for the Mind* (Wiley-Blackwell, 2007), and *Football and Philosophy: Going Deep* (2008). He is a runner who converted to cycling, and is a passionate newbie who doesn't care that the only carbon fiber on his bike is in the fork.

GREGORY BASSHAM is professor and Chair of Philosophy at King's College (Pennsylvania), where he specializes in philosophy of law and critical thinking. He is the author or editor of seven books, including *The Lord of the Rings and Philosophy* (2003), *The Hobbit and Philosophy* (forthcoming, 2011), and *The Ultimate Harry Potter and Philosophy* (forthcoming, 2011). A runner as well as a biker, he has completed ten marathons, including Boston. When it's sunny, he just puts on the sunblock and goes.

RAYMOND ANGELO BELLIOTTI was born at a young age. A poor but honest barber's son, he yearned to play shortstop for the New York Yankees. When it became clear after high school that he was not going to replace Phil Rizzuto, he turned to other pursuits. Summers spent working on construction crews and toiling in nursery fields convinced him that there was no percentage in hard labor. Seeking an undemanding, frivolous, yet exciting career, he stumbled onto philosophy. Belliotti joined the SUNY Fredonia faculty in 1984. That pretty much ends his story. He ran some marathons, got married, wrote some books, sired two children, coached a lot of baseball, lost most of his hair, and sulked as the remaining strands turned gray. Belliotti never owned a bicycle.

ANDREAS DE BLOCK is an assistant professor in the Institute of Philosophy at the Catholic University Leuven. Andreas's primary research interests are in philosophy of biology, biomedical philosophy, and philosophical anthropology. His papers have appeared in philosophy journals such as *Biology & Philosophy*, *Philosophical Psychology*, *Studies in the History and Philosophy of Science*, and *Perspectives in Biology and Medicine*. He thinks that cycling is much more important for humanity than philosophy.

BRYCE T. J. DYER is senior lecturer in the School of Design, Engineering, and Computing at Bournemouth University in the UK. Bryce's primary research interests are sports technology, product development, and the humanistic and technological balance of design. He is currently progressing through his PhD, which attempts to create an ethical approach to developing assistive technology for Paralympic athletes. He still dons lycra as a competitive time trialist and triathlete, and believes that happiness is 30 mph and a disc wheel.

TIM ELCOMBE is an assistant professor in the Department of Kinesiology and Physical Education at Wilfrid Laurier University (Ontario, Canada). His research focuses on applying pragmatism to sport philosophy issues and the connections between human movement and culture at large. In addition to academic journals and books, he has published in popular philosophy works including *Basketball and Philosophy* and *Soccer and Philosophy*. Tim recently climbed Mont Ventoux while on a cycling trip in France with his wife, yet still wears baggy shorts over lycra while riding as an homage to his basketball background.

RUSSELL ARBEN FOX is an associate professor of political science and director of the Political Science program at Friends University in Wichita, KS. He has lived and ridden bicycles in every place he has resided: Utah, the DC area, his current (hopefully lasting) home in Kansas, Washington state, South Korea, Germany, Mississippi, and Illinois. He has never raced (for money), nor attempted to gauge the carrying or hauling capacity of any bicycle he has owned. When not busy with the usual academic duties, blogging (inmedias.blogspot.com), commuting to work, or riding for fun with his wife and four daughters, he researches American politics and history, East Asian philosophy, comparative political theory, populist, localist, and communitarian political movements, romantic and Christian political thought, and more. His essays have appeared in *The Review of Politics, Polity, American Behavioral Scientist, The Responsive Community, Theory and Research in Education,* and *Philosophy East and West.*

ZACK FURNESS is an assistant professor of cultural studies at Columbia College Chicago, a Pittsburgh native, and the author of a book on bike activism and the politics of automobility called *One Less Car* (2010). Despite being a staunch advocate for bicycle transportation, he thinks bike corporations get off the hook too easily and he is far more inspired by old ladies on cruisers than macho hipsters with no brakes. Furness never feels "vehicular" when he's on a bike, and he would love to see 1 out of every 10 Chicago streets depaved for community gardens and playgrounds. His body looks nothing like the models featured in *Bicycling Magazine* and he owns no lycra.

JOHN GLEAVES is a doctoral student in the Department of Kinesiology at the Pennsylvania State University focusing on the philosophy and history of sport. He earned his BA in philosophy from Carroll College and has studied at the International Olympic Academy in Olympia, Greece. His cross-disciplinary research focuses on understanding the philosophical issues of doping and performance enhancement by incorporating diverse fields such as physiology, medicine, bioethics, and legal theory along with philosophy and ethics. When not studying doping, John continues to race bikes and is always searching out sprint finishes either on the velodrome or at a local crit.

STEVEN D. HALES is professor of philosophy at Bloomsburg University. He was recently Visiting Professorial Fellow at the Institute of Philosophy, School of Advanced Study, University of London. His work in popular philosophy includes *Beer and Philosophy* (Wiley-Blackwell, 2007), *What Philosophy Can Tell You About Your Dog* (2008), and *What Philosophy Can Tell You About Your Cat* (2008). His serious boring work is in epistemology and metaphysics, like *Relativism and the Foundations of Philosophy* (2006). He needs to get on his Cannondale R800 Sport more often.

ROBERT H. HARALDSSON is a professor of philosophy at the University of Iceland. He received his PhD in philosophy from the

University of Pittsburgh and has mainly worked on nineteenth-century philosophy and literature. Under the influence of such thinkers as Ralph Waldo Emerson, Henry David Thoreau, John Stuart Mill, and William James, his interest has increasingly turned to philosophy as a way of life, most recently to philosophy and cycling. He has published accounts of his cycling trips through the interior highlands of Iceland.

JOHN RICHARD HARRIS is an assistant professor in the Department of Philosophy at Texas Christian University. John's research interests focus on applied ethics, political philosophy, and the philosophy of law. When John is not biking off to work to avoid mowing his lawn, he likes to ride his racing bike as fast as he can along Fort Worth's Trinity Trails, play with his three cats (Thom, Ethel, and Cal), or just do anything with his wife, Tracie.

PETER M. HOPSICKER is assistant professor of kinesiology at Penn State Altoona. His research interests include philosophy of mind in skilled motor behavior, moral development through sports, the pursuit of the strenuous life through physical activity, and the historical development of sport and recreation in the Adirondack Mountains. A devoted non-racer (and proud of it!), he has been accused by those in the peloton of being a "non-cyclist who rides a bike really well."

JESÚS ILUNDÁIN-AGURRUZA, born and raised in Pamplona, Spain, ran with the bulls for a number of foolish years. He is an assistant professor of philosophy, and Allen and Pat Kelley Faculty Scholar at Linfield College in Oregon. His main areas of research and publication are the philosophy of sport and the philosophy of art, and he has published in journals such as *Sports, Ethics, and Philosophy* and *Proteus*, as well as in anthologies on sports and risk, soccer, childhood and sports, and others (some in Spanish). His big philosophical appetite, which also helps fuel his motivation to pedal, ranges from ethics and metaphysics to philosophy and literature, Eastern philosophy, and more. He races as a category 2. Jesús's best days are probably behind him, but that's OK because what he enjoys most is riding hard for its own sake.

YANNICK JOYE is a huge fan of the late Belgian rider Frank Vandenbroucke, best known for humiliating Michele Bartoli on the 22 percent Côte de La Redoute of the 1999 edition of Liège – Bastogne – Liège. Vandenbroucke fans thought he was the best cycling had ever brought them since Eddy Merkcx. Doctor Joye was often laughed at because of this, especially since Frank became a shadow of the winner he once was in his later years. To be taken more seriously, Yannick studied philosophy and eventually got a philosophy doctorate (which many saw as a reason to take him even less seriously). If Yannick isn't hammering his racing bike, then he's doing research on environmental aesthetics. Currently he works as a postdoctoral researcher in the Institute of Philosophy at the University of Leuven, Belgium. He has published in peer-reviewed journals like *Leonardo*, *Review of General Psychology*, and *Environment and Planning B*.

CHRIS KRALL, MBA, is a technologist at the University of Scranton (Pennsylvania), where he toils in relative obscurity. On the weekends, however, he becomes an avid cyclist, marathoner, and triathlete who has competed in events around the US and Europe, run the Boston Marathon, and made the podium in an Ironman event. A cancer survivor, he is grateful for all that Lance has done for the cause.

STEEN NEPPER LARSEN is an associate professor of philosophy and sociology at Research Initiative – Mind and Thinking, GNOSIS Research Centre, Aarhus University (Denmark). He wants to combine and renew critical theory and phenomenology and is engaged in establishing a meeting point between philosophy and the neurosciences. He wonders if there are any limits to neuroplasticity, our learning brain. He is also concerned with critically assessing contemporary "cognitive capitalism," which is so bent on swallowing creativity, social cooperation, the will to share and communicate, etc., and turning them into commodities. As a racing fanatic he's "eaten" over 120,000 km of asphalt in the last 20 years on his customized Danish red and white Schrøder (a must at 6 ft. 7 in.). He also dips his body in the sea (Øresund) every morning, all year round.

MIKE McNAMEE is professor of applied ethics at Swansea University where he teaches medical ethics. He runs and plays football and tennis. No stranger to sports injuries, he hops on the bike on sunny days only, and largely as therapy. His last book was *Sports, Virtues and Vices: Morality Plays* (2008) and he is the founding editor of the journal *Sport, Ethics, and Philosophy*.

HEATHER L. REID is professor and Chair of Philosophy at Morningside College in Sioux City, Iowa. She works in ancient Greek philosophy, philosophy of sport, and Olympic studies. Her first book,

The Philosophical Athlete, was published by Carolina Academic Press in 2002. *Contests of Truth*, a comparative study of athletics and philosophy in ancient Greece, will be published in 2010. She is a former member of the formidable Winning-Peugeot cycling team, and has competed in most major US races as well as the women's Milk Race in England. She qualified for the final Olympic trials in 1984 and 1988 and has been national collegiate champion on the track and vice-champion in the road race.

PATA SUYEMOTO is an independent scholar with interests in feminist approaches to education, research, and issues of race and diversity. She earned her PhD in reading, writing, and literacy from the University of Pennsylvania. She is also a bicycle riding teacher with the Bicycle Riding School and an avid cyclist who finds that cycling provides many metaphors for life – balance, freedom, and revolution.

SETH TICHENOR teaches philosophy at Linfield College, Oregon. His many interests include classical South Asian philosophy, comparative philosophy, philosophy of religion, of culture, of pedagogy, and whatever else comes up in an interesting conversation. He's written for such journals as *Asian Philosophy*, *Philosophy East/West*, and *Dao*. Nowadays most of his energy goes into teaching – he's been named twice Outstanding Educator at Linfield – and building philosophical communities – Seth has worked in Honolulu's Philosophy in the Schools Foundation (one of the best teaching gigs of his life), as well as ENCORE, which brings philosophy to different Oregonian communities. Having done a number of triathlons, it turns out he's a lot better in the water than on land, but he loves cycling hard – even if it means watching half the field spin right past him after the swim leg is over.

SCOTT TINLEY is a lecturer in the Exercise and Nutritional Sciences Department at San Diego State University and the founder of the Institute for Athletes in Retirement and Transition. He has authored five sports-related texts and a collection of short fiction. Tinley won the Ironman Triathlon World Championship in Hawaii in 1982 and 1985 and the Ironman World Series three times in the early 1990s. As a seventh-generation Southern Californian, his first love is surfing and other ocean sports. Admittedly, he would rather pedal his 1978 Schwinn Cruiser along the boardwalk than race his five-figure carbon fiber/unobtanium custom bike. He is fascinated by the role that the bicycle played in women's liberation.

JILL TRACEY is an assistant professor in the Department of Kinesiology and Physical Education at Wilfrid Laurier University (Ontario, Canada). Her research focuses on the psychology of injury and rehabilitation. She also works as a sport psychology consultant with various teams and athletes. Her research has appeared in numerous journals including the *Journal of Sport Rehabilitation*, the *Journal of Applied Sport Psychology*, and *Quest*. She has been riding a bike since she jumped on her big brother's banana-seat bike at three years of age and has never looked back – except to check for traffic. She holds the position that there is never enough lycra and is equally at home and happy on the road or mountain biking.

PATRICK VALA-HAYNES was born in Oregon. And, yes, things do look a little different there. He is a 2008 Sundance Screenwriting Fellow, whose short fiction, essays, and poetry have seen print in numerous literary magazines and newspapers. He has freelanced for the past 25 years as a sword fight choreographer and dramaturg in the Northwest, including work for Oregon Shakespeare Festival and Tigres Heart Shakespeare Company. He admits to being a scrambled Renaissance man who knows more about plumbing, carpentry, and cannons than he wants to. For a real living, he owns and runs a bicycle shop near the foothills of the Oregon Coast Range. His greatest cycling experiences have all ended in utter, physical defeat. He is not deterred.

CATHERINE A. WOMACK is associate professor of philosophy at Bridgewater State College near Boston. Her research in philosophy of public health focuses on how personal identity and behavior change are connected through social connections and environmental influences; she is currently working on how individual eating and activity habits are shaped by workplace social groups. Her two-wheeled activities, when not avoiding potholes, car doors, and renegade cabs in Cambridge, include mountain bike racing, cyclocross riding, organizing a women's road ride, and yelling at cyclists who run red lights.

LENNARD ZINN is a former US National Team rider who, disappointed with the ride quality of bikes for the tall crowd, and armed with a physics degree, became a frame builder to improve the riding experience of the extra tall crowd. The number and breadth of his multiple endeavors has grown to match his 6 ft. 6 in. frame. He has written several successful books (such as the *Zinn and the Art of Bicycle Maintenance* series), produced DVDs, and is the technical writer for *VeloNews* magazine. He also owns *Zinn Cycles* (www.zinncycles.com), for which he designs and builds frames, components, and clothing, all tailored to make cycling more enjoyable for those vertically blessed *and* cursed. This makes for a dream job that takes care of any regrets he might have about stopping his racing days early … after all, past 50, he's basically *still* getting paid to ride a bike to this day!